A STORY OF FAITH, ~~FAITHFULNESS~~
AND LEARNING TO TRUST GOD EVEN IF ...

JOURNEY OF A

Legacy Man

A MEMOIR BY
W. DALE REVELL
WITH JANE REVELL

JOURNEY OF A LEGACY MAN
A Story of Faith, Faithfulness, and Learning to Trust God Even If ...

ISBN (Print): 979-88384294-2-1

Library of Congress Control Number (LCCN): 2022912397

Published by W. Dale Revell. Argyle, Texas

Prepared for Publication by: www.palmtreeproductions.com

To contact the author: journey.of.a.legacy.man@gmail.com

PRAISE FOR JOURNEY OF A LEGACY MAN

I have been privileged as well as personally challenged walking with Dale through the past 38 years of this amazing Jesus journey. He has repeatedly walked the depths of dire health prognosis, yet he continues to press on with contagious hope, which is the evidence of the presence of our Lord and Savior. Dale's calm assurance was evident throughout his Ford Credit career as a leader of people, often in the public eye. Even more significant, he remained the same when no one was looking. Dale and Jane have never wavered—they are fully devoted followers of Christ.

Their life together reflects a sweet legacy built upon God's promises moment by moment. They have experienced countless medical decisions, constant prayer, abiding faith, and enduring trust in God's plan .... no matter what. As I have been, you will also be captured and uplifted by this heart-filling story of what only God could have done. Thank you, Dale and Jane, for your Christ-likeness! Oh Lord, guide us to be as faithful all the days and decades ahead until You come.

—REV. RICHARD S. DEWITT

Plano, Texas

Acknowledgments

There are many who deserve my public thanks for their encouragement, prayers, meals, kind words, and help throughout my life. There are hundreds of friends, work colleagues, church folks, extended family members, and medical professionals who have touched my life in some way or another. Unfortunately, space will not permit me to name them all so I say a simple, but heart felt, "Thank you!"

That brings me to a very special group of seven people who deserve to be singled out as I express my appreciation for their presence in my life.

- My Mum and Dad—Glen and Elda Revell—who gave me physical life, but more importantly, an unwavering legacy of trust and faith in God. They were unselfish, caring, patient, firm but loving, and always covered my family with prayer.

- My children—Cindy Revell Washburn and Matthew Revell—who have travelled with me through every mile of my health struggles, first as young children then as adults. They have been with me in the good times and the not so good times. They have demonstrated their love for me, been my constant encouragers, and gifted me with joy as they walk daily in their relationship with Christ Jesus.

- My wife—Jane Revell—who took my memories of growing up, and combined with God's awesome miracles, wove them into this amazing legacy story of my life. Because of her efforts and love for me, I can now gift it to my family and friends. She is an amazing gal and a great writer.

- My Texas friends—Gary and Teresa Phillips—who encouraged Jane and I as we travelled through the maze of writing a book. Teresa's expert editing and Gary's knowledgeable assistance in the publishing process helped us take our vision and create the legacy we hope will bless every reader.

CONTENTS

How does one define a legacy man? Should he be known for what he achieves or what he has had to endure? Dale Revell could have found his identity in any number of situations from his life. He could have been seen as just another small-town boy whose only future was the local garage, or he could have been known as Kingston's next great hockey prospect. Many saw him as an important executive in corporate America. Even more know he was a cancer survivor multiple times over. But the man you will read about in these pages, who has overcome so many challenges and achieved great success, is known by me as a generous and loving father, a faithful friend, a victorious warrior, and a man of God. That is how my dad is defined, and that is the legacy that he passes on. It is an honor to know Dale Revell as my father, my friend—the *Legacy Man*.

—MATTHEW REVELL

Riding in a car is quite an experience. You perceive significantly different views of the world (and life) depending upon where you sit and which window you look through. On journeys as a back seat passenger, one has limited views through a small window and restricted access to front-seat conversations (especially fighting against the radio noise). But from the coveted front seat, the world is more visible, and you can see where you are going! It is the source of entertainment, snacks, instruction, direction, and wisdom. This is how I read my Dad's memoir. From the different views of the car, I see different parts of our story and how God's grace, mercy, and direction was with him (and us) throughout our adventures.

—CINDY REVELL WASHBURN

The human mind cannot comprehend the millions and millions if not billions of roads which encircle and crisscross the surface of the earth. In the USA alone, there are nearly 6 million miles of paved and unpaved roads. This number does not include all the cow paths covering the fields of Texas.

There are wide expanses of expressways swirling around huge cities and single mountain passes only wide enough for one person's carefully placed steps. There are two lane country roads meandering through small towns and villages. There are places even in the Midwest where the wheel marks on rutted trails formed by pioneer wagons are still visible. There are straight stretches of roads just waiting for that sudden burst of combustion which will push a Mustang's speedometer to 120 MPH. There is an unbelievable road aptly named The Dragon's Tail because of its 311 curves packed into 11 miles—a nightmare of switchbacks! Even the seas and sky have invisible paths through which man journeys as directed by navigational tools.

And for the protection of all travelers upon most roads, there are signs—Stop, Proceed With Caution, Sharp Curve Ahead, Road Divides, S Curve, Express Lane, Double S Curve, Yield, Slow Moving Vehicle, No Shoulder Ahead, Road Work Ahead, Do Not Pass, Road Closed, or No Outlet. The list is endless.

Regardless of the destination of each road, there is always a beginning point—a place where one's journey begins.

What is a journey? What does it look like and feel like? Is it different for each person? As a believer, should my journey appear in a pattern which is clarified at every turn or twist? Should it be spur of the moment experience? Such questions have prompted me to consider my own life journey. Looking back, what was God orchestrating through the details surrounding my life? What roads lay ahead of me? What legacy would I leave?

When Jane and I travel, we spend considerable time pre-organizing as many details as possible—dates, airfare, hotels, car rentals, restaurants, and entertainment. We leave very little to chance. It is our desire to be in control of as many details of the trip as possible to ensure there are few moments of surprise, hesitation, disappointment, and/or insecurity.

How does that apply on life journeys where every twist and turn presents a unique challenge, an adventure, and experiences of highs and lows? What does God want to teach us about our insatiable desire to be in control? What does He want to teach me and my family?

When my wife was coaching, she relied on a whistle to keep control of those under her direction. It was loud and sometimes harsh as she may have needed to stop a negative behavior or skill set which would be detrimental to the health of a person or success of a team. Her whistle is an attention getting method which she used, not as a punishment, but as a direction changer. What follows then is better direction, corrective teaching, safety, and refocusing on purpose.

Now, lest someone think I believe God always uses the shrillness of a situation to gain our attention, let me add that I believe He also chooses to whisper in tones so softly my human ear cannot comprehend the meaning. And even if He is silent, the question still remains: can I trust Him?

How does that translate when one is walking through a difficult time or situation? Am I willing to release control to God through every detail of my life? Am I willing to not see the bigger picture, not know what is around the next corner, not program my personal GPS to lead me in the safest, fastest, most direct route through pain, decisions, and consequences?

Am I listening for my God's whistle, His whisper, or even His silence and then be satisfied to wait upon His direction? Can I accept His journey for me as my own?

It's interesting to study all different types of miracles appearing in such varied shapes and sizes in the life journey of a human being. Do I perceive something which gets me out of trouble in my youth to be a miracle? Is a miracle orchestrated by my choices or by a power outside of my control?

One can see I have many thoughts traveling around my mind as I begin this task of sharing my life's journey with whomever opens this manuscript. I have a legacy to leave and a story to tell. So, I begin!

—DALE REVELL

June 2022

"FOR GOD HATH NOT GIVEN US THE SPIRIT OF FEAR; BUT OF POWER, AND OF LOVE, AND OF A SOUND MIND."

2 TIMOTHY 1:7, KJV

1962 AUSTIN HEALY BUGEYE

VERONA, ONTARIO

Everyone's life journey begins somewhere. If I calculate correctly, to this date in time my life odometer has recorded 72 years, 864 months, 3,756.78 weeks, 26,297.46 days, 631,139.04 hours, 37,868,342.4 minutes, and 2,272,100,544 seconds. The great thing is that the device is still counting!

The story of my life journey began on February 11,1950 in a small Canadian village called Verona. It consisted of one main street, no stoplight, four churches, five gas stations, one doctor in residence, one school, one pool hall, no bars, two grocery stores, two car dealerships, and one big swimming spot on the shores of Rock Lake. Verona could boast of 650+ people, all of them being well aware of each other's business. It was an idyllic setting where children were free to roam every inch of land and lake from dawn to dusk with no concern for their safety. My mom's only rule was for me to be present at the supper table-washed up and ready to eat.

Every town has its own quirky elements, and the town of my youth had its fair share. Because everyone was so familiar with everyone else, a person's individual birth name was seldom used. Many of the residents had nicknames which tended to be the only name by which they were referred. Snapper, Chief, Allie Oops, Dudley, Dicky, Babs, Fuzzy, Casey, Stump, Hermie and Knoxy were well known nicknames. I was dubbed, Rev, probably not in reference to a prophetic vision of a pastoral calling in my future, but more than likely referring to my "revved up", highly energetic, exuberant enthusiasm for fun and adventure.

I would be remiss here if I did not mention that I was the second born of three children of Glen and Elda Revell. My arrival on the family scene came two years after Glenda and two years before Sandy. They were by all accounts nearly perfect while I was not. One specific event stands out as a tribute to my "all boy" nature.

Upon arriving home from an evening out with friends, our parents were not at all pleased to discover my sisters locked in the master bathroom. I was reclining on the couch happily watching my favorite television show. It probably was not a good idea for me to have waved that knife around and threatened them if any channel changing occurred. No, it was not one of my finer moments and the consequences were probably well deserved. In those days, slap therapy was acceptable!

Like many businessmen, my business career began with delivering newspapers and my route included the whole village of Verona. I made pretty good money, but I loved Christmas as I received generous tips from my customers. To facilitate a better delivery system for me, my dad put a big basket on my pedal bike for me to carry newspapers that would not fit in my canvas carrying bags that I slung over my shoulder.

To my personal advantage (and sometimes disadvantage!), my persona was very well known all up and down Main Street and every connected side road as I was the only paperboy delivering the Ottawa Journal and the Kingston Whig Standard. It was a very big thrill for when, as a result of all my hard peddling and consistent delivery service in the rain or snow and the heat or cold of Canadian living, I won a trip to the NHL Allstar Game in Toronto at the famous Maple Leaf Gardens. Me, a skinny 13-year-old paperboy from small town Verona sitting in the expanse of "The Gardens" watching my childhood heroes storm up and down the ice in pursuit of that small round puck and a victory.

What a thrill! Hard work does pay off.

One of the grocery stores was established in the 1920s by my grandfather, Samuel Wesley Revell. Being a businessman always looking at future investments, he also established the Revell Ford Motor dealership in 1936. My father, Glen Wesley Revell and his brother Harry, became partners with their dad in the business which is still in operation over 80 years later.

My earliest memories through the childhood journey were visiting the dealership with my mother and sisters to see Dad who worked very long hours. Whenever we came, Dad would get us a pop out of the Coke machine which at that time was a very special treat. Some days he managed to come home for lunch and in the winter, he would bring a tractor from the dealership. I am sure the entire village could hear our screams of delight as he pulled our toboggan behind the tractor.

I remember the original, one car showroom with several big front glass windows and a bench outside where each day found many of the older gentleman in town resting as they observed the local traffic and village life occurring around them. Their agenda usually was a deep discussion of local politics, lifestyle choices, stories from their pasts, and of course, village gossip.

As I got older, I spent many hours with Dad at the dealership serving gas, cleaning the rest rooms and service bays, detailing cars for customer deliveries, tagging along on trips to tow people out of the ditch, or taking a parts run to Kingston 20 miles away. I guess one could say that I learned the car dealership business from the ground up.

I LEARNED THE CAR DEALERSHIP BUSINESS FROM THE GROUND UP

By getting me involved at the dealership at a very young age, Dad did not realize he would be handing me the opportunity of experiencing my very first car accident—as a driver no less! After one particularly heavy snow fall had blanketed the car lot and messed up the laneways, Dad enlisted my help in backing out new cars so he could plow the area. Sounds like a simple maneuvering operation which required an open driver's door, a light touch on the gas pedal, and a firm grip on the steering wheel. Well, combined with years of driving experience, those elements should have resulted in a successful procedure. However, when the driver was only 8 years old with no previous backing up experience, disaster was inevitable. The open door plowed into the next vehicle and it was not a pretty sight!

OOPS!

Typical of my dad, he did not respond with anger but assessed the situation and used it as a teaching moment. One more job for the Body Shop.

At that time, I could not have realized the blessing that my dad, whom God specifically planned to be my parent, chose to include me in the family business in order to develop within me character and integrity. He was the greatest example of that in my life.

Throughout my years of "Tom Sawyer" living in Verona, I spent countless hours in various types of youthful amusement. Winter found me engaged in outdoor hockey games at the village ice rink and ice fishing with my friend, Gary Stinson, on Rock Lake. One such fishing session resulted in our hooking a fish which was so large we had to increase the size of the ice hole in order to extract our prized catch! You can imagine our delight when the fish weighed in at 18 pounds! I know that sounds like a Big Fish story, but Gary's dad had said beast, a Northern Pike, mounted as a memento.

This same friend and I always had some adventure which must have caused my guardian angel fits as we engaged in innocent activities. On one occasion, we used Gary's Dad's small tractor to pick up a trailer from a neighbor. I rode shotgun on the fender as we motored up Main Street and all went well until I fell off where upon said trailer ran over my body! My mum's close examination revealed a wide tire mark running across my stomach and chest areas. I had been protected from serious injuries, so we agreed not to tell Dad who tended toward excessive worrying. Mum probably stepped up her prayers for my safety after that.

Summers found me playing road hockey in front of the vacant Fina gas station with Alley Ops (Al), Chief (Larry), and Lynn Revell, or organizing an all-day game of baseball behind the Free Methodist Church. Ever the good buddies, Gary and I always teamed up to launch his wooden rowboat for fishing trips on Rock Lake, anxious to try our luck again for another big catch.

Of course, there was always an element of danger worked into the adventures of the Verona young lads as we often engaged in activities which would have created immense consternation with our parents had they been aware of our plans. Almost every spring, when the ice had just barely melted, Chris Walker and I would sneak into his family's boat house and, after lowering the motorboat down into the frigid water, don a pair of skis to skim across the cold surface for a couple of turns. Hopefully, we could get close enough to the shore so as not to fall into the water but land on the beach. Usually, we were successful.

The fun and frolic of my carefree Verona life always came to an abrupt end each September by the arrival of the dreaded first day of school. Gone were the hours spent in youthful pleasure with cousins and friends. Gone was freedom in its purest form! Instead, I found myself once again bound by the ringing of the morning bell from Prince Charles Public School which was directly across the street from my home. Wasn't I lucky? So instead of grabbing a fishing rod or baseball bat and riding off on my bike for a day of adventure, I snatched a piece of toast and ran like the wind to not be counted late.

To be perfectly honest, I hated school. Not just because it meant the end of all my fun, but also because it was never a pleasant experience. I did not enjoy reading for pleasure or studying. So, when it came time for reading out loud in class, I was terrified. Many of my academic struggles could be tied to my difficulty in reading. (God does have a sense of humor as my wife is a college English major who devours reading material like candy. Opposites do attract, I guess) And I should mention that those were the days when an error on a spelling test resulted in a leather strap hitting on the palms of my hands. Hard to believe I know.

My entire public-school journey was not a total disaster as I did enjoy and excel in sports and recess. For the majority of Canadian youth, hockey was the mainstay of our sporting experiences both as spectators and players. My first recollection of strapping on skates, putting on a leather helmet, and grasping a wooden stick was when I was about 7 or 8 years old playing in the Pee Wee League in Kingston. My dad and Gill McMahon were my coaches, and it was fun beyond measure. My love of the sport continued until I was 36 when my life journey took an abrupt switchback and hockey became strictly a spectator sport for me. More on that later.

When I reflect on my hometown and all its eccentricities, my heart is drawn to a very prominent place right on Main Street, the Free Methodist Church. Physically it resembled a rectangle shaped structure formed from warm red bricks. Its window frames encased stain glass designs of colored shapes which captured my attention whenever the sermon became boring or was on a topic in which I had no interest. Or I could gaze just behind the Pastor's head to view the front wall where some artist had painted a large picture. It was the portrayal of Christ kneeling beside a large rock with His hands folded and an expression of deep sorrow upon His face. I think He was in the Garden of Gethsemane. The colors were extremely muted, and I always wondered if it was a Rembrandt. Probably not.

There were several family groups of Revell clan in this church and my parents chose to sit on the right side second row from the front. Somehow this changed because years later, my parents started sitting on the left side of the church. I always wondered if there was a problem on the right side and they were excommunicated to the left!

Because we sat so close to the front, Mum was always very concerned about the appearance of my rambunctious behavior. If I felt the desire to wiggle too much or act up because the sermon was too long or boredom had overtaken me, she had a way of using her two fingers to pinch the skin on my arm. Even though the pain was intense, I dared not show any signs of suffering or the trip down the aisle out the back door would have been even more intensely painful!

Our Sunday School rooms were in the basement of this building, and it was there that one of my embarrassing moments of youth unfolded.

The guest teacher that morning was none other than our Senior Pastor, Reverend Ball, a fine and distinguished man I greatly respected. During his discourse, my eyes began to droop, and I found myself nodding off. More than likely this was due to some harmless late Saturday night activity which required my attendance or maybe because it was an early morning class. Regardless of the reason, I just could not stay awake which resulted in my abrupt disruption of the entire class by falling off the chair in a sleepy stupor!

Can one say, "Awkward"?

For my family, the "Church" experience was deeply woven into our life journey. In the early days, this specific denomination did not allow any musical accompaniment for singing as the leaders felt that was too worldly. I remember when it was finally decided to add organ music and it created a lot of angst with some of the older members who felt that a sacred rule had been broken.

And trust me! There were lots of rules!!!!

The "don'ts" and "do's" were strongly reinforced and it was often hard to grasp mercy as a gift or to see the joy of my salvation. Of course, I was looking at faith through the eyes of a young fellow wanting a little more freedom and a whole reduction in the number of behavior rules!

Whenever the church doors opened for Sunday School, Sunday morning church, Sunday evening service, Wednesday night prayer meeting, Vacation Bible School, Christian Youth Crusaders, visiting missionary presentations, and youth group gatherings, we would be in attendance. Sometimes I did not attend such programs with great enthusiasm, but I will forever be indebted to my parents for their dedication in keeping my youthful vision continually refocused on the teachings of Christ.

Because my parents felt the importance of directing their children toward God, they were very involved in our church. Their desire was to give us a strong spiritual example so that a firm foundation would be there when we took ownership of our faith. Mum taught Sunday School, Christian Youth Crusaders, served on Women's Christian Temperance Union committees. At one time, Dad was the Sunday School Superintendent.

Their home became a gathering place for guest preachers and visiting missionaries. Mum had been given the gift of hospitality and she delighted in preparing our home for social times around good food accompanied by cups of steaming tea and amazingly delicious butter tarts—a staple in any Canadian diet! There was always room for all ages of people—young or old—and she would make everyone welcome.

Now, lest the reader form an opinion that my spiritual journey in its earliest years was filled with only negative experiences, I can recall great memories of much anticipated times spent at church camps. Stittsville Camp in Eastern Ontario was a super cool place where new friends and I could sleep in grass floored tents, construct crafts, play field games, and swim in a real swimming pool. It was always a week of fun and faith building centered in youth interests. I even spent one summer as a life guard there. Of course, I had no training for the job, but at least I could swim. Got me a lot of attention from the young ladies!

During the summers, my church denomination also held a Family Camp Meeting for seven days at the Light and Life Campground only 15 miles from Verona. Our family attended each service to be a part of the corporate worship led by special musical groups and then listen to speakers who opened the Word of God to instruct us in righteous living. Everyone sat on hard wooden benches with wood shavings under our feet. Meals were served cafeteria style in the dining room and the crowds were always large. My extended family unit had four tiny but uniquely designed cabins on the property where many hours were spent visiting and making great memories with cousins, grandparents, aunts and uncles.

It was also a spot where as a twelve year old, I was able to once again practice my driving skills by using a standard shift Volkswagen to chauffeur some of the older gentlemen to the restrooms. For the reasonable cost of ten cents, they could experience a round trip!

After camp meeting week was over, my Mum would extend our mini vacation into another week of adventure and fun right at that special place. There was even a moment of high excitement when one evening we heard that a convict had escaped from the Kingston Prison. At about the same time, a strange vehicle pulled up in front of our cabin on this relatively deserted meeting grounds. Mum was alone with three young kids, no phone, and no way of leaving so her tool of defense was a semi-filled chamber pot (an old-fashioned term for a pee pot)! The crisis was avoided when the car drove away! It would have been exciting to see Mum accost the wayward fellow with the full contents of the pot! What a story that would have made for the local paper.

For me, life in Verona moved along at a pretty steady pace and my days at Prince Charles School soon drew to a close. The next stop along my education journey was at Sydenham High School where a whole new world of opportunity was open for me to become involved in sports and studies. By this time, I had acquired my driving license and was tooling around town in a 1962 Austin Healey Bug-eyed Sprite. It was a dream to drive, and I enjoyed every moment behind the wheel. I bought it from the dealership, and it was my first car.

My commitment to sports was very evident as well as my struggles in the academics which were not a priority for me. However, I did excel in Mischief 101. My buddies and I did not fall into drinking or late-night party going, but we were creative in our activities. Probably the one I am most famous for was the time when Lynn Revell and I decided to NOT get off the morning transportation bus but precede on into Kingston to spend the day. This was the perfect day to skip school because when I left home my Mum had been sick in bed. The way was clear for a free day.

All went as planned so we could have lunch at the Superior Restaurant across the street from the movie theatre before our show started. At the end of our meal but before we could pay, much to our shock, into that very restaurant walked my mum and her friend—ready to enjoy their shopping day lunch! She had been healed. It was a miracle! Unfortunately for me, she saw us and proceeded to fill the entire air space with my name—"William Dale Revell!" In front of all the diners present, an unpleasant scene unfolded. We had been caught!

In no time at all with my mum leading the way, I found myself presented to the principal who enforced the punishment I was so familiar with by now. One week at lunch time standing along the wall right outside the office in plain sight for all who passed that way! It should have been named the Dale Revell Wall of Shame.

This incident was followed shortly by another stellar moment of stupidity when another friend and I conspired to open the window on the third floor of the high school and promptly launch the dreaded French exam papers out into the wind.

You're right! Another week holding up the Dale Revell Wall of Shame. Followed by a week of after school detentions. I'm sure by now my parents wondered if I would ever learn my lessons—academically and socially.

I am sure their prayers included many pleas for a miracle!

There were many bumps along the road during my high school days and mostly brought on by myself.

However, there were several positive times in my high school years when I had the privilege of attending an amazing youth camp just 15 miles from my home. Echo Lake had been the dream project of my Aunt Joyce and Uncle Earl Sears along with two other Christian couples. When they formed the basic structure of the camp on the shores of Echo Lake in 1956, they could not have realized what a key component of my spiritual journey this special spot would become. I enjoyed every detail of camp life—water skiing, intense team sports, midnight runs, campfire, home cooked meals which always included Chelsea buns, enthusiastic worship times, and speakers chosen to challenge us as young people.

Even the harshness of our Canadian winters could not deter us from gathering together at camp to renew friendships, play hockey or ice skate on the lake, take snowmobile rides, challenge each other in board games, eat those famous Chelsea buns, and be refocused in our walk with Christ. The staff dedicated their holiday vacation, summer vacation, and weekends to create a special place just for youth.

A highlight of my youthful journey.

On a side note, I especially enjoyed becoming acquainted with many of the young ladies in attendance.

My senior year, or as it is labeled in Canada, my Grade 12 year, finally arrived and graduation was an eminent event. People around me were making their future plans for marriage, vocational training, and college. My guidance counsellor met with my parents to advise them as to my future endeavors. He politely but firmly expressed his opinion that I did not have the academic ability to be successful in college. He felt my best chance at success was for me to continue at the dealership in job settings more suitable to my skill set. Mum and Dad were not pleased with his assessment, and they were determined that I should give college a try for at least one year. They asked me to follow my sister Glenda's choice to attend Spring Arbor College, a small liberal arts Christian college in Michigan. That sounded like a really exciting opportunity for me—college in America!

So, one fine fall day in August 1968 found me driving my aqua colored 1963 Ford Falcon west on Verona's Main Street, heading out of town to begin the 500-mile trip on a new part of my life journey. I was more than ready. Let the fun begin!

"THERE IS MEANING IN EVERY JOURNEY
THAT IS UNKNOWN TO THE TRAVELER."

—DIETRICH BONHOEFFER

1963 FORD FALCON COUP

SPRING ARBOR, MICHIGAN

Never in a million moments could I have imagined just what an amazing journey was ahead. Me—Dale Revell from small town Canada, driving unto the campus of an American university with a freshly issued Student Visa Card, my own gas credit card, a dorm assignment, class schedules, and FREEDOM!

Now, God was wise to have my older sister in place that year as she kept a close eye on my activities.

For that freshman year, my roommate was a fellow Canuck from Toronto area and our new friendship was a real blessing as he shared my enthusiasm for sports. He introduced me to soccer which I discovered was a popular sport on campus and one I thoroughly enjoyed.

We played together on the Varsity Team—the Cougars—and enjoyed traveling to other college campuses. There was a close camaraderie amongst the players as we were like a band of brothers within the parameters of the Christian setting. There were some pretty interesting characters on the team, but under the leadership of Coach Cliff McGrath, we developed into a cohesive unit and experienced great success over the four years I played.

Staying true to our Canadian heritage, Don and I, along with another fellow Canuck, also joined the Jackson Generals hockey team. Jackson was a small city just east of the Spring Arbor campus. The hockey team was a semiprofessional team composed of ex-players from Michigan State University and the University of Michigan. Many of our games were in various parts of Michigan and the state of Illinois. The team had a large following of fans locally and the arena was always packed for our home games. The local newspaper followed our season faithfully and it was exciting to read about our successes. Oh, yes, we had our share of losses too!

Probably one of the biggest highlights of playing for the Generals was the two games we played against the Detroit Red Wing Oldtimers which at that time included Gordie Howe, Ted Lindsey, and Jerry Able, son of Hall of Fame player, Sid Able. It was a thrill just to be on the ice with such great names from the sport I loved.

My new team also had its share of "characters" whose lifestyles and choices were certainly different from my upbringing. This was probably one of the moments when I was beginning to understand why my parents stressed the importance of developing a close walk with God. It saved me from a lot of bad choices which could have swerved me off the best road on my journey.

In the third year of playing for the Generals, I suffered a major shoulder injury and was unable to play that season. It was a discouraging time for me. In their wisdom, my folks had continued to pay my health insurance and I was able to have the corrective surgery. I will explain more details later of God's attention to every concern of our lives. My hockey days at that time were on hold until I could heal so I was honored when the management for the Generals asked me to take over as coach for the team. Suffice it to say, it was very intimidating as most of the players were older and more experienced than me. But it worked out well. Looking back, I can see that it was my first introduction to becoming a leader who could have a positive influence on others.

Of course, all college life was not composed of just sports events or social gatherings. My parents were working hard to make it possible for me to attend college, so I soon realized I would need to make some adjustments in my personal approach to academic learning. Class attendance, completing assignments, reading the material assigned, and preparing for exams were not to be ignored. It became very clear to me that if I wanted to continue to be eligible for soccer, I would need to take learning seriously. Now I knew I would never be an Einstein nor as smart as my sisters, but I definitely could apply myself better than I had done in high school. I can honestly brag that I was never on academic probation, a miracle of God's doing coupled with the fact that I was determined to prove my high school guidance counselor wrong. Believe it or not, I even frequented the library. And not just to check out the latest edition of the *Sports Illustrated*!

Building on the business example set by my father and my mother (who in later years established Glynelda Fashions, a very successful ladies fashion boutique in Verona), I chose Business Administration as my major. Once the basic required Liberal Arts courses were behind me, I could then concentrate on building a foundation for business leadership. Because of my lifelong interest in sports, a minor degree in Physical Education seemed an appropriate addition to my overall degree. The journey of a college experience was in full swing.

College life fell into a nice routine. Attend classes, play hockey and soccer, keep my car shiny clean, eat regularly in the dining hall, recruit my sister to do my laundry, and join the fellows for late night runs to Parma Truck Stop for steak sandwiches. Those trips were designed as study breaks, or at least that was the reason we gave to everyone who wondered where we were headed almost every night! There was some form of educational pursuit during these breaks but certainly lots of laughter and frivolity.

Now, you may be wondering why there were no gals present at our late-night trips. Well, the college had a curfew for the ladies at 10:30 pm during the week and midnight on weekends. It was the opinion of those in authority that we fellows would not get into as much mischief in the late evening hours if some sources of temptations could be controlled.

Just ask Adam! Everyone knows how much havoc a woman can cause. That is a joke, folks! I know better than to put that in print.

To say I enjoyed my freshman year would be an understatement! There was a freedom I relished, not to stray from my Christian heritage or convictions, but one which allowed me to experience decision making on the journey of taking ownership of my own personal faith separate from my parents. Weekly Chapel attendance was a requirement for each student, and I discovered that the speakers concentrated their efforts into presenting discussion topics and messages geared to young adult minds. The college church offered an additional avenue for faith building.

Now, lest the reader form the opinion here that I was on the path to celibacy, let me assure you that a healthy interest in the opposite sex was still clear on my radar. Like many young people experiencing college for the first time, I had a rather preconceived notion that, although I was now hundreds of miles away from "home" and involved in a totally different lifestyle, it would be possible to continue in the relationship with my high school gal. We would just have to write and call each other to keep the bond strong. My naivety was very evident as my parents even brought her to campus that fall to celebrate Homecoming and the crowning of my sister as Homecoming Queen! It seemed like the perfect arrangement in spite of the many miles between us.

Alas, during Christmas break, I was handed my walking papers and our relationship ceased to exist. It was an abrupt swerve in the road of my life journey which saddened me.

But just like He always does and as I was beginning to better understand, God had someone different in mind for my life. Earlier that fall, I was introduced to a young lady who was one year ahead of me. She was cute, funny, athletic, spunky, opinionated, and dating someone else. We immediately formed a friendship which was nothing I could have previously imagined. Our talks contained discussions on sports topics, class assignments, the differences in our church up bringing, and our present romantic interests. I remember lounging around the Student Union Switchboard area after hours while she worked the main campus phone exchanging laughter and campus gossip.

It was quite humorous to the other students when we adopted the habit of yelling greetings across campus by addressing each other by our last names. "Mawdesley!" and "Revell!" Her shopping expertise even came in handy when I had to select a Christmas gift for the Verona girlfriend, pre-break up of course.

It was great to have a friend who was a young lady I could respect and share a thought or two with apart from any romantic notions.

The Holiday school break found us each at our respective homes enjoying family and friends. Upon our return for the start of second semester, imagine my surprise when we both exclaimed, "Hey, you won't believe what happened! I got jilted!" We shared our stories of loss, shrugged our shoulders, had a good laugh, and then slid back into the comfortable friend relationship where we had left off. It was a nice feeling to have the security of Jane's friendship at this time.

Our mutual God must have had a pretty good chuckle as He watched us spend more and more time together over the next few months and be totally oblivious to the plans He had for our lives. It took a quick kiss initiated by Jane for me to realize we were more than comrades and I needed to step up my game. Wow! That was the beginning of a great journey which continues to this very day!

Of course, my parents were very interested in the details of my new sweetheart's personality and background. I supplied them with needed information on her years on the farm as a child, her educational interests, her family members, and her Baptist upbringing. There was some consternation over her belief of Eternal Security, but it was a minor difference once they had an occasion to meet her. And meet her they did on their next visit to campus.

During that winter season of my sophomore year at Spring Arbor, my parents motored down to visit with me. By that time, I was playing regularly on the Jackson General Hockey Team and Jane, and I were definitely considered by everyone on campus to be a dating couple. The initial plan was for my parents to meet my new girlfriend during the hockey game on the weekend they were there. As fate would have it, the game was being played on a Sunday night and this did not bode well with the parents as they had never agreed, while I was living at home, that Sunday hockey would be part of my activity schedule.

Therefore, they chose to remain at the hotel until the hockey game was over. However, as in all the plans of man, events can change at a moment's notice. While playing during the game, I unfortunately received an injury to my hip which required me to be transported to the local hospital in extreme pain. That left my new girl, my sister Sandy, and a college friend the wonderful task of returning to the hotel room to inform my parents of my predicament. I had fully intended for Jane to meet my parents over a very nice dinner and a setting in which they would have a chance to visit with her. It was not to be.

While someone else escorted my mom to the hospital, Jane had to meet my father in the parking lot of the hotel. Being a man of very few words and with Jane sitting beside him in the front seat, my father said absolutely nothing to anyone in the vehicle while he mulled over the playing hockey on Sunday dilemma. It was a very quiet ride for everyone in the car! One can only imagine my embarrassment and the awkwardness of the setting when I, lying on a gurney covered in a white sheet, had to introduce my parents to my new special gal. The ridiculousness of the entire situation was only compounded when my Mum embraced Jane and exclaimed, "Oh, Joan, Joan! What a way to meet you!"

Can someone say, "Awkward!" again?

Jane was a good sport, and we have all had a good chuckle over the whole event. I will add that she and my parents developed a deep love for each other over the ensuing years. I was blessed by their strong and loving relationship.

By this time, a new road sign had been posted along the lane of my life journey, "Thru Traffic" and I motored on ahead in confidence.

The remainder of that first year of college raced by as the days were filled with studying and classes, additional hockey games where my fan base had increased by one eagerly supportive blonde gal! There followed numerous social events on campus, and several weekend trips to our respective homes to continue establishing family connections. I had now been welcomed by Jane's relatives into a large, supportive family base comprised of many siblings and extended members. Their gatherings were always filled with much laughter, vigorous political discussions, great food, unsweet iced tea, green olives, and the occasional reference to my "Canadian" accent! All in good fun!

It was with mixed emotions that I greeted the approach of summer break that May '69. I was rejoicing in the successful completion of my first year as a college student but facing an abrupt change in the dating arrangement. It was to be a very long summer as both Jane, and I had to return home to pursue job opportunities. Once again, I traveled the road East while she headed North and pledged to continue building our love for each other through phone conversations, letters, and quick weekend trips back and forth. By this time, I was able to pilot a pretty sweet car—a 1965 soft yellow colored Mustang—and it could fairly fly over the 500 miles between Verona and Vassar.

For employment, I did not have far to search as my dad offered me a position back at the dealership and it was a good fit. When I was not planning my next Michigan excursion, playing ball with the Davey Drillers, or cruising up and down Princess Street in Kingston, I was filling various work openings at the garage. I remember one particular glitch in my plans when, in my youthful exuberance for Mustang speed coupled with a clear stretch of road in front of me, I gave the Pony her head and she promptly responded with a burst of energy which proceeded to cause a major malfunctioning within her engine. There might have been a partner in crime challenging me to a street race, but he shall remain unnamed.

Bummer! A blown engine was my reward for that moment of need for speed and a straight highway. And this right on the eve of that much anticipated first summer trip to see my gal. Well, once again with his calmness of spirit (He may have been reminded of his youthful experiences behind the wheel of a car!), Dad handled the moment with mercy and had the shop technicians again quickly fix the problem. I was soon on my journey westward and hopefully, a little wiser in my choices, or at least more aware of and heeding the "SLOW DOWN" sign being frantically waved by my assigned Guardian Angel.

I am sure my parents once again renewed their fervent prayers for my safety and for an increase in my maturity level.

By this time, I knew I wanted to commit Jane and I to a lifelong pledge to traverse whatever roads my life journey ahead would undoubtedly cover. It was with no hesitation that I used Glenda's wedding weekend to present Jane with a beautiful pearl commitment ring and rejoiced when she agreed to a more permanent arrangement at some point in the future. Our young ages were of some concern for both our parents, but they trusted in our decision.

Once our engagement was unofficially announced, it was brought to our attention that we just might be related!

What? How? When?

The answers to our questions could actually be proven on paper. Through the diligent research work and creativity of Jane's beloved Aunt Marion Barbour, there existed a family tree scroll complete with small oval photos of my future mother-in-law's ancestors. Its details were amazing and could trace back many generations with accurate dates of births, marriages, and deaths.

Imagine our surprise when there in black and white was my name, William Dale Revell, four generational lines below another Revell who also married into this huge family group. That wise fellow, Fleming H.

Revell, had fallen in love and married a young lady, Josephine Barbour in 1872 who was the great aunt four times removed of Jane. By becoming his wife, Josephine also became the sister-in-law of Emma Revell who was the wife of Dwight L. Moody, the American Evangelist renowned for his commitment to sharing Christ's plan for man's salvation through his many revival meetings in the USA and Britain. He also established the Moody Bible Institute in 1886 and Moody Publishers in 1894, both located in Chicago, Illinois. These two fine Christian men had jointly founded the Revell Publishing Company in 1870 to bring the Christian faith into the common man's life through printed material.

My side of that olden day's connection comes through my Dad's family who were distant cousins of those American Revells. There was even a family reunion in Kingston, Ontario which my grandfather remembered as having brought those Yankee and Canadian cousins together.

Thankfully, the kinship of my future bride and myself was through marriage. Not that I was concerned, but it does add an interesting detail to our mutual ancestors. And to think we even have a tie to the great, Dwight L. Moody. Interesting indeed!

And so, the crisp fall '69 weather found me once again heading West out of Verona, back to SAC, to begin training for soccer, adjusting to the studying routine, applying spit and polish to the Mustang, and escorting my gal around campus. When I realized that marriage was on the horizon, I began to take my education even more seriously with a definite focus on the Business major choice. Scholarly wisdom did not suddenly descend upon me, but it sure did help to have an English Major by my side who could assist me in that old nemesis—reading to understand content. Her only required reimbursement was the occasional toasted tuna sandwich from the Snack Bar or pizza from Sir Pizza in Jackson.

Ice Hockey once again filled my activity calendar when soccer season ended, but this time there was one spectator who was extremely special to me. Jane had grown up listening to the Detroit Red Wings on the radio as her family did not have a television, so it was fun to explain the rules and demonstrate the techniques. She quickly caught on to the action on the ice and added her voice to the crowd noises. It was a good season— both on the ice and off!

School ended and another summer found me back in Verona planning for Jane's next visit when I had plans to officially confirm our engagement. Humorously, I made my proper proposal request in the middle of the Kingston Grand Theatre as Sound of Music was playing on the screen. Not such a romantic spot with hundreds of other movie goers, but the moment was right. We began to make plans for an August '70 wedding in Michigan. Well, she and her mother made plans! I was just required to show up on time, say the right words, and not pass out!

After another busy summer of work and sports, I packed up the Mustang for the very last time, backed out of the driveway to head West, and returned to the familiarity of college life with the prospect of marriage some 13 months down the road. Classes progressed well and life seemed to be settling in on a steady, straight course.

When May of 1970 rolled around with the wedding scheduled for August 22nd, I decided to stay in the States for summer work. Fortunately, Jane's father was able to procure for me a position working on the assembly line at the General Motors Engine Casting Plant in Saginaw.

That was quite an experience for a young Canadian fellow who had never before worked in that type of setting. I certainly received an education of a different sort from my previous three years! Unfortunately, the only hours available were on the night shift. It was very good money, and I knew we would need every cent we could save as I still had two years of college left and Jane would be in her senior year of Education courses followed by unpaid student teaching.

For most of that summer, I spent more time during the day with my future mother-in-law than I spent with my future bride as Jane was hired on as a teacher's aide for a very intense daily educational program for children of migrant workers in the area. Our paths crossed when her work time was over and mine was just starting! Talk about a strange dating schedule.

But the end result was a joint bank account with enough money in it to allow us to purchase in Spring Arbor an 8x50 foot older mobile trailer complete with fiberglass drapes, wooden crates for storage, green appliances, a lovely (?) floral couch, an Antique Morris Chair, garage sale lamps, and a front door which would not lock. We referred to the decor as Early Salvation Army. The oil furnace was a rather interesting experience as it required one to fill the bottom with oil then light it by throwing in a burning piece of cloth. If we ran short of oil, we could always sleep on the kitchen floor in front of the gas oven. There was no telephone, but we did have a 12-inch black and white television.

The broken door lock was no problem as we just used a long rope to tie it shut by connecting its knob to the refrigerator handle before we exited outside through the back hallway door which required a huge leap as there were no stairs.

A humorous side note here—after our August 22, 1970, wedding reception, we left the celebration in grand style when Dad loaned me his gleaming, green Mercury Cyclone Demo complete with a high-performance engine and a sleek design. The road ahead was looking great as we headed to Detroit for our reservation at the sumptuous Dearborn Holiday Inn.

Imagine our panic, when shortly after leaving Vassar City limits there appeared in the rear view mirror the image of a familiar car which belonged to my Uncle Eldon Sears. For the next 50 miles or so, we played cat and mouse with him as he seemed to be enjoying the pursuit of the newlyweds. Could he possible follow us all the way our hotel? Finally, after reaching speeds in excess of 100 MPH, he turned off and we could breathe a sigh of relief.

We moved into our first home in Spring Arbor after a week-long honeymoon in—of all places, Verona. Our family cottage on Rock Lake was a perfect spot to introduce my new bride to the lake and community where all my extended family and boyhood friends resided. (And it was a free place which fit our tight budget well!) She fell in love with the place and the people. For that, I will always be thankful!

And so it was that I began my 3rd year of college with a new wife, a bright orange Volkswagen Super Beetle which my "older wife" had to sign for, and new roads to journey upon as I anticipated the future. My class schedule was much more enjoyable now as the topics were centered on my degree choices. Each credit earned brought me closer to accomplishing what I so desired. The proof that with the proper encouragement in the right setting (and lots of prayer!), anyone can achieve some success. All the miles of my life journey to this point had been leading me to a realization that the seemingly impossible can become the possible with the Father's steady guidance and a willing heart.

I am not sure what I imagined the married life journey would be like, but it certainly met and exceeded my expectations that entire year. The routines of my single young fellow days were altered to accommodate the amazing addition of a fun loving, spunky, creative, and happy (usually!) partner. We shared that old trailer in the Deering Road Park as if it was a luxury condo with a view of the Amalfi coast! Our financial budget was pretty limited, but who cared?

Grocery shopping together replaced Parma Truck Stop trips and I did not even mind. I had never been much of a chef or hung out in the kitchen, but now there was a better reason to frequent that area! There was always lots of laughter as we experienced the blending of two different family styles of cooking—the basic comfort foods from The Betty Crocker Cookbook used by every farmer's wife and those Canadian delicacies of lard pastries, sweet squares, and butter tarts.

If I made one big mistake in the early months as a husband, it occurred the evening I came home from soccer practice to discover Jane had spent the afternoon creating a pie—her first ever! Imagine my shock when said pie came hurtling across the kitchen in my direction and hit the window screen above the sink, slide into the dishwater, and finally came to rest submerged in dish soap bubbles! All I had just

"DOESN'T TASTE LIKE MUM'S PASTRY!" said was, "Doesn't taste like Mum's pastry!"

Believe me, those words have never been uttered by me ever again in 52 years of marriage! I was a fast learner in that department.

Our social calendar revolved around entertaining or being entertained by other married couples. Such evenings saw us playing intense card games while feasting on whatever foods we could all contribute from our kitchen cupboards. It was either a feast or a mini meal depending on who had what to offer. Some of our fondest memories of that year center on our dear friends, Danny and Paula Dutton, who shared with us many a night of rousing ROOK games. It was always girls against boys which brought out Danny's famous line, "You girls are going down the river road!" Rook enthusiasts will understand this one. These were always nights filled with laughter and good fun! Sometimes, the girls actually won!

Soon the fall semester started, and that year was a full academic schedule for both of us with Jane carrying the heavier load during the fall semester of demanding Education courses. Then would follow her second semester for Student Teaching one hour away in Marshall, Michigan. We fell into a pattern of classes, library work, soccer practice and games, part-time employment at Dowley Manufacturing, and the occasional movie when the budget allowed.

Now what the fledgling budget DID allow for was the addition of my first motorcycle—a sleek red 1960 Suzuki 250! What fun we had motoring around the Jackson area covering new roads full of twists and turns. Our sense of adventure far outweighed the usual dangers attributed to two wheels, no seatbelts, fast speed, and youth. Our Guardian Angel must have been very busy on those journeys! And once again my parent's prayers were ratcheted up for our safety.

Fall slipped into winter with the usual blasts of cold Michigan air and plenty of snow. Soccer season ending and I once again dug out my ice skates, hockey stick, and uniforms to take up the sport I had loved since childhood. The road between Spring Arbor and Jackson became very familiar to me as I traveled its route in great anticipation for an exciting season of breakaways and goal scoring.

Little did I realized that the first really big U-turn on my life's journey, one which would seriously sideline me, would come in the form of a broken collarbone and subsequent major surgery to graft hip bone to the site. On the hospital admissions day, imagine our shock when the pre-surgery down payment was $900! It might just as well have been $9,000 as our bank account was pretty meager. Some would say that as luck would have it, my Canadian insurance policy had been continued by my folks, but I know it was my God's provision.

The surgery was a success and I have already mentioned the coaching which allowed me to continue as a Jackson General until the next fall. It was the first really big challenge of trusting God, laying claim to my own faith, and walking through a crisis with my sweet wife who took on the role of caregiver for the first time.

The spring of 1971 found the Revell and Mawdesley families gathering for Jane's graduation. By this time, our bank account was in desperate need of refueling!

The answer came in the form of two jobs at a private golf course in Jackson where Jane worked during the day shift in the ProShop office, and I became the nighttime grounds keeper in charge of physically turning on the huge watering heads for each green. She was required to hand write monthly bills for 200 plus members as well as meet customers in the shop while I spent entire nights surrounded by eerie silence broken only by the rhythm of swishing sprinkler heads as shadowy animals emerged from the woods to frolic on the greens.

We both soon tired of this split work schedules and handed in our resignations in the dead of night after working together one dark and spooky shift. I am sure there was some surprise the next morning when the grounds keeper and the Pro Shop manager read our large "We quit!" message scrawled on the maintenance shed blackboard. It was a strictly impulsive immature move which left us with the question, "Now, what do we do?"

Well, the straight road to Verona beckoned us and we headed home once again to spend the remaining summer month with family at the lake. The best news came for us when Jane was offered an English and Physical Education teaching position for the fall at a high school some 60 miles from Spring Arbor. It would require her to drive one hour each way but was a real blessing to have such a good job in the areas she loved to study and teach. A minor downside to the long journey was the fact that our VW Beetle had no radio. Dad Revell saved the day as he supplied us with an 8-track player and many tapes of Christian quartet groups. We became very familiar with the Oakridge Boys and the Bill Gaither quartet as our road trips took us between Spring Arbor, Sand Creek, Vassar, and Verona.

The long drive, as well as her teaching responsibilities, became extremely tiring, so we took a big leap and relocated to Adrian, Michigan, closer to Jane's school. The actual move from the trailer to apartment was placed in the capable hands of myself and another college friend. Dan and I proceeded with abandonment and placed all our worldly possessions—dishes, clothes, furniture, etc.—into large black garbage bags which were then loaded into his Studebaker for the trip down south. Not sure how impressed Jane was with our packing skills but not one item was damaged. Miraculous!

Now it was my turn to do the long drive back to campus for classes and so out of necessity, the first motorcycle was traded in on a newer, bigger model—a Honda 350 to be exact. Well, at least that was my reasoning as explained to my wife! These bikes would become just the first two of seven motorcycles I have enjoyed while traveling down the journey trails of my life. If the Guardian Angel from my youth thought there would be a respite in the responsibility of providing protection once I got married, it was not to be. And when Jane strapped on a helmet for weekend rides, I am sure my parents once again increased the intensity of their prayers for safety as now there were two of us zooming around on those two wheels.

I must mention our apartment here! It was very big, brand new, and had a dishwasher! The Early Salvation Army decor received some additional pieces of antique furniture from a local shop, and we could even boast of air conditioning.

My last year at college was pretty sweet as I now had a new cool motorcycle, a healthy body to play sports again, and a working wife! Jane jokingly reminds me that she WAS the bread winner that first year. I think over the years I have paid my dues and then some. Good thing we have a sense of humor together!

Knowing this was my last year to be a college student, I enjoyed the times spent in class and with my buddies. Finally, in the spring of 1972, my parents were able to shout, "Praise the Lord!" as I walked across the stage to receive my college degree! It was the culmination of their prayers and trust in God's faithfulness, my wife's encouragement, and hard work on my part.

My folks were so proud that they posted a graduation announcement in the Kingston Newspaper back home. You can imagine their surprise when the high school counselor, who was so sure their son was not college material, saw the article and contacted them with an apology for doubting my abilities and dedication to higher education. If there is any good to have come from this type of pigeonholing it is in that, over the years, I have been able to use myself as an example of how unfair it could be to misread a person's potential and therefore possibly discourage growth or advancement. It was a dream realized. A personal goal accomplished. A new stretch of road ahead!

And what a journey that would prove to be as I had received an amazing job offer in Toronto, Canada with Ford Motor Credit Company! Unbeknownst to me, my dad in his wise manner as a businessman and father, had mentioned to the Ford Credit sales rep that I would soon be finished with college. After an interview at World Headquarters in Dearborn, I was thrilled to receive the offer for employment to commence in August.

I look back down the road I have come and am amazed at the faithfulness of my Heavenly Father to guide me along all of those twists, turns, potholes, and detours in my life journey in spite of my immaturity.

Thus, it was with great anticipation, some trepidation, and a sense of excitement in the future, we once again packed our Early Salvation Army household goods (this time in a U-Haul), headed across the Ambassador Bridge in Detroit due East on the 401 toward the big adventure in Toronto!

"GOD MADE THE WORLD ROUND
SO WE WOULD NEVER BE ABLE TO
SEE TOO FAR DOWN THE ROAD."

—ISAK DINESEN

THE FORD ROAD

DALE'S EXECUTIVE SUMMARY

NOTE TO THE READER

In my response to the next road sign to appear in front of me—"Alternate Route," there shall now appear in front of you my first 12 years of employment with Ford Motor Credit Company of Canada.

FORD MOTOR CREDIT COMPANY

- TORONTO OFFICE—August 1972-1974

- ADJUSTER—auditing dealer vehicle inventory for several months

- CUSTOMER SERVICE REPRESENTATIVE—collecting delinquent vehicle loans from customers and physically repossessing their collateral (money or vehicle) if unwilling or unable to pay monthly payments.

- BARRIE OFFICE—1974-1977

- ASSISTANT BRANCH MANAGER—manage office operations staffed with 15 persons. Responsible for all facets of dealer inventory financing and collection of all outstanding customer loans.

- OAKVILLE CANADIAN HEAD OFFICE—1977-1979

- MEDIUM AND HEAVY TRUCK FINANCING ANALYST— responsible for analyzing Medium and Heavy Truck financing requests received by Canadian Branch Offices from dealers and large fleet accounts.

- KITCHENER, WATERLOO—1979-1981

- FORD CREDIT DEALER SALES REPRESENTATIVE—responsible for all financing needs (inventory, facility loans, individual customer vehicle loan arrangements) of a select group of Ford and Lincoln Mercury Dealers in the K/W area.

- HALIFAX, NOVA SCOTIA—1981-1984

- BRANCH MANAGER ATLANTIC CANADA *(Nova Scotia, Prince Edward Island, New Brunswick, and Newfoundland)*—manage all facets of branch operations including dealer loans, customer/dealer vehicle financing, all loan collections, etc. with 20 employees.

- BUFFALO, NEW YORK—1984-1988

- BRANCH MANAGER—manage all facets of branch operations including dealer loans, customer/dealer vehicle financing, all loan collections, etc. with 25 employees for Western New York and Northern Pennsylvania.

That's It!

Well, after in-depth discussions with my writing partner, it has been brought to my attention that the previous summary, albeit concise and accurate, falls a little short of the intended purpose of this personal retelling of the journey of my life to date. Hence forth, the Executive Summary shall be expanded to include all those fascinating details which allow the reader to travel roads I have traversed. The retelling shall now commence!

"YOU LIVE LIFE LOOKING
FORWARD, YOU UNDERSTAND
LIFE LOOKING BACKWARD."

—SØREN KIERKEGAARD

1965 FORD MUSTANG

TORONTO, ONTARIO

What an amazing place! Toronto is a city of perpetual motion, mazes of streets shuttling millions of people coming and going, a streaking subway underneath looming skyscrapers of steel and glass, immense green spaces where folks of all ethnicities gathered to relax, museums and hospitals covering entire city blocks, countless apartment buildings intermingled with expansive neighborhoods, and shopping centers whose footprint could contain my hometown and still leave room for parking.

It was into all of this bigness, Jane and I entered—two young persons clutching college degrees and embarking on a great adventure upon which only God could possibly know the route ahead.

Housing was our first order of business, but where to look in such an immense city? The answer came from a least expected source—a

Loblaws Grocery Store. While looking over some apartment rental flyers at the checkout counter hoping to get an idea of where to start the search, we noticed a handwritten ad posted on the bulletin board. Someone was seeking to sublet their apartment and the address was practically right across the street from where we were standing. Two bedrooms, one bath, galley kitchen, hardwood floors, one parking space in the basement, and a big balcony directly overlooking the Don Valley Parkway. The tenth-floor location would afford us a wide-angle view of Toronto and keep us above the constant noise from the freeway which never empties of its contents! We snatched up this good deal and agreed to the sublet rental sum of $160 per month—a fee which seemed astronomical but necessary.

How exciting to move our "stuff" into this spacious spot with the assistance of Uncle Alfie Ball, Uncle Carmen Newcombe, and Dad Revell. They proved to be pretty good at packing the freight elevator from top to bottom while bantering back and forth about our newlywed status! The entire process of hauling our belongings from storage at Kingsview Free Methodist Church parsonage to a new home was quickly accomplished with relatively few broken pieces. Well, maybe not totally unscathed but then, one must never criticize volunteer help, especially when it is free and family.

The next step in our settling into city living was to locate a church where we could find our "spiritual" home. God had that all figured out so instead of us finding a church, the church came to us! The first night of our new living arrangement found us returning from a quick swim in the apartment pool to be warmly greeted by a couple and their two daughters with a welcome invitation to attend their church the next morning and come to Sunday lunch at their home. (Their son was at home recovering from consuming too many strawberries!) At that moment, little did we realize how very deep our friendship with Jim, Esther, Stephen, Laura, and Martha Elliott would become over the ensuing years.

These precious people became our adopted family, our soul mates, our wise mentors, our comforters, our secret keepers, our traveling partners, and most importantly, our dear friends. That first dinner led to countless meals together, Sunday afternoon model home viewings, Warden Avenue Free Methodist Church youth group gatherings, Echo Lake Youth Camp staff work, two mission trips to Haiti, good deal car shopping, Canadian Tire store excursions, and endless laughter. Our tears have blended together over sickness and sadness, but each painful experience has been balanced out by wonderful moments of joy over baby births, young people's salvation, family weddings, and always, laughter.

Their initial invitation to be a part of their church and share in their family life became deeply valuable to us and to this day, remains a precious treasure.

And so, with housing determined, friendships initiated, and a spiritual community to draw from, I entered the doors of the Forrester Building on Don Mills Road to begin my career at Ford Motor Credit Company. My expectations of what was to come in the development of my business employment escape me now, but I can assure you that I could never imagined where my work journey would take me over the next 33 years. For sure, I was nervous, insecure, eager to prove myself, and very thankful to have such an opportunity afforded me at such a young age!

What would the workplace look like once I exited the elevator on that specific high-rise floor where all the eyes of my fellow workmates would greet me? Ah, the new man on the job! Just a young buck with no experience starting on the bottom rung of a very tall ladder.

I took a deep breath, mumbled a quick prayer for courage, and found my desk. Thus began the next stretch of my journey introduced by that big, bold green light signaling—"GO!" God was giving me the go ahead to proceed full throttle and trust Him to help me weave through the unknown of the workings in a business I had witnessed first-hand growing up from the dealer perspective.

And start at the bottom I did as my first assignment was Collections! Everyone desiring to advance in this prestigious finance company was required to serve their time in this humbling, demanding position. Personally contacting car loan customers to inquire as to their intent to meet the requirements of the loan for which they had signed. In other words, "Pay up or give it up!"

For a young fellow like me who had never reneged on any debts, it was quite a shock that this type of behavior warranted an entire department staff. But I tackled the challenge of the position and forged ahead to be the best Collector in company history. My workday always started with a bumper-to-bumper drive from the apartment to the office—the usual journey for a Toronto business worker. There were no Starbucks or Tim Horton baristas offering early morning Joe along the route, a fact which will surprise all the coffee loving youngsters in the family. (That Canadian icon—Tim's—became popular several years later.)

We were a motley fraternity of collectors—all males, mostly college graduates, hard workers who understood the importance of self-motivation. No one was going anywhere up that corporate ladder without first proving he could handle telephone collections to reduce loan delinquencies and personal collection calls out in the field.

I quickly learned that, even though I was a Christ follower who embraced mercy and grace, my job would require me to hold folks responsible for their failure to complete their financial commitments to the company.

My bosses strongly reminded me that my future promotions would be determined by the extent to which I could help reduce delinquent accounts—either by payments or repossessions of vehicles.

At that time in the automobile business, collectors actually made "house" calls to retrieve payments or take possession of vehicles. One can only imagine what interesting situations we junior collectors found ourselves in when physically covering the expansive city and surrounding countryside. Often our solo calls were made after office hours into low rental apartments or government housing projects.

There were many times when I was extremely nervous and wondered about my safety. This uneasiness was the direct result of a disturbing experience I had one afternoon on a collection call. A young man had been repeatedly withholding his payments, so I was tasked with the job of receiving his funds or removing his car from his possession. Finding the correct home address on a one-way street in the city, I approached him by leaning into the open car door as he was sitting in his car which was parked in the wrong direction with engine running. He was not willing to rationally discuss the situation and immediately threw the car into reverse with the intention of escaping. In a surreal moment, I found myself being dragged under the car door as he accelerated rapidly. Only God saved me from serious injuries, as during the struggle I was able to turn off the ignition key and halt the car's progression. My previous skill at elbowing in hockey may have contributed to the success of my effort!

The tow truck driver who accompanied me saw the whole fiasco transpire and had called for police backup. I was a bit of a mess with torn clothes and bloody shins, but very thankful to be alive! After an arrest was made and car towed away, I limped my way to Jim and Esther's house where I was to meet Jane for supper. She was pretty shocked at my condition and not at all impressed with my current job requirements. She even suggested that danger pay should be included in my wages.

It was an eye-opening experience for both of us! People really can have a careless attitude toward others.

The driver? He was convicted of intent to cause bodily harm and deported to his native country after he stated in court that it was my problem if I had been seriously hurt. The judge was not impressed!

This crazy collection experience was soon to be followed by another one which may sound like something out of the movie *Deliverance*. Traveling back from a weekend visit to family in Verona, I received a phone call from the office to alert me to the location of a gentleman who had skipped out on his car loan payments and possibly had said car at a remote cabin near Algonquin Park. Would I be able to recover the car on my way back to Toronto?

Sure!

So, Jane and I drove into the area in the dark of night, found the cabin at end of long driveway in the deep woods, located the vehicle, and like characters from *Mission Impossible* and with the keys in the ignition, we legally stole the car! My last words to my blonde-haired accomplice were, "When you see me driving out the driveway, you take off and don't stop until we get to Toronto!"

LIKE CHARACTERS FROM *MISSION IMPOSSIBLE* AND WITH THE KEYS IN THE IGNITION, WE LEGALLY STOLE THE CAR!

Another successful repossession!

And all this was done with NO cell phones in hand! We would need to travel down many more roads for the next 20 years before cell phones assisted us on our adventures.

It is of importance here to mention that today Ford Credit Collections are handled at large call centers all over North America and repossessions are completed by licensed repo agents specifically trained.

We were a breed of Mavericks in those early days!

It was interesting work with strong levels of adrenaline rushes as we searched, located, and legally "stole" cars! There was always a degree of celebration in the office when repossessed vehicles were returned to the company compounds or overdue accounts closed with funds received from our rookie efforts. These celebratory after-hours gatherings would at some point include a six pack of some libation which would be welcomed by almost everyone. Well, almost everyone.

Now, this brings me to make a bold statement regarding my personal involvement in the above mentioned celebrating with alcohol. In my early youth, my parents had strongly encouraged me to refrain from the consumption of any form of alcoholic beverages as they had observed too many negative effects on individuals and families. It was not that they did not appreciate a good time of fun and fellowship. They were the epitome of fun, laughter, and good times. Because I respected their feelings, I did not drink.

Now, as an adult with the responsibility of forging my own set of behavioral guidelines, I once again decided to not drink. This decision did not in any way affect my attendance at company functions where I enjoyed the camaraderie of fellow workers. They were comfortable with my decision and always included me in whatever was planned. They even went as far as to include in the liquid refreshments the Lincoln of all ginger ale—Vernors. Just for me!

In fact, said drink was the root cause of a very humorous story which transpired during the company Christmas party our first year in Toronto.

Jane and I had a great time attending the event and were very appreciative when the hosts offered us our usual drink—Vernors—as an alternative to any stronger drinks. It filled the bill and smoothed over what could have been an awkward moment for us. My mum was interested in the party details and Jane shared with her the amount of Vernors we had consumed over the course of the festivities. Mum was immediately upset and shared with my dad that she could not understand why Jane would tell her that we had been excessively drinking at the party! Nothing was mentioned to us until Christmas morning during gift opening when mum presented me with a full length, handsomely designed leather coat with the promise that it was mine IF I stopped drinking!

Well, I did promise and then informed her, amidst gales of laughter from the rest of the family, that Vernors was a nonalcoholic ginger ale brewed in Detroit. She felt foolish and I got to keep the coat anyway! Another moment defined by laughter for years after. My mum was always able to share a laugh over some faux pas she might have committed!

My career at Ford settled into a productive pattern of collections and paperwork. It was challenging, rewarding, and stressful all at the same time. I will always be appreciative of those early years with the company when my bosses, observing my potential, created an environment where I could mature (remember I was only 22 years old at the time), and possibly move into a management role someday.

I am sure by now it is very plain to anyone reading this life journey that cars have always played an important role in the fabric of who I am. With this new position at Ford, I was able to drive vehicles from the company carpool thus eliminating the need to use a personal car during the week. Well, now I could seriously step up my car styles and models.

Soon a British Racing green Mustang Mach 1 Fastback with 351 Cleveland engine and Hurst four speed transmission replaced our copper colored 1971 Maverick Grabber.

The only thing which travelled up Young Street faster than that car was the wind. What a thrill it was to hunt out other unsuspecting drivers of lesser powered vehicles and give them a taste of speed. I thoroughly enjoyed that car. For sure, it was not to be my last new car!

Next to fill the parking spot was a 1974 Silver Cougar—speed replaced by comfort. Then full luxury came in the shape of a Silver 1975 Thunderbird with wire wheels and red leather interior. That was a classy ride!

Back on the road again.

Keeping true to our choice of staying connected to our spiritual roots, Jane and I had chosen to make Warden Avenue Free Methodist Church our faith center. It was such a great home for an amazing community of believers who worshipped together, accepted and served each other, and sought out people who needed special care. Our pastor was a young leader who had a missionary's heart which led him to organize a Spring Break mission trip for 30 parishioners to assist the church community in Port a Prince, Haiti. Jane and I were privileged to be a part of the planning team which organized the trip ahead of time and then later accompanied the entire team of 30 which included my sister, Sandy and her husband, Chet.

It seems as if from the moment we disembarked from our plane and proceeded into the city depths, God had definitely posted along the route the same two signs over and over, "STOP" and "LOOK OUT AHEAD." He wanted us to stop our Western lives for a moment in order to actually experience the people. It was an eye-opening experience like nothing we had ever experienced before or since. The obvious poverty under which these precious people were living gripped all our hearts as we worked side by side with locals to repaint and repair major structures on the mission station, hold teacher training sessions for their church school staff, sort donated clothing, and whatever else needed to be done.

The Haitian people became very dear to all of us and our concern for them continues to this day as it is evident that their daily lives are still in precarious states due to natural disasters, political greed, and illiteracy. It has been our privilege over the years to support Haitian children through several ministries.

Another added blessing to our Toronto living was it allow us to become staff members at Echo Lake Youth Camp near Verona. Yes, the same camp of my youth. Imagine how excited I was to return to that deeply treasured spot and introduce my wife to the all-volunteer staff who had witnessed my youthful exuberance, innocent shenanigans, and faith seeking moments. They welcomed her with open arms and lots of Camper Dale stories! She fit right in with her usual rambunctious enthusiasm and became an expert at mopping floors, whipping cream, peeling potatoes, and doing dishes.

Those years we served as staff members were so rewarding and gave us a totally different perspective on the deep commitment each person in leadership gave to each teen who came for long weekends and summer camp sessions. God richly blessed us with mature Christian adults who exemplified what true servants of Christ do—sacrificially serve, generously give, pray for, and accept young people searching for significance just as we had been only a few years prior.

Now back in Toronto, imagine my surprise just a few months after our mission trip, when my bosses approached me with my first offer of a managerial position at a small Ford Credit branch in Barrie, Ontario—up the 400 Highway, north of Toronto, and setting along the shores of beautiful Lake Simcoe. Wow! Such a chance for a young fellow only 24 years old. Assistant Manager! The new road sign read, "Express Lane," as God had my life plan in full speed ahead mode and Jane was in agreement that we should proceed to the next adventure.

"WE MAY GO TO CHURCH ONCE
A WEEK, BUT OUR CHRISTIAN
LIFE IS DAILY—STEP BY STEP."

—DAVID JEREMIAH

1971 FORD MAVERICK GRABBER

BARRIE, ONTARIO

So, one fine early summer day we headed out to travel up Highway 400 north of Toronto for our new assignment. This would be our very first company move and by that, I mean the company would send in professional packers who would pack our entire condominium and transport everything to our new home. No more U-Hauls or black garbage bags!! It was exciting for us to shop for a house and find a fairly new back split on a fenced lot that had three bedrooms, one and a half bathrooms in the middle of a family-oriented neighborhood. It was to be our first exposure to community living outside of apartment and condominiums. As soon as we were settled in, I began working in the office and Jane was able to locate a job for the fall teaching grade six.

Compared to Toronto living, residing in the delightful community of Barrie was an adjustment but not unpleasant. As always when we settled in a new area away from family, we immediately located a church which would offer us biblical teaching and Christian fellowship. The Barrie Free Methodist Church fit that bill to a T!

An extra special blessing at this church was the presence of a young pastor who in his youth had spent time with my family in Verona and was well acquainted with Echo Lake Youth Camp. We found him to be personable, caring, a seeker of God with sensitivity to Holy Spirit's leadings. For the duration of our short stay in Barrie, that church family as led by Pastor Carl Bull anchored us in the importance of service, laughter, and unconditional acceptance as well as firm biblical truths.

Probably the extra reason this church and pastor were so special to us was that they welcomed our first-born child, Cynthia Elizabeth Revell, into the world with great jubilation and excitement. Little Miss Cynthia decided to make her appearance on December 7, 1976, which also happened to be her mother's birthday! It was a crazy, exciting day which culminated in the delivery of our chubby, blue-eyed baby girl proceeded immediately by her father's prompt fainting in the delivery room. It was a bit chaotic to say the least! And I should note here that no one knew about such fainting until I mentioned it first several years later. My wife was true to her promise not to share this until I did.

At 26, I had now been blessed with the wonder of fatherhood with all its joy and mystery. What kind of father would I be? Was I capable of helping her grow up? Was I wise enough to identify her strengths and weaknesses as her life unfolded? Would she see me as a role model? Reflecting back on my early years, I suddenly realized that this parenting road I was turning unto had been traveled by my own parents with similar trepidation and doubt. How much more did I now appreciate their attention to my social and spiritual development. Just as they had bent a knee in earnest prayer for wisdom, I would need to do the same.

And what of the stunning Thunderbird you ask? Well, it was soon replaced by a beige 1975 Ford Granada four door which Jim Elliot and I purchased, along with three other "Good Deal" cars from a dealer bankruptcy. Don't ask me how happy my wife was going from luxury to a legitimate family mobile in beige no less! Necessity required adjustments.

And so, the learning curve began. Fatherhood and Work. It was like drinking from a fire hose!

My responsibilities at work ratcheted up as I was in charge of managing the office staff as well as the collection delinquency and repossession accounts. Sometimes it was extremely intense as I would need to make decisions about closing car dealerships that were forced to go out of business. That entailed selling their inventory and the mountains of paperwork which followed.

This part of the journey was often filled with many small curves and twists as I was learning to supervise personalities within the office, work more closely with upper management, and socialize with dealers and their staff at various functions.

Of course, at many social opportunities through my job position, there was always the offering of alcoholic beverages. For me it was not an issue to refrain from the consumption of alcoholic as I had made that decision many years back. In no way did I find myself judging others as I believed it was a personal preference either way.

However, my choice to not drink did seem to offend one gentleman in upper Ford Credit management, and he addressed his thoughts to me in the form of a reprimand that I made others feel uncomfortable or I might be offending them by not participating. There was even a suggestion that my career would not advance in the company if I continued to take the non-drinking stance. It saddened me that my personal convictions were being scrutinized, but I trusted my God to continue to lead me down the path he had laid out and designed specifically for me. If my choice to not drink affected my future advancement at Ford Motor Credit Company, then so be it.

I am jumping ahead in my storytelling here, but at this point I believe it would be appropriate to mention that at my retirement dinner in Omaha, Nebraska many, many years later, this same upper management executive apologized to me for his criticism of my unwavering commitment to refrain from alcohol consumption as he publicly acknowledged his respect for my integrity in the company setting. I don't share this smugly or with pride but rather as an example of how my God honored my decision.

Soon, we settled into an enjoyable pace of life with church activities, work, occasional trips to Verona for vacation, entertaining a host of family and friends, and the comfortable small city living that the Barrie area offered. I was expecting to remain at that branch for several years so you can imagine my surprise when I was offered another promotion back to the greater Toronto area.

As I matured in the company, I was beginning to see that others were recognizing my managerial potential. It became quite clear to Jane and me that we would need to adjust our thinking and adapt to the likely possibility that there would be many address changes ahead of us. Her mother humorously commented several years later that her address book under the letter R was like a flow chart for all our relocation moves and she only penciled in each new address as it would more than likely change before any ink had dried. So true!

1973 FORD MUSTANG GT

BURLINGTON, WATERLOO, ONTARIO

Soon on the horizon loomed the Burlington city limits sign marking our next assignment. Burlington is a city by its own right but falls under the greater Toronto area geographically. Once again, the road we would be traveling upon was interwoven with the hustle and bustle of big-city traffic as well as tourists heading to and from the Niagara Falls area which was not far from our new location. It was not an unpleasant area in spite of being in a city setting as its southern boundary was the waters of Lake Ontario.

My job assignment was at the Oakville Head Office for all of Ford of Canada and it was extremely exciting to be a part of this vibrant, progressive company. I assumed the position of the Manager of Fleet accounts and had many opportunities to interface with senior Ford Credit management. Before long, this position metamorphosed into regional sales manager through the Hamilton branch and my territory enlarged to include the area around Burlington, Toronto, Hamilton, and Kitchener-Waterloo. It was my responsibility to call on Ford dealers to arrange training for their sales staff in handling retail finance and leasing for vehicles. Dealer mortgage and inventory financing also fell under my responsibility in the assigned territory. It was a fascinating time and challenging as I interfaced directly with dealers and their staff. That kind of personal involvement required that I also attend golf tournaments, hockey games, and entertain dealers outside of the workplace. That wasn't all bad!!

By this time Cindy was a very active, cheerful, and delightful toddler. Jane and I made the decision that there was not a need for Cindy's mum to work outside the home, so my two girls enjoyed wonderful days of exploring the Burlington area with its beautiful parks, playing together at home, and entertaining family and friends. As a family, we enjoyed worshipping and serving at the Free Methodist Church in Hamilton where we were privileged to become involved with the youth program and Jane enjoyed singing in the choir.

It seemed like an almost perfect life until we were confronted with a fairly serious health situation in our little girl's life. Without much warning, Cindy began to experience petit mall and grand mall seizures which on several occasions required hospitalization. It was a very frightening time for us as there did not seem to be any recognizable cause. At that time the standard treatment for childhood seizure issues was continuing observations paired with daily anti-seizure medications.

As relatively new parents, we learned very quickly to do our research, ask questions, and stay keenly aware of our child's medical history.

To be sure we were challenged by the "Why?" of our child's condition but chose to hide our fears behind a mask of resolve that God was in control. It seemed to be the face that Christians with all the answers in verse form through Scripture would project in times of suffering. Little did we realize that there would be many more severe twists and turns ahead for us which would even more strongly challenge the very foundations of our faith.

Because more and more of my dealer responsibilities required me to travel on the road Monday through Friday, it was decided by management that our home base should be in the Kitchener-Waterloo area. So, six weeks before the arrival of our second child and in the middle of a wild snowstorm, we moved to Waterloo—65 miles west of Toronto. The area was fringed by Amish Communities with large farms, quaint markets, small town atmosphere, and very friendly people. What a nice break from the traffic snarls of Toronto. The Hamilton office became my command center so I could now interact with the dealers in a more relaxed setting and still make it home in time to be a part of the family activities.

And active is the word! For not long after settling into our white and rose-colored two-story cookie cutter square house with the little front porch and the chain-link fenced backyard, we welcomed with great delight a chubby faced little boy! He was christened "This Baby" by his curious sister but we settled on the name—Matthew Dale! He was a very handsome little fellow with extremely blue eyes and chubby, chubby cheeks. I am very proud of the fact that with this birth, I did not faint!

He was the very calmest of babies who observed everything his sister did and usually responded with squeals of laughter. He greatly enjoyed watching from the safety of his walker as his high-flying sister entertained him with cartwheels, clownish antics, songs of joy, and the occasional sharing of her treats. Great was my blessing at the end of a long, long travel day dealing with Dealer issues, when I pulled into the driveway to be greeted by their little, sweet faces pressed to the front door glass just watching for my arrival knowing there would an evening of time together. Cherished moments for sure!

Our new life in Kitchener-Waterloo settled into what would become the pattern of our relocation moves with the company. After determining the area for housing and potential school choices we immediately sought out a church where we could become active members of a believer's community. Because so many of our moves required us to be away from family, these fellow believers became our friends and support system. Within the setting of the Kitchener-Waterloo Missionary Alliance Church we found people who invested in us as a family and helped us carry burdens during our stay in that area.

My work at Ford Credit continued at a steady pace as I travelled many, many miles to call on dealers and work on situations which would come up in their business plan. This would require me to be on the road away from my family, but I was very thankful that once again Jane was able to stay at home with the children and create a positive, all be it loud and crazy sometimes with two small children, home atmosphere where there was an acceptance on my wife's part for the long hours which my position required of me.

The road upon which we now travelled seem to be on a pretty steady course with few bumps under our wheels. However, this was soon to change as shortly after Matt's first birthday and on a sunny Easter Sunday morning we set out for Toronto to spend the day with Jim and Esther's family. Upon arriving at their home after the one-hour trip from Waterloo, we were shocked to awaken the children from their slumber in the backseat and discovered that the entire side of Cindy's face was completely swollen. It was as if in front of our eyes she had transformed from a slim little gal into a swollen shape as the fluid retention moved into her tiny little tummy and legs.

The very next day we sought the medical attention of a doctor in Waterloo who was as stumped as we were about her condition. His suggestion was for us to force-feed her due to protein loss and wait and see what happened. In our extreme fearfulness we asked God what we should do when it seemed as if she was progressing even further into some unknown condition.

In great desperation, we made the decision to drive to Toronto Sick Children's Hospital and present her to them for immediate help in determining what was happening. That is exactly what we did.

THE SIGN ON OUR ROAD JOURNEY DEFINITELY SAID, "DETOUR AHEAD"

The sign on our road journey definitely said, "Detour Ahead."

It became obvious to the physicians that this was not an ordinary case and under their direction we would embark on a one-month journey of intensive medical investigations, testing, and consultations. Sick Children's Hospital is a teaching hospital where physicians from all over the world come to study. And over the course of that month many physicians studied our daughter.

Words cannot describe what kind of experience this was for all of us as I had to continue in my work position traveling around Ontario, Jane needed to be with Cindy at the hospital, and Matt needed daily care. The housing situation for Jane was resolved by Jim and Esther's offer of her staying with them while my mother-in-law arrived to spend that month with Matt at home.

It was a very difficult time for me as I was torn between my responsibilities at work and my concern for my family. I did my best to be at the hospital in the evenings to relieve some of the pressure on my wife and then to travel back home the hour and a half to two-hour trip to reassure Matt with my presence. The hospital staff determined that Cindy could come home on the weekends as it would be easier for our family to manage. It for sure was a great mystery to all who were involved in her care.

Our families and friends in the US and Canada stood beside us and surrounded us with their prayers as everyone waited out the results of testing and medical opinions. To say that our faith was tested sounds trite and yet it certainly was. When there are no answers to our questions, we often are tempted in our human weakness to begin to question our Father's care and concern. Many a night I asked the Lord for His direction and for a miracle. Sometimes on a journey you just have to keep plugging along and hope that answers will appear. Step followed weary step.

It seemed so unfair that this little girl had to go through this experience without any rhyme or reason. At the end of that one month, the doctors gave us a rather broad diagnosis and we took our little gal home. Our faith had been shaken, but in some ways deepened because we had no answers and we're beginning to see that even though we had both been raised in deeply religious homes and supposedly knew all of the answers to the usual faith questions, we didn't really have a handle on the "Whys" of life. What we had learned through all of this was how extremely important family, church, and community are when one is facing a crisis. Once again, this was one of the steps in our journey to take possession of our own faith and understand the workings of the Holy Spirit as our Comforter in daily living.

Over the next year, Cindy's health fluctuated between the ebb and flow of fluid retention, so her physicians established a wait and see pattern. In spite of her diagnosis, she continued to develop into an active, positive youngster who never let anything stand in the way of enjoying life! Nothing was going to stop her from grasping hold of every moment and, regardless of the risks, run with the wind in her hair and fun in her laughter.

Then, shortly upon the resuming of our life as a family, my company offered me an unbelievable opportunity. Would I be willing to accept the position of Branch Manager for Atlantic Canada operations which would include Newfoundland, Nova Scotia, New Brunswick, and Prince Edward Island? This was a huge step for me by which, if I accepted the position, it would make me one of the youngest Branch Managers in the history of the company.

I called Jane on a Friday after receiving the offer and asked her if she'd like to move. She is always up for an adventure so agreed that it seemed like a good idea. Her question was, "And by the way, where would we be moving to this time?" My answer was Halifax, Nova Scotia, Canada—1,100 miles east of Toronto! Without a moment's hesitation, she announced, "You're on, let's go!" I have always been thankful for my wife's enthusiasm for the development of my career and her willingness to handle our relocation processes.

That very Monday morning and typical of corporate moves at that time, I left for Nova Scotia knowing that she would arrange for the move, pack up the kids, and join me as soon as possible.

Wow! What an adventure was ahead for us.

"HEALING DOESN'T MEAN THE DAMAGE
NEVER EXISTED. IT MEANS THE DAMAGE
NO LONGER CONTROLS OUR LIVES."

—UNKNOWN

1975 FORD THUNDERBIRD

Seven

NOVA SCOTIA, CANADIAN PROVINCE

Maritime Canada is a uniquely vibrant spot bordering the Atlantic Ocean with its crashing waves, fishing communities, bustling cities, and people proud of their heritages. For many years, there was an unspoken term given to anyone born outside of the Maritimes. That person would be considered as a person from "Away" who would not understand a Maritimer. And here I was, a man born in Ontario and married to an American woman! I soon realized I would have to adjust to some of these reasonings and prove to them that I could be trusted. This is spoken with some humor also!

Living in the Maritimes for our family was an absolutely wonderful experience. Having come from a land loving family and especially Jane with her farming background, to have the ocean at our disposal was phenomenal. When we first moved in, actually upon the first night in our home which I had purchased without my wife's viewing, our two small children came rushing into the house at nightfall yelling at the top of their lungs, "Call the fire department! There's a fire down the street!" We all rushed out and discovered that it was not smoke but rather fog literally rolling up the street. That evening we lay in our beds and listened to the mournful sounds of fog horns echoing across the expenses of Halifax Harbor.

Much to my relief Jane approved of my housing choice and immediately set about settling us into our new community. Because Newfoundland was one of my territories, within the first month or so of my family's arrival, I had to make a visit to that fascinating island. It was like nothing I had ever seen before. Fishing village upon fishing village upon fishing village filled with houses painted in very vibrant pastel colors. I was struck by the friendliness of the people and their creativity in their lifestyles. If someone wanted to open a bar, they simply hung out a sign, moved their furniture around, and opened their door for business.

I have learned over the years being a businessman who was required to be away from my family that a man's wife carries a tremendous responsibility to maintain the family mental and physical health. My wife was required to make many decisions without being able to contact me because at that time cell phones were still non-existent. That first trip I took to Newfoundland proved how resourceful my wife was in emergency situations.

One day only a few weeks into our new neighborhood the children were outside playing in the backyard on an old swing set left by the previous owners. Somehow in the action of Matt swinging on one of the swing contraptions and the children climbing all over the structure, Cindy almost completely cut off the end of her finger. Jane did not have any idea where the closest hospital was nor how to get there, so being a resourceful person, she called 911 to get an ambulance for transportation to the hospital (which was across the harbor in Halifax proper).

That left Matt by himself, so she promptly scooped him up and ran two houses down to pass her son off to the lady who answered the door. The ambulance whisked my girls off to the hospital where a plastic surgeon reattached the tip of Cindy's finger.

From that moment on, there developed a deep friendship between Jane and Bernie Burgess, the woman who had graciously watched our son in the hour of need. They became fast friends! God has a way of supplying for us at exactly the right moment the exact person we need.

Once I received word at the office in Newfoundland and determining that things were under control, I proceeded with my business, and then made plans to head home. However, or as luck would have it, nature decided to throw a curve into my plans by shrouding St. Johns in dense fog so I could not fly home and then placing an iceberg in the Harbor so I could not take the 17-hour ferry ride back home. Definite roadblocks on those two lanes of travel—sky and sea!

Obviously, the weather finally cooperated, and my trip home followed after a few days of experiencing Newfoundland's friendly hospitality.

Our family's time in Nova Scotia is rich in memories of picnics on rustic beaches where we searched for shark egg sacs, sea urchins, whole sand dollars, pieces of colorful sea glass, pearl lined oyster shells, and smooth driftwood. We even were able to pick wild cranberries growing in bogs nestled along Lawrence Town Beach where the surf was extremely strong and powerful.

Of course, there was always fresh fish. Our first experience with that came one evening when a man in a truck drove slowly up our street offering fish for sale. Jane's parents were there, and we decided to treat everyone to fresh Atlantic fish. It wasn't until the man delivered to the front door the newspaper wrapped fish that we realized it was the whole thing. Not fillets like we were accustomed to in Ontario from the grocery store! A whole fish! It is a good thing Jane's father knew how to fillet the whole fish because I sure didn't know how to do it in spite of all the fishing done on Rock Lake in my youth.

I don't think our family will ever forget the time our dear friends, Gary and Pat Langley, invited us to take our very tiny travel trailer with them along with their great big trailer down to the ocean where his father lived. We spent an entire weekend right on the ocean and had the amazing opportunity to visit Goat Island directly off the shores from the house. Gary's dad rowed all of us out to the island in his wooden dory where we spent the better part of the day investigating the riches of this abandoned island. We even discovered an entire seal skeleton devoid of flesh and bleached white by the sun. At my wife's request, Gary's son hauled a wooden lobster trap all over the island and back to shore where it became part of our material possessions and accompanied us on several more moves over the years. A trophy of our successful ocean trip with no lifejackets for any of us!

During our three years in Nova Scotia, Cindy eagerly started school which allowed Matt and his mum special time to explore the area even more! Their morning routine was structured around a daily trip to the nearest Tim Horton doughnut shop where the manager would greet them and offer Matt one of his special creations—a Tim Man roughly shaped like Mickey Mouse!

One early morning, they parked near Halifax Harbor where they could claim a spot along the route of Britain's Prince Charles and Lady Diana who were visiting Canada for the first time as a married couple. The royal motorcade rapidly approached their curb side perch, then slowed down almost to a stop. Much to my wife's delight, Lady Diana leaned around her husband to wave at Matt. As the limo moved away, Matt promptly said to his mother, "Now can we get our doughnut?" (Doughnut love is an inborn trait of all Revells I am convinced!)

These times were very special for mother and son as preschool was not to his liking which was perfectly ok with us. Matt was a sweet natured lad who loved to ride his bike and play Dukes of Hazard with our pastor's son, Andrew. They were often observed (and caught!) re-enacting the climbing out the car window scenes-just like on the TV show—using Jane's cars! Many an adventure was lived by these two as they were joined by another young boy from down the street and roamed the neighborhood spying on the six girls who they claimed tormented them.

WE ALL FELT FATHER'S CALLING TO USE OUR TALENTS IN VARIOUS WAYS TO ENCOURAGE OTHERS IN THE FAITH

Speaking of the pastor's son, I am reminded of the great times we had at our church of choice, Hillside Wesleyan Church. The folks there became dear, dear friends as we all felt Father's calling to use our talents in various ways to encourage others in the faith. It was my pleasure to drive the church bus every Sunday to pick up children and families interested in attending services. A fast-paced Junior Church Program was developed for children ages 5 to 12 years with the older youth serving as music leaders as well as puppeteers. Jane enthusiastically headed it up and I served as the official crowd controller. Some Sundays we could have as many as 120 energetic youngsters, and I knew then why God had not called me into the teaching role—at least not with children and they were sometimes squirreling around! My teaching skills rested more successfully with adults.

Our three years in Nova Scotia were rich in work related experiences and the fellowship of great friends as well as many visitors from "Away." We enjoyed entertaining folks as we never tired of driving along the ocean, serving fish chowder, exploring historical sites, and just embracing the lifestyle of the Maritimes. By 1984, I was ready to continue my upward corporate climb and explore new territories open to me. During one visit to our branch by Ford Credit CEO at that time, I inquired of him concerning the possibility of any management opportunities in USA operations. He responded, "If you can get a work visa and a green card for entrance into the States, then let me know." At that time, this was not a normal career path for Canadian Ford employees.

I think there was some amazement on the part of Senior Management when, after a successful lengthy immigration process, I did receive a ninety-day window in which to obtain a permanent job in the USA! There immediately followed my interview for the position of Branch Manager in Buffalo, New York. It was a great day of celebration when I was offered the position and officially accepted!

We were heading to Buffalo!

Well, at least, I was.

For some reason, it took my family a bit longer to get clearance, but after many glitches, they each received their passports and began to put together plans for the moving vans to once again park in front of our home ready to receive our worldly possessions for the long journey across the border. This would count as our 5th company move, so Jane was getting very experienced in directing moving companies.

My new position commenced January of 1984 before the house sold so the family stayed behind until March. Because of the currency exchange rate between the two countries, this move would personally cost us over

30% of our home equity. Despite that expense, we were still very excited to proceed down the road only God could have opened up for us.

Before I travel down the next stretch of road on this journey to share the steps I have traveled, I would like to pull over at the "REST AREA" sign and reflect on all these years you have been reading about. Other than some occasional sputtering of disappointments, physical setbacks, and unfortunate happenings, my life journey had been up to this point a relatively smooth one. My Christian faith had been based on memorized verses of Scripture, short seasons of prayer, the occasional mission volunteering opportunity, regular church attendance, and my personal attempt to walk a nearly perfect path of faith drawn from what I believed the Lord required of me to earn that, "Well done, thou good and faithful servant" award someday. I was not a boastful man, just proud of my work ethic, family values, amazing children, adventure loving wife, and my role as a business leader.

But no previous job, family, or faith experience could have ever prepared me or my family for what was developing right around the next corner.

"GOD NEVER SAID THAT THE JOURNEY WOULD BE EASY, BUT HE DID SAY THAT THE ARRIVAL WOULD BE WORTHWHILE."

—MAX LUCADO

2012 CHEVY CORVETTE

BUFFALO, NEW YORK

Situated at the eastern end of Lake Erie and most famous for its proximity to that great natural phenomenon of Niagara Falls, the city of Buffalo was going to be a fascinating place for our young family. Our excitement at relocating there was magnified by the closeness to our families and friends on both sides of the USA/Canadian borders. No longer would we be required to travel great distances by car or plane to spend quality times together. There were new places to explore, foods to enjoy (beef on weck, those famous Buffalo wings accompanied by a huge rectangle shaped pizza, and Polish paczki (donut like pastry covered with powdered sugar or icing) just to name a few family favorites).

Wait, I am getting ahead of myself here in the story salivating over the area's delicacies!

As I have previously mentioned, my arrival in Buffalo was several months before the family arrived, so I was given a corporate housing allowance and booked into the locate Red Roof Inn. Now, I will only comment on this housing arrangement to mention that it was at corporate expense. That will leave much to the reader's imagination as to my satisfaction at the conditions under which I resided. Adequate, but not the Ritz Carlton!

Without a moment's hesitation, I accepted the challenges of a new work environment in a new country and a new set of employees whose working environment and job security would depend upon my role as their Branch Manager. Would I be ready for a new problem-solving paradigm in the setting of the USA Ford operational processes and procedures?

It seemed amazing that 12 years before, I had left the States as a fresh out of college newly married fellow and now was returning as a 34-year-old father of two young children who had worked his way up the corporate ladder to reach this landmark spot.

Once again, I was reminded of all those past years in my youth and college days when my parents, with their great wisdom and lifestyle examples based on a deep personal walk with Jesus, had encouraged me to make decisions and choices based on biblical teachings. I am sure there were many times when they felt like some of their instructions fell on deaf ears, specifically my ears!

These precious parents of mine were never afforded the opportunity to attend college. In fact, their educational endeavors academically ended after ninth grade as both of them needed to secure permanent full-time jobs to support themselves and assist their parents. My heart will always be indebted to them for their dedication to encouraging me to take life seriously and examine my daily decisions based on wisdom they had acquired through a dedicated reading and following of Holy Scripture.

Proverbs 16:10-15 (MSG) falls into place here.

> *"A good leader motivates, doesn't mislead, doesn't exploit. God cares about honesty in the workplace; your business is His business. Good leaders abhor wrongdoing of all kinds; sound leadership has a moral foundation. Good leaders cultivate honest speech; they love advisers who tell them the truth. An intemperate leader wreaks havoc in lives; you're smart to stay clear of someone like that. Good tempered leaders invigorate lives; they are like spring rain and sunshine."*

One of my first challenges on the new job setting was to evaluate the working conditions of my staff. The Buffalo Ford Credit Branch was definitely outgrowing its present physical working facility, so I proposed to corporate management that we consider relocating to a new facility which could accommodate our expanding business. They agreed with my wisdom in this decision and gave me the go ahead to proceed with locating the new spot for the office and actively engaging the renovation process of said facility. It was an exciting time as we were able to acquire a brand-new office space and design it to the specifics of what we needed to continue our best business practices.

I think at this stage in my career development, I was beginning to understand the importance of process improvement. I enjoyed the challenges of studying a situation, laying out all the options, and actively moving in the direction of new programs of operation and yet staying within the boundaries of practicality and budget.

My role as Branch Manager was definitely a challenge, but one that I embraced with enthusiasm. The Branch Manager's responsibilities covered all staff development, increasing volume of dealer business for existing dealers, recruiting new dealer business, assisting in the training of dealership staff, and analyzing dealer financial strengths or weaknesses. Was it without serious problems? Of course not! But I found that I enjoyed going to work almost every day with an understanding that I had the backing of my praying family, a heritage of workplace integrity, and the assurance that the Lord was directing the path upon which I was traveling. There were some nice perks also to my new position as I was able to select a company car for business and pleasure use as well as car lease options for my family.

By this time in my life story, it should be obvious that cars have always been an attraction to me. So, I was very pleased when a sleek black and gold Lincoln Continental Mark 1 graced my driveway! It was a dream to drive for luxury and style. It was definitely a step up from the Crown Vic "boat" I had been issued in Nova Scotia.

IT WAS A DREAM TO DRIVE FOR LUXURY AND STYLE

It was with great anticipation that the date arrived in March when my family would be joining me as we would receive the keys to the new house we had purchased on McNair Road in Williamsville, New York, not far from my office location. This residence represented the tenth new mailing address for Jane and me in our married life so far! At this point I think Grandmother Mawdesley just went out and purchased a separate address book for the Dale Revell family as her current book was becoming tattered and torn with all that erasing under the letter R!

Now, as I have previously mentioned, I am very fortunate to have a wife who loves new adventures and, I might add, especially house hunting. In the car business, there is always a sense of humor about people kicking the tires of the car upon inspection with the intent to purchase. Well, my wife has developed and perfected that specific process of house hunting into a new art form complete with her own style of "tire kicking."

After purchasing a house once in Ontario where, when you sat in the living room and someone flushed the upstairs commode, you were positive that the entire contents of that rushing water sound cascading through the drain pipe embedded in the wall directly behind your head was going to wash you entirely out of the living room; my wife became an expert at testing all toilets in any homes she was considering. She is too classy of a lady to have people think she "used" each toilet in every home; she just announced beforehand that she was performing flushing tests. Much to the chagrin of many a real estate agent, she would open windows, turn on water taps, check behind refrigerators, inspect foundations, check all closets, and talk to neighbors if possible. Many a raised eyebrow was projected in her direction, but her method worked!

For sure fixer upper homes were never on the list as neither one of us was willing to tackle anything beyond occasional paint projects. We are true supporters of all local trades men who can accomplish any renovations with our financial support.

The task of judging a neighborhood is often difficult with just the quick sweep of an eye, but somehow Jane seemed too able to know what would fit our needs each time.

Our family has certainly benefitted from that skill set and the Buffalo home was a winner for sure. I had set a maximum budget for our purchase as we had lost quite a bit of investments with the exchange on our Canadian dollars coming across the border. Our real estate agent had set up several houses to look at on McNair Road and after checking out one house, Jane observed a beautiful home directly across the street that had just come on the market. Said house was of course at the top of our budget. Undeterred, Jane and the real estate agent entered the home and there was no going back. Every other viewing appointment for every other house in Buffalo was canceled. From front door to back door, from top to bottom, from side to side this house captured my wife's heart and before I knew it our move-in date was upon us.

Such excitement as we waited at the empty, new house for the first sighting of the moving truck pulling down our street to deliver all of our worldly possessions! According to the official paperwork from the moving company, we could expect this process to take all day and possibly a few hours the following day.

Well, the noon hour came with no truck in sight. The afternoon hours crept along and still no large, lumbering vehicle approached our location. There soon arose a bit of concern on our part as to the delay, so a quick call was placed to the moving company for an update.

A very long silence greeted us as the dispatcher was rendered speechless.

There was no truck present at 125 McNair Road, Williamsville, New York, and men scurrying around unloading an entire household of the Revell Family treasures. At that point, even the moving company did not know where their truck was!

The evening hours brought us the realization that somewhere in the contiguous United States of America was an extremely large motor vehicle pulling an oversized moving van completely off course and basically LOST (at least to us)!

The Buffalo relocation move would go down in the books as our most unusual and stressful one! But the next morning brought good news. The mystery was solved! Seems our two drivers had never been outside the

Maritimes and had discovered that one of them had relatives in Upstate New York. So, for the past two weeks our possessions had been safely parked in a driveway where a family reunion was being held.

Dispatch quickly reissued delivery orders and soon our house was bustling with activity. Needless to say, there were many apologies handed out from everyone connected to the moving company. Sometimes one just has to take life in stride and make the best of it.

With that crisis behind us, we settled into a nice routine for the duration of early spring. I headed off to work, Cindy scurried off to finish first grade at local public school, Matt and his mother roamed the local neighborhoods in search of donuts (and other interesting spots!). The entire area of Buffalo proper was filled with amazing

THE ENTIRE AREA OF BUFFALO PROPER WAS FILLED WITH AMAZING PLACES TO EXPERIENCE ...

places to experience, and each weekend found us doing just that. There were even some excursions by my wife and kids to several famous cemeteries which encouraged visitors with tour guide manuals of the famous and infamous buried there. One side trip found them standing in the cremation building whereupon they quickly exited when it was realized the posted sign said, "Keep Out!" and certain processes were happening right before their eyes. Some paths are best not traveled!

Downtown Buffalo was in the beginning phase of reconstruction after the closings of many steel plants. It was interesting to see the progress of new parks, marinas, and businesses.

Of course, it was super great to entertain our Verona/Kingston/Michigan families as well. We were blessed to have a house which could accommodate lots of folks. Pizza and wings were always on the menu!

Nothing beats a house full of company exchanging laughter, good food, or day excursions out and about.

Summer of 1984 was soon upon us, and we geared up for more family time together. One very warm early summer day, Jane and I had a brainstorm session and came up with the idea to add a backyard swimming pool to take advantage of the swim season without dragging everyone and everything to a beach.

Well, we did our homework and visited several pool companies who specialized in large above ground pools which would, in my opinion, work quite well in our spacious backyard.

I want to especially draw your attention to the emphasis on "my opinion" in the previous sentence. Finally, I believed we had reached a consensus on the type of pool we would purchase for our swimming enjoyment.

Humm, not sure where my assumption had taken me! Several days later I arrived home one evening to see a large rectangular shape had been brightly spray painted on the grass in the entire half of our backyard. Bright yellow paint to be exact!

Well, my wife had also done additional research and her personal shopping which had culminated in her decision to invite a local INGROUND pool company to assess the backyard and make the proposal for adding a pool flush to the ground, a much bigger and tad bit more elaborate pool complete with diving board and cement decking.

Wow! Somehow, I missed that part of the original discussion and plan. In her defense, she was right on this one, but it took me a while to admit that!

Shortly thereafter, our yard was crawling with workers gripping shovels and pushing wheel barrels ready to clear away the dirt rubble piled up by the mini backhoe which had snaked its way between a neighbor's fence and two beautiful trees we wanted saved.

The pool was not going to be ready for several weeks, but somehow our two little people missed that detail, so the second day of digging, a work man pointed out to me the sight of Matt and Cindy sitting on the back step clothed in their swimsuits and clutching towels! They were very excited, but very disappointed that swimming was delayed just a bit.

Finally, the day arrived in early August when the pool was finished, filled, and ready for swimmers. The "On your mark, get set, go" command was presented to the children, and they jumped into the shimmering water ready to enjoy the rest of the warm Buffalo summer. The timing of the decision to install a swimming pool was perfect for our family as we greatly enjoyed swimming together, entertaining family and friends, and just relaxing around the pool. It was a time we can reflect back when the Lord knew we needed those special moments together and those memories of good times because of what waited for us around the next sharp corner of our journey along life's path.

Nearly every day, all day, and into the night, our backyard air was filled with the shouts of, "Hey, watch my dive!" or "Marco Polo!" Much to our relief, none of our neighbors objected!

As I have previously mentioned in each one of our other moves, our goals were to choose a solid neighborhood close to good schools and, more importantly, be near a church which would complement our family values while offering us programs for our children's ages and friends for each one of us. The first church we selected in Williamsville was a very large established traditional church recommended by a couple of neighbors. Our first impression of this body of believers was relatively favorable and we attended several weeks. Because our policy is to get involved almost immediately, we attended Sunday schools, placed our children in the children's ministries, and even opened our home for casual fellowship.

It is not my attempt to speak disparagingly about this established church which will go unnamed here. Suffice it to say, for some unknown reason, we did not feel comfortable in this very traditional Christian setting. Their welcome of us was pleasant for the most part, but we discovered the road we travelled on searching for our home church appeared to have some potholes in it and a few bumps. There just seem to be many closed groups amongst the members, thus we found it very difficult to feel accepted. Looking back, we can see now God knew exactly the Christian community that we needed, and He soon proceeded to lead us down the right road.

Also, sometime during that month of August 1984, Jane and I discussed the possibility of our children attending a private school centered on the teachings of Scripture and the reinforcement of the values we felt important for our children's spiritual development. While still wrestling with that uncomfortable "church" question, we were able to be on the receiving end of the recommendation of a certain Christian school based right there in Williamsville. It came highly recommended. Without any delay due to the fall school season quickly approaching, Jane made an appointment to take the children over to Christian Central Academy for new student interviews for Cindy who would be entering second grade and Matthew who would be a kindergartner.

I don't think I was quite prepared at the end of their interview day for all the children's excitement and enthusiasm for this school. They gave me all the details of the classrooms, the two gymnasiums, the real cafeteria, and the auditorium which look like a movie theatre with velvet seats! It seems that they passed their entrance testing with flying colors much to their relief.

It was only after their excitement had entered a calmer state that I realized my wife was a little quiet. Their attention span was exhausted explaining all the details of the new school, so they got their bathing suits on and went for a swim. At that time, Jane and I could actually discuss what had transpired that day. It seems the children were correct. Their interviews with several teachers went well and their testing accomplished the desired result for their acceptance into the school. My wife believed it would be a good fit for the children to attend if we could afford it.

It was at this point that I was made aware of another interview that had taken place at the school. During the admittance meeting with the administrative assistants in the school's main office, the question was presented to Jane, "You don't by any chance have a teaching degree?" Always being an honest person, my wife shared that she did indeed have a Bachelor of Education with endorsements in English and Physical Education and several years of teaching experience in elementary, junior high, and high school.

For them, it was as if the heavens had opened, and angels were singing! Her parent interview promptly turned into a teaching position interview with the high school and elementary principals! Would she even be willing to consider filling the position of girl's physical education instructor for grades K through 12 as well as high school women's sports coach?

IT WAS AS IF THE HEAVENS HAD OPENED, AND ANGELS WERE SINGING!

The salary was not a tremendous amount, but the opportunity to be part of the education community in which our children would be involved was extremely enticing. If she chose to accept this position, it would require a huge adjustment to our family and personal time. The coaching position alone would require many, many hours outside of the classroom and the sacrifice on our young children's part of sharing their mother with hundreds of other children had to be considered.

Unfortunately, or possibly fortunately, we needed to make this decision as a family quickly because school was soon to start. Because we have always prayed for wisdom and believed that the Lord had led us to this specific school, Jane accepted the position and immediately put into motion an entire restructuring of her priorities in order to be prepared for the first day of school in September.

I think at this point she may have also felt that, suddenly on our traveling down the Buffalo Road, a huge and daunting hill had arisen in front of us, and especially her. This new position would require a tremendous volume of energy and high-level organization skills in order to balance family life, school, and church.

And speaking of church, she was informed that the policy of Christian Central Academy was to require every staff member to attend at least one weekly service at the church which had assumed the responsibility of the struggling school in August 1978. This church was The Chapel on North Forest Road in Williamsville—a large, nondenominational community of believers under the leadership of Pastor James Andrews—its founder. We needed to consider this requirement seriously.

Was God leading us to this place?

And so it was, that on the fourth day of September in 1984, my little family stood on our home's front steps for first day of school pictures before heading off on another new adventure. The kids were so proud of their required uniforms while their mother looked all the part of a Physical Education teacher in her stylish athletic pants with matching jacket. Around her neck hung a very valuable teaching tool—a silver whistle gifted to her by her beloved high school PE instructor who had encouraged her to be a teacher. This day would mark a decided speedy escalation on our family's life journey as we zoomed ahead down the clearly marked road of "Freeway Entrance Ahead." It was to be a very busy time for sure!

I too was ready for that new fall day as I left the house attired in my usual professional work attire consisting of a professionally pressed dress shirt under a custom-tailored suit, hand selected tie, and shoes polished to military perfection. The picture of that day reflects the order, planning, structure, personal accomplishment, and excitement all be it tempered by a twinge of fearfulness that always accompanies something new. We were all embarking on a great new adventure!

Over the next six weeks, while I continued in developing positive working relationships with my staff, while adjusting to US business practices, and continuing to meet the needs of dealers in the Greater Niagara area, our household settled into a pretty steady pace on a forward moving path. CCA's high school women's soccer season kicked off with great enthusiasm on everyone's part in spite of the player and coach's inexperience's. The children settled in very successfully to their classrooms and immediately fell in love with their teachers who were extremely gifted Christ followers deeply committed to providing excellent educational opportunities as well as encouraging spiritual development.

There was a huge adjustment for our family as Jane's teaching assignments as well as coaching responsibilities resulted in very early morning departures from home, morning staff meetings, rigorous teaching assignments, and the intense sports team after-school practices. Home and away games required my three CCA Crusaders to extend their long days even farther into the evening hours.

However, our children became adept at finishing their homework while their mom was working with the athletes or in the car traveling to and from competitions. They often roamed the amazing old building with other staff children creating hide and seek games, engaging in the occasional shenanigans common to children playing outside on the equipment, or embracing the role of team assistants. To this day our children continue their love of sports and physical fitness which I believe they were gifted with through the time spent at CCA events. Of course, there is the heritage passed on to them through their parents love of physical fitness, sporting activities and competition, but those precious days, weeks, months, and years spent at this unique place certainly contributed to their development as athletes as well as Christians.

The entire concept of Christian education that my family became involved in at that time was refreshing, vibrant, and would forever create for us wonderful memories.

The beautiful old traditional style building which contained CCA became far more to us than classrooms, chairs, black boards, books, school bells, class schedules, recess, lunchroom, and every other physical component contained in that corner of Williamsville, New York. We were embraced by an extremely loving community of men and women dedicated to providing excellent educational foundations upon which we could construct solid bases for decision making throughout life experiences. It was a well-rounded approach when combined with solid spiritual doctrine and teaching as led by the pastoral staff of the sponsoring church, The Chapel.

Adhering to the school requirement that each staff member attend at least one weekly service at the mother church, our family did just that within the first week of school. What an amazing experience from the very minute we entered the front doors of that modernistic building on North Forest Road. Every person we met greeted us warmly—parking lot attendants, door greeters, ushers, staff members, and fellow worshipers. There was a feeling of excitement as we entered the worship center with people who seemed to be anticipating something different than we had felt at the other local church we had attended. Even the music seemed to come "alive."

At this point in our family's physical and spiritual journey, we could never have imagined the wonderful blessing this community of Christ followers and fellow believers would have upon our lives for the next four years. After service on our way home, our young children ages five and seven vocally determined that this is where they wanted to go to church. Something had captured our hearts from the very first greeting through the entire message and especially at the conclusion of the service that morning.

As was his custom at the end of each service, Pastor Andrews would stand at one of the lobby doors to personally greet as many people as he could. With our young children in-tow, we patiently waited in line to receive an introduction to this man who was actually my wife's boss as well as possibly our new pastor.

I need to mention here a small incident that had occurred the previous week at CCA during the student's chapel time. Each staff member was required to supervise these chapel times and on this specific day, it was Jane's responsibility to be in attendance. The speaker that day was none other than Mrs. Joan Andrews, wife of Pastor James Andrews whom we had not met and only knew as the Pastor of The Chapel Church.

Because it was a very warm September day, the windows of the classroom in which this particular session was being held were wide open to allow some type of air circulation. Of course, that also allowed for the entrance into the room of every flying creature in nature's existence. As Mrs. Andrews was beginning her message to the students who were seated in rows directly in front of her, a very large bumblebee decided to make his entrance into the room and proceed to rumble his way up and down each aisle which incited not the least amount of squirming and wiggling on the part of the attentive students. As he made his labored approach down the aisle my wife was seated in, she grabbed the closest tool by which to administer a behavioral correcting motion upon the invader when it came near her location at the end of the row. One can only imagine the destructive sound such tool of attack made as it descended upon the unsuspecting intruder perched on the chair next to Jane's seat.

All eyes and ears were no longer focused on the distinguished speaker but rather upon the commotion caused by Coach Revell and her red attendance book. A collective gasp from the other staff members in attendance filled the room followed by resounding peals of laughter from each and every child. Once order was reestablished, Mrs. Andrews continued with her inspirational talk. The students then exited the room to return to their classes. Coach Revell proceeded with her daily responsibilities. The staff had a good chuckle, and the incident was stored in everyone's memory.

That brings me to the very moment our family was introduced to the man who would become our new spiritual leader as we exited on our very first Sunday at the Chapel. Another staff member was present who introduced us as the Revells whereupon Pastor Andrews immediately identified us as "The Bee Lady and her family." He further commented that his wife was very amused by all the commotion one little flying insect and a red book weapon of correction had created on that very warm day at the school.

What an introduction!

Pastor and his family would from this moment on become our dear, dear friends. The cementing of our relationships was solid and secure as our God brought us together and covered us with all the laughter, love, and tears the approaching life experiences would require of us.

In retrospect, my family and I were in this church, enrolled at this school, living in this neighborhood, settled in this city, located in this state, and positioned in this country at exactly this moment which had been ordained for us. In His loving way, God knew that our faith was heading for a very bumpy journey along an extremely frightening and treacherous highway.

This then brings me to the part of sharing my story with you, as family, friends, and acquaintances, that is oftentimes emotionally difficult to remember and clearly express. I have attempted to carry you along on many of the roads I've traveled from my earliest days as a young lad in Verona to the present time in storytelling when I am now at age 34, successful by all of the world's measurements, deeply in love with my wife of 14 years, enthusiastically enjoying my young children's antics, and pretty much settled into a very agreeable lifestyle that my present status in the executive business world could offer me.

By anyone's observation, the highway in front of my family and me was one which looked smoothly surfaced and well-marked by properly posted signs of directions. Life was good, even great!

Nine

THE PAVEMENT ENDS

L et me take a moment here to ask a question about life. What does the Bible say about life, more specifically, about milestones in a life? Rest assured I do have an answer.

Psalm 90:12 (NIV) is pretty clear.

> *"So teach us to number our days, that we can gain a heart of wisdom."*

Let me further expand on this Holy Scripture quote.

It has always been an unspoken tradition within the span of a person's days, months, and years of existence on planet earth that there is recorded at some specific spot, whether it is in a family Bible or a mother's journal or even a personal diary, details and dates which serve as reminders, milestones, or turning points for some momentous event that happened and through which time is marked.

This is not to imply that every date in the family's history such as births, marriages and even religious experiences are not milestones to be recognized as important, but there may be one or two that rise above all the others in the memory moments. An event, whether large or small, which has a marked moment for remembrance.

October 16, 1984 is a date on the calendar which holds that distinction — the personal mile marker by which I now reference all past and future events of my entire life journey. To set the stage for what unfolded that day, I need to share some details.

Having enjoyed an active physical life—ie; baseball, hockey, soccer, golf to mention a few examples, I have always been in good health with only the occasional ache or pain. A broken collar bone here. A broken leg there. Nothing beyond the scope of human tolerance and understanding. Just accidents with quick healing times.

That was all about to change for me and my family.

The unexpected happened as the state of my overall health began to deteriorate to the point that during the daily yard cleanup as the pool was being finished, I noticed extreme tiredness and excessive sweating. Even the smallest effort to assist my family in physical exertion caused me to experience weakness unlike anything I had ever felt before. It was a struggle to keep pushing myself at work and at home, but I did not mention it to my wife. Better to remain silent and wait it out. I fell into that typical male response to health issues. Ignore it and all will be well.

Finally, on the first Sunday night in October 1984, I admitted to Jane that I was not feeling well and wondered what we should do. Thankfully, she strongly encouraged me (as only a wife can!), to get to the doctor on Monday for a checkup. By then, even the usual process of food elimination was not functioning so my physical problem list was growing.

Surprisingly, I was able to visit our new family physician that very day. Having not required his services as of yet, I went into his office as a stranger unaccompanied by my spouse who was teaching. After all, it was just going to be a quick overall exam, a prescription to fix the problem, and then a fast exit to return to work. I left his office with the diagnosis of constipation and the instructions to use an enema solution that evening. That was it.

I should be better by morning.

Well, following the doctor's treatment order did not solve the problem. In reality, that next morning my pain level was extremely elevated, and we were beginning to be seriously concerned.

After having sent my family off to school in order to keep the kids and Jane to a routine so as not to frighten them—I presented myself at the Emergency Room in a small regional hospital less than half mile from our home.

Following all the usual ER procedures within which I explained my symptoms and the previous diagnosis, I was ushered into an ER room and examined by a new doctor who immediately addressed me with these confusing words, "I believe that someone has missed your problem. There is something abnormal in your abdomen and I am immediately ordering a CT scan which can't be done at this hospital. You will need to go to our main hospital in downtown Buffalo. I will arrange transport for you now. We will then be informed of the results after it is read by a doctor."

By this time, my anxiety level was mounting, and I realized I needed my wife to be present. This was confirmed when a nurse announced to me that my insurance would not pay for the ambulance to transport me. Could I call someone to do that? So, I called CCA, to remove Jane from class, and instruct her to come pick me up for the drive downtown. Of course, this only heightened her concern as she prepared to leave school not knowing what was happening.

In retrospect, this was, for my wife, one of those milestone moments I mentioned previously. As she was hurrying to depart school, she was stopped in the hall by Ruth Adams, her principal, who spoke these words into the space between them as they hugged—"God does not promise tomorrow. He only gives us what we need for this moment, for this day. Trust Him!"

Words shared from an understanding of Matthew 6:34 (MSG),

> *"Give your entire attention to what God is doing right now, and don't get worked up about what may or may not happen tomorrow. God will help you deal with whatever hard things come up when the time comes."*

An interesting side note here was that there had been an error in processing my insurance and my coverage DID provide for ambulance transportation which would have saved Jane and I that drive to the downtown hospital. And yet my Lord knew what was best because I was able to share with her what had unfolded already that morning. I do not remember much of what was said other than we knew this was potentially something neither one of us could have foreseen three days before. At some point, I'm sure we prayed that it would be a clear CT scan and our lives could return to some type of normalcy once again involving family, work, school, and church.

I don't remember much about the procedure nor what transpired shortly after, but I was quite aware of the fact my wife was strangely quiet as we were heading back to the hospital near our home with the instructions that the doctors there would be meeting with us.

Many, many times we have all heard the saying, "The Lord works in mysterious ways." It seems that one of those mysterious ways had occurred for us immediately after the CT scan when the attending technician sat down with my wife and shared with her that, in spite of the privacy laws regarding someone's personal health, she felt led to inform Jane that she could see in the CT scan that there was a large tumor present in my abdominal cavity. She very kindly broke the news even before the scan had been officially read. It was within that moment in the stillness of the waiting room that Jane realized this was a bigger problem than we had imagined. We never knew the name of this technician, but we will always be thankful that she stepped outside of standard practice to personally comfort my wife and give her a chance to formulate a plan of action to notify my Canadian family. That is probably one of the hardest phone calls she has ever had to make in her life.

By this time, our anxiety had deepened, and we knew we would need to reach out to family and friends quickly. Upon receiving our distress call, my parents immediately made plans to be with us. At this point in their lives, my dad had retired from the dealership and with my mother, established a very fine ladies fashion boutique in our little village beside Rock Lake. It had become a family affair as my two sisters ably assisted Mum in the managing and operating of Glenelda Fashion. So, Mum and Dad were able to almost immediately leave Verona for the long drive to Buffalo, New York. I was not a passenger in that vehicle, but I am sure that the air space in that car was filled with my parents' prayers spoken with great fervor as they interceded with their Lord on behalf of their beloved son and his family.

Once more I found myself admitted to the Millard Fillmore Suburban Hospital in Williamsville, New York and waiting for test results to be officially shared with me and my family. By this time, I knew this was more than just a minor bump in the road, a slight curve, a rough patch of gravel, or a minor pothole along the journey of my life. I felt like the whole direction of my life had suddenly entered into some long, dark tunnel and I had absolutely no control, in spite of how hard I gripped the steering wheel.

At this extremely low point in my mind, with my physical body failing and confusion all around, there entered into my hospital room a very distinguished but somewhat intimidating doctor who had the test results from the scan as well as blood test and needle biopsy results. In no uncertain terms, with firmness in his voice, Doctor Cooper explained to me the diagnosis:

"Tests revealed a nodular, poorly differentiated lymphoma with a huge intra-abdominal mass which measured some 17 centimeters by 14 centimeters, as well as a 3-centimeter spleen and 2 centimeter left supraclavicular node area," he said.

I had full blown, life altering Non-Hodgkin's Lymphoma—a malignant cancer. It was well advanced and included several locations above and below my mid-section. Time stood still! I was stunned! Cancer!

It is a good thing Jane was present as I did not hear any of the other words swirling around the room that day. Without realizing it, we had just learned our first lesson in the handling of all health issues—always have someone else present who can actually remember the doctor's words!

How can this be? Where did this come from? How did I get caught up in this horrible diagnosis?

It felt as if I had been cruising down the road in a bright red Mustang convertible enjoying the sunshine full on my face when my vehicle had been forced off into a deep ditch by a sudden, powerfully strong rain storm which washed over me to the point that my very breath was limited to gasping for air. I had lost control in a raging wave of confusion and shock.

I HAD LOST CONTROL IN A RAGING WAVE OF CONFUSION AND SHOCK

What will happen to my family? What will happen to my job? What will happen to my future? Did I even have a future?

How was I, the man trained to problem solve and lead others either at home or work or church, going to handle this news?

I did not have any answers. My office shelves were filled with operational manuals for problem solving, but none of them were marked, Cancer Procedures. Nothing in my past training as a young man, husband, father had ever focused on what to do when faced with this—Cancer!

Where was Father God in all of this confusion?

Somewhere in the very back of my consciousness, I could hear that last question whispered into existence to be repeated over and over.

The remainder of that day was lost in a fog of confusion and shock.

Unfortunately, we had decisions to make regarding the immediate protocol for my cancer care, so many of our thoughts and questions were put aside to be struggled through later. Even years later!

We have learned over the years that the Lord is never late nor early with the timing of His plans as they unfold in our lives and this became very evident as my family and I realized that our recent relocation to

Buffalo, New York was not an accident. Dr. Ruth Adam's softly whispered words to Jane about God's timing rang so, so true.

The attending cancer care doctor was a lymphoma specialist who had designed a rigid chemotherapy regiment for treating my specific disease. It was extremely aggressive and my only hope at that time of surviving much longer. It was not a hard decision for us to make as I was determined to fight hard for my future. Protocol treatment plans were put into motion immediately. It was even suggested that we prepare a Last Will and Testament if we had not already done so. This was a serious situation and there were no guarantees of my survival beyond six months.

Returning home that evening, Jane had the awful task of trying to explain to five-year-old Matt and seven-year-old Cindy what was happening and why Daddy was not at home yet. After settling them into bed for the night, my exhausted wife sat down with her Bible and wept, seeking a word, something of encouragement from her Father God. A milestone moment occurred when her eyes fell upon a verse which to this very day has become our family's Coat of Arms, our motto, our watchword, our formula, our battle cry!

2 Timothy 1:7 (KJV),

> *"For God has not given us the spirit of fear; but of Power,*
> *and of Love, and of a Sound Mind."*

The timing of God's revealing that verse to us was perfect! In fact, my wife declares she believes He added that verse to her Bible at that very moment. I am not arguing that point. Over and over even to this very day, the truth of this one verse has saved us from despair, comforted us in the night struggles, eased our confusion, calmed our weary minds, and given us hope!

It was heartbreaking all around as the hospital had an antiquated policy that children under the age of fourteen could not visit any patients. Our children were pretty confused and frightened, so the very next morning their mother engaged the nursing staff in a discussion centered on making an allowance for our kids to see me. Receiving negative rebuff, Jane marched into the Nursing Supervisor's office to calmly but firmly request that an exception to "the rule" be made in regard to our children who needed visible confirmation their dad was still ok.

It was another one of those milestone moments which would determine the course of my wife's involvement in my overall cancer care for the many, many years to come. The lady looked into Jane's pleading eyes and said, "Your children can visit their dad! In the future with your husband's journey ahead, you need to remember that the squeaky wheel gets the oil! Stay calm but be forceful for what he needs and what your family needs."

Through those words and at that moment, my own personal Pit Bull was created to be unleashed upon anyone associated with my care. Jane has learned to fight for me with dignity, knowledge, firmness; all born out of love, since that day in October 1984!

This began the gruesome process of fighting for my very survival. My first treatment began on October 25, 1984 and was repeated every third week over the next five months. Due to the intensity of the chemotherapy, my body would need the three weeks between infusions to stabilize and recover somewhat. Words become inadequate in describing the reactions I had from the chemo, but it is enough to say, it was extremely difficult both physically and emotionally for me as well as my family.

Fridays became treatment days and then the entire weekend was spent in vomiting as well as extreme exhaustion. Nothing could have prepared me for the price I would have to pay while I fought this invading disease which resided within my body. Nor was my family prepared for the extent of the physical care I would need while struggling through the side effects of the necessary chemotherapy.

That rigorous chemotherapy was soon followed by seemingly endless rounds of radiation. Not the pinpoint style many would be able to receive years later to prevent unnecessary cell damage, but the all-encompassing kind which often injured more than just the designated cells.

But praise God, my wife and children never left my side or complained when I could not eat, or the nausea became continuous. Even in those days of their young years, Matt and Cindy always tenderly cared for me, comforted me, wrote encouraging notes, shared their joys and fears, cried, or laughed with me, and tried to act as normal as possible. It must have been exceedingly confusing for them to see their once strong dad reduced to a weakling curled up on the couch of our family room. In their own way, they attempted to handle all that was transpiring around them daily. They were so very young. In their understanding of hurts or pain, skinned up knees and cut fingers were quickly attended to by that dreaded hydrogen peroxide and a smiley face Band-Aid! This now was a wound they could not see—an invisible hurt no bandage could cover.

MY WIFE AND CHILDREN NEVER LEFT MY SIDE OR COMPLAINED ...

I tried my very best to not be a complainer which often resulted in me silently suffering. That may be the moment in our marriage when my wife wisely determined that just because I SAID I was ok did not always translate into me actually BEING ok. She could quickly recognize the degree of my pain or nausea level and work very hard to get me the relief I needed.

My cancer doctor was the leading expert at that time in Buffalo for my disease, but not the leader in bedside manners if you get my drift. He saw his job as administrator of my treatment and left the personal touches to his office staff, so my Personal Pit Bull had to often times step in to intercede on my behalf for better nausea meds. One more squeaky wheel moment for the records. Another provision of God's detail planning for me.

On this same thought of His infinite planning for our protection on those dark roads, it is interesting to realize how very important my wife's second sense was in my care as she could always recognize when I was in physical trouble by hearing me make a very small sigh deep in my throat. A noise I was not even aware I made in times of deep physical stress. Several times it alerted her that I needed prompt relief in the form of more pain meds or, in the extreme case, immediate medical attention. I will always be grateful to my Lord for His gift to me of my Pit Bull.

He also gifted me with two amazing children who never expressed to me any reluctance at caring for me nor any complaints when our family plans were altered due to my physical needs. Their expressions of love for their dad were sincerely based on a deep tenderness and affection for me. With every faltering step I was forced to take, they were right there, not demanding any special attention or demonstrating any impatience at the limitations my disease wielded over me. This expression of genuine love would never end and still exists to this present day.

Their prayers as children were so precious and even more so now, as in their adult years they have both grasped a deep faith which gloriously manifests itself in every part of their lives. I have many, many times been on the receiving end of their powerful words of faith and trust in Father God's power to heal and comfort me. And in addition to them, I am loved and prayed over by their spouses, Wendy and Chris, who are added blessings to Jane and me. Well, I can't leave out our grandchildren for sure either as they too surround us with their prayers along our journey. A legacy of prayer warriors started all those years past!

And so, our family's new journey began.

Where once we experienced long trips over smooth, relatively straight roads through countryside's resplendent with rich details of color and familiar scenery or along well-planned city streets filled with the hustle and bustle of others engaging in their individual plans, our road became a narrow one filled with shallow ruts, sharp rocks, mud-filled pot holes, and deep crevices threatening to swallow us up in despair, confusion, and fear.

There was no room to turn around or bypass the hard parts. There seemed to be no sense or reason for this sudden and abrupt change. In my mind, I frantically searched for the cause of this major malfunctioning of my human body. My well-trained business mind immediately shifted gears to maneuver around all the hazards looming in my path. Surely there was some reason why such a breakdown in my well-oiled life had occurred. Perhaps I was not faithful enough in my tithing, my support of missions, my witnessing, or my church attendance. Maybe I wasn't even a true believer and sin in my life had caused this misery.

I knew the Holy Scriptures.

Had I not been raised in a Christian family, practiced all the proper behaviors under the threat of losing my salvation, and fully believed that the success of my life reflected God's blessings for righteous living?

Somehow and very abruptly, the supposedly solid structure of the road in front of me crumbled under the heavy weight of all my doubts and fears. I was not alone in all this darkness as Jane too was struggling to find rhyme or reason. I would like to share that we found understanding and clarity immediately, but there were to be many foggy moments ahead for us as we crept along making our way through the hazards. Sometimes we could barely make any forward progress in our spirits as nothing made sense and Father God, the God of all peace and healing, seemed to be avoiding us in Buffalo, New York. The only road sign we could see ahead was one which cautioned, "Dangerous Road Conditions."

Fortunately, our children were too young to fully understand or comprehend the severity of my health situation nor the uncertainty of our future as a family unit. They were content to play with friends at school, attend their Mum's sports team games, spend time with family, cavort around in the pool or on our boat, and embrace all that our new church offered. As I mentioned, their questions of my health were answered as honestly as possible, and we did not deny the severity of the cancer. They learned early that sometimes Dad was not functioning well, and Mum was occupied with his care.

And there was always humor!

Some might have been disturbed at our family's adoption of humor as a coping skill, but it certainly worked for us to relieve some of the tensions surrounding nausea, hair loss, tiredness, and despair. Our kids learned along with us that there were appropriate times to use humor and we all became very skilled at keeping respect for the right time to use a laugh or two to lighten a moment.

The very first time we experienced this "behavior" relief was when, after my first round of chemo, the reality hit that neither my hair nor mustache would survive the drug side effects. After a private appointment with a wig specialist, my new expensive human hair wig was soon firmly residing on my head as I came home one evening before Christmas. We had warned the children that my hair was falling out, but I don't think they were quite prepared for the shock of no hair or mustache which they had never seen me without. Well, their first and only question was, "What is under that wig?" I removed the said wig (which was ugly!) and after an extremely long moment of silence, they both erupted into waves of laughter, nervous laughter, but still laughter.

That laughter helped to lighten the moment of our adult dejection and filled us with a child-like freedom to find the lighter side of sadness.

That wig humor continued even as I abandoned it for the next hair loss experience. But it was not wasted as it was used as a wig for many a Halloween costume or a snowman's head covering over the years. It still resides somewhere in our house just in case a grandchild might be in need of a prop. Money well spent!

So many memories are imprinted in our minds from our years in Buffalo during my initial cancer care, but there are some which rise to the top as very special ones.

Over the years we have been beyond richly blessed with wonderful friends, neighbors, work mates, and family. During the first shocking days of my diagnosis and while I was still in the hospital, my childhood friend (the water skiing in early May chum!) made the long roundtrip from Verona to Buffalo to sit by my bedside and comfort me. Chris Walker declined to stay overnight which then required another long journey back home. I will always cherish those hours we were together. We had shared many an adventure in our youthful days, but this one cemented our friendship in a much deeper sense.

In fact, over the years since those first frightening days in October of 1984, other brothers in Christ came along side of me, some driving hours to sit by my side in hospital or at home. Their unselfish sacrifices of time with their families were blessings I never could have imagined as they shared laughter, tears, tearful prayers, a Bible study, or sometimes just silence—the silence of men when words don't need to be spoken.

Another memory we will always carry with us occurred once again in that same hospital late one evening several months down the road. It was determined that I had developed an additional small maxillary tumor under my jaw line which would need to be removed. Now, it should be mentioned here that there seemed to be a pattern developing with my health issues whereby nothing was ever just an uncomplicated process. Nothing was nor ever would be a classic textbook diagnosis or procedure. This has been proven to be true many times!

What was a pretty simple, tiny malignant tumor removal surgery continued late into the evening hour and Jane waited with growing concern as the clock hands slowly crept along. Finally, the doctor met with her, and with tears in his eyes informed her that not just one tumor had been removed but seven, each intertwined around glands and tissue.

Not what he had expected!

By this time the hospital halls were silent and dimly lit as she waited for me to be returned to my assigned room. It would be her responsibility to break the news to me that in-spite of all the previous wretched chemo and extensive radiation I had endured, more cancer had been discovered. A dark moment for sure and not just due to the nighttime shadows.

Then there occurred another "Father God" milestone moment in our lives as the silence of the darkened, deserted hallway was broken by the opening of an elevator door and footsteps proceeding in the direction of Jane's waiting post outside my room.

Our Pastor, James Andrews, had been led by Holy Spirit to make a late night stop to check up on us. It was perfect timing as my wife was overcome by the surgeon's unexpected words and was having a cry of despair—alone and feeling somewhat abandoned. In a Christ-like embrace, Pastor allowed her to cry out her emotions onto his immaculate suit jacket as she verbally expressed to him the unfairness of more cancer.

There was no condemnation, wise council, or Biblical words spoken. Only this:

"Are you finished now? Then let's go tell Dale together."

In the quiet of my room, the ugly news was shared, and I began to weep, realizing the rough road just continued to loom in front of us. Then, as Jane would tell me later, it was if Christ himself had entered the room!

Pastor reached into his pocket to extract his perfectly pressed, monogrammed white handkerchief and proceeded to wipe my weeping eyes as well as the bloody residue on my lips.

God's touch through man's hand!

The beauty of this moment continued several nights later when I decided I wanted to go to the Sunday night service at church, even with my heavily bandaged face. My family needed to go.

We could not wallow in self-pity.

And that decision was another example of the immense measure the love our Heavenly Father has for us as well as His power to meet our deepest needs.

It was Communion night at The Chapel—a regular occurrence surrounded by quiet reflection and prayer. Pastor always stood behind the wooden table holding the elements, spoke softly words from

Scriptures, paused for private prayer, then dispensed the juice and bread with the aid of the deacons. This night he spoke not a word, unveiled the elements tray, took it in hand, and proceeded to serve Jane and I our communion himself. It was a defining moment for us!

Not only did it remind us of God's presence, but it also cemented our relationship with this dear, dear man of faith.

God was showing us that He could see our pain, feel our anxieties, accept our questioning the path we were trotting upon, and He still loved us!

He did not, nor ever would, abandon us to this broken-down condition of anxious fears, physical pain, mental confusion, and hopelessness. That was not, nor ever would be, His perfect plan. I will readily admit that many times the windows of our traveling vehicle were often fogged over as we sat in falsely perceived abandonment on the side of life's road.

But He always provided (and still does) at just the right moment an encounter, an experience, or an opportunity to receive an inspiration, a reassurance, an incentive to keep trusting. Not one second of my life was without His watchfulness.

I will ever be thankful to Him for His directing our steps to The Chapel and the amazing staff who served there as not only did they pray for me, but through their faithful and unselfish obedience to God's directions, I was able to be a part of an amazing Easter Pageant event which helped to renew my trust in my Savior's unending love for me and my family.

For several years, The Chapel staff had, through phenomenally creative minds joined by an all-volunteer crew of church members, been presenting an amazingly beautiful and moving play visually unfolding the events leading up to the death, burial, and resurrection of our precious Savior. There were no professional actors. There was no Hollywood generated script. What was present throughout the arduous planning stages was the blessing of amazing creativity God had gifted to the Pastor, the Director, the Set Designers, the Music Leader, and the actors who came from the common ranks of all persons and professions. Teachers, doctors, nurses, students, lawyers, mechanics, truck drivers, corporate executives, business owners, retired, self-employed, unemployed, wealthy, poor, the list is endless. Everyone united together to present to the hurting, seeking world a chance to encounter and experience the Love of Christ.

And encounter we did!

Even as a crew member, I was richly blessed.

God's timing is never off for at just this moment in my struggling life, I was asked to become one of the 12 disciples in the Last Supper scene. This was not to be a speaking role which was a great relief to me, but rather a silent portrayal of the sharing of their final meal with Christ and the raw beauty of His love for them. As the narrator verbally painted the story directly through the words from Holy Scripture and we physically re-enacted our responses to Him while seated together around the table, it was a moment suspended in time. A very special moment within which I could be reminded that I now lived on the other side of Easter and death was defeated through my Savior's own personal pain. My struggle with the cancer could be covered by His compassionate and never-ending mercy.

An added blessing here came in the brotherly love I felt from the other "disciples" who shared those last supper moments with me. These were men who had been faithfully praying for me and my family. We were held together through that divinely designed plan of God to merge our daily lives as a strong bond of believers. The sign in front of me said, "Lanes Merging."

Now, I scramble hard here to find just the right words to express the great blessing our family experienced through Christian Central Academy and The Chapel. It just is not possible to properly give credit to the wonderful people God surrounded us with during those difficult four years.

I can only compare it to what must happen in the design studios of an auto maker. Challenge—to design each component of that car to best protect the occupant as he/she rides incased in the framework of steel, plastic, and fiberglass. Seatbelts restraint motion. Airbags cushion impacts. Shatter resistant glass deflects flying objects. Bright lights illuminate roads ahead. Lumbar seats add comfort. Tinted windows block glaring sunlight. Fog lights cut through denseness. Climate controls dispense heat and cold to aide in well-being. The list could be endless, but each part is especially designed for the good of the entire package.

Here lies the beauty of this comparison!

My life, as in all lives, was created by The Master Designer even before I was born. Each part of who I am, who I know, where I have been, and where I am going has been designed in the very smallest detail for a purpose. Not one moment has been by accident! This had never been more evident to me than in our association with the staff at CCA and our involvement with the community at our new church.

After that milestone day in October of 1984, our family was fully embraced by so many people. Encouragement came from many sources. Church folk sent cards. Young CCA students created loving messages in crayon or marker. Teenagers wrote prayer notes scribbled on notebook paper. Teachers unselfishly covered Jane's classes during times I needed her extra attention. Our children were enveloped by the love of others who often cared for them when we were exhausted or overwhelmed. Lovingly prepared meals were delivered to us. Who could ever forget the aroma and taste of Debbie Fillmore's homemade chicken noodle soup! Delivered at just the right moment when I could not eat anything else.

Cards and letters expressing concern and prayers arrived from literally all over the world. The news of my diagnosis soon spread, and many people reached out to my family to encourage, offer help, and pray. Even to this very day, casual acquaintances tell me they were praying for us. It seems the rallying cry for comfort and healing prayers had been sounded. It was truly amazing to receive such an outpouring of love and concern! Many precious lifelong friendships began in those days of uncertainty and suffering.

Some may have wondered where God was in all of this. I believe that He was reassuring us of His presence through the outpouring of this love in action by so many wonderful people. Even in my doubts of my survival, I was beginning to see God's hand working.

EVEN IN MY DOUBTS OF MY SURVIVAL, I WAS BEGINNING TO SEE GOD'S HAND WORKING

There is another milestone worth mentioning here which was a very valuable experience for us. It came in the form of one small boy's honesty.

In the year following my diagnosis, Matt entered the first grade and was gifted with a young teacher who deeply loved her students. This lady was caring, kind, thoughtful, organized, and creative throughout her task of teaching these precious souls entrusted to her. It was her desire to not just "teach" them but also to lead their hearts along a path to grow spiritually.

With that thought in mind, imagine with me a day when Jane was in her office between classes and the door opened to allow this weeping gal to quietly enter with something in her hand. Upon the desk she placed a crumpled piece of white construction paper accompanied by another tiny yellow shape. It had obviously been cute once and wholly intact. Through her tears, our son's dear teacher said, "I think I made a mistake here."

It seems her original plan for her class's Spiritual Development unit was for them to discuss prayer and its role in our daily lives. The theme was that God promised to answer all prayers. If they so desired each child could select a precut white candle base to tape on the wall. Whenever they had a request, they could write it on the base. When the answer came, they could then attach the bright yellow paper flame to signify that their Heavenly Father had definitely been listening to their smallest requests as shared in group time and He had answered.

Well, Matt made a verbal request one day that his father would be healed and have no more cancer! Simple, heart-felt plea. He was thrilled (as we all were) when the next month went by and there were no new cancers discovered to add to the present ones. Because he believed his prayer had been answered, he told the class and then proudly taped his tiny yellow flame to his candle.

Prayer answered!

However, within a few days, my cancerous maxillary tumors were found, and it was another flat tire added to our already crippled family car.

The very next day, Matt stormed into class, grabbed his candle with his flame of hope, wadded it up and throw it on the teacher's desk. The following words were uttered from a very dejected little soul, "This is wrong! God doesn't answer our prayers!"

Well, one can only imagine the tenderness of the moment between his mother and his teacher, but Holy Spirit had the whole picture in full view as to the plan of God. He was ready to teach a truth and they were open to "hear" and listen.

Jane shared with this distressed fellow believer that she too was learning that God does answer prayers.

He really does!

But to be more specific,

He often says, "Yes!"

He often says, "No!"

He often says, "Wait!"

He often says ... nothing!

Or so it seems at the very moment one is struggling to make sense of a perplexing situation, find an answer to a despair, conquer a crippling fear, seek reassurance, or simply find hope!

Even King David of Israel, the apple of God's eye, lamented thousands of thousands of years before our little boy expressed his disappointment, that he felt abandoned.

Psalm 22: 1-2 (NLT),

> *"My God, my God, why have you abandoned me? Why are you so far away when I groan for help? Every day I call to you, my God but you do not answer me. Every night I left my voice, but I find no relief."*

But just as quickly as these verses unfolded in Scripture, they were proceeded by stronger words to give our son (and us) a "Rest Stop" within which to park a troubled spirit. A moment of respite from the worrisome road our family was stumbling down.

Psalm 22:24 (MSG),

> *"He has never let you down, never looked the other way when you were being kicked around. He has never wandered off to do His own thing; but He has been right there, listening."*

My young son's prayer request and the simplicity of his honesty was a powerful, Holy Spirit led moment which opened up an opportunity for deeper spiritual teaching in his classroom as well as in our home. Bible stories and truths were studied in greater depth as we all realized God's plans don't always align with our desires. His way is always the best—even when we don't understand. We would carry that truth over many a rough spot in the years to follow.

Even today, both our children and their families cover us with their prayers, boldly asking but also knowing He will answer in His time and with His purposes. Our lives exist to glorify Him!

In her book, *God Did Not Do This To Me: Finding Hope, Courage, and Faith to Face Our Toughest Challenge,* Lisa Stringer presents her family's struggle with her husband's cancer and shares her husband's quote which is so appropriate.

"Our personal crucibles of experience can often become a tutor along our life's journey. Each life experience can become a life lesson that becomes a part of our life message."[1]

My family and I were learning so much about prayer, suffering, compassion, and sometimes just the very basics of how-to daily maneuver around or through those hazards which seemed to always block our roads.

Oftentimes we were (and still are) reminded of many stories from our childhood days spent under the teaching of Sunday School teachers, youth workers, camp counselors, Bible study leaders, and pastors.

Stories about people who were human beings full of character weakness and flaws, but whom God used to reveal so much about Himself and His purposes.

A few of these ancient individuals remind me of my own personal struggles.

- King David sought answers, found strength—1 Samuel 22-24
- Moses sought wisdom, found trust—Exodus 4
- Job sought reason, found comfort—Job
- Paul sought relief, found praises—2 Corinthians 12
- John the Baptist sought clarity, found His Messiah—Luke 7
- Stephen sought ministry, found courage—Acts 7

Even as ... caves became shelters from anger, plagues encompassed a nation, life fell apart, physical affliction never left, a beheader's axe fell, and stones rained down.

There was (and is) always a life lesson around every bend if we are willing to "see" it through the vision of our soul's windshield.

Pastor Andrews reinforced this truth for us once when he stated,

"You may shake on the rock ... but the Rock will never shake under you!" (May 1986)

That small but powerful quote was printed on a wooden plaque and has been displayed on my wife's desk for all these years. A great reminder of Psalm 40.

As I have already mentioned just as Matt helped us with his honesty regarding the candle and prayer, Cindy created another milestone marker early in my treatment days when she confronted her mother, who was scurrying around the kitchen getting our evening meal ready after being delayed by several well-meaning phone calls. She had overheard snippets about my health status. She planted her hands on her hips and stated,

"Why do you tell everyone else all about Dad and how he is doing but you tell us nothing! We want the truth! Is our Dad going to die?"

Well, after recovering from the shock of such a stark question expressed by our precious eight-year-old, Jane realized that tempered honesty with the children was needed. They deserved the truth as we knew it so that their fearful thoughts or imagined scenarios could be shared, discussed, and prayed over.

I believe these early moments of my cancer years were moments my family and I would never have learned without first experiencing the fear, frustration, and weariness which accompanied the sharp curves and deep valleys of our life journey.

Endnote

1 Lisa Stringer, *God Did Do Not This To Me,* Page 109, Whitaker House, 2020.

Ten

WELCOME ABOARD!

In case it seems that all our days in Buffalo were weighted down with sickness and struggles, I will mention here the gift our Creator designed for us when first He spoke, "Let there be ..."

With those words, He formed the great water ways of the world, invisible streets for nautical vessels piloted by the hand of man. Cloud-covered mountains sent their snowy waters down winding creeks and rivers to fill vast lakes which, in the order of natural motion, steadily pushed their liquid contents into bodies of oceans. A phenomenal example of power and purpose. These icy waters often cascaded down extreme rock formations to plummet into whirlpools of churning splendor. One such raw beauty in motion is represented by the great and mighty Lake Erie and the swiftly moving Niagara River. Together they converge to throw their energy and contents violently over the rocks of the spectacular falls pressed between New York State and Ontario.

To judge their ages is useless, but to give them respect is vital. Their invisible currents are captivating and challenging for the best of boaters. These were not the tranquil waters of Rock Lake, the playground of my youth! No gentle lapping waves nor slowly crawling currents. This was serious boating not for the faint of heart!

And to this group of adventurers our family joined when, with Pastor Andrew's encouragement, we purchased a motorboat. Now, his idea was for us to slowly start out in the boating world with an eighteen-foot bow rider big enough to accommodate our family of four.

Imagine his surprise when our new boat was HIS old boat of twenty-three feet—a sleek beauty he had traded in for a newer model. No small boat for us! And of course, it had to have lots of speed to carry on my reputation for a love of horsepower and zip!

Remember my childhood nickname—"Rev"?

I should mention here that my buddy, Dick DeWitt who was an avid sailor, always wondered why I did not choose the sailing life with its calming pace, noiseless cutting through waves, and serene capturing of winds in woven sails. Well, once again that adolescent label above said it all. I was never built for slow movement under my feet—either on land or on the high seas! Fast, and his cousin Faster, were my companions! In the future, motorcycles, Corvettes, and Ford Mustangs would duplicate the velocities I enjoyed.

I am pleased to note this difference in our boating styles never interfered with the priceless friendship Dick and I shared and continue to do so even to this very day. Ours is an Old Testament David and Jonathan relationship—one of loyalty and compassion in suffering, celebration in victories, and a deep-seated faith in Jesus Christ, our Defender and King. Dick has walked with me down many rough lanes as well as along paths of great joy. And always by his side has been his amazing wife, Marvel.

She has blessed our family so much over the years with laughter in the high ridges and heartfelt tears in the very lowest valleys. Friends through it all!

Now, once again, back to boating!

Having been raised "on the water" so to speak, I could boast of some knowledge regarding boating safety and rules of navigating. However, the amount of knowledge required to operate a vessel upon these swiftly moving, larger bodies of water was extensive and challenging. There are no natural signs on waterways marking location, travel distances, a specific route, or all hazards.

So, over the centuries, man has used his intellect to design aids of navigation in the form of buoys, day beacons, lighthouses, flashing lights, fog signals, and channel markers just to name a few. Each is a sign of caution or direction for boaters traveling upstream, downstream, or zigzagging across bodies of water moving toward the sea, the final destination for all waters. There are masterfully designed maritime charts for water depths, current routes, the location of unseen hazards, and much more. Just as road maps and operational rules guide our land vehicles in their comings and goings, seafaring aids assist boaters to arrive safely at their intended destinations.

Well, isn't this a perfect moment to share a little Senior wisdom born from years of living and learning?

Since the beginning of man's existence way back at the early steps of Creation, God established a simple fact. Humans would always need directional guides. We would never survive without rules of behavior.

Our souls would drift away from Him every time we ignored the perfectly placed markers, beacons, warnings, stop signs!

God's absolutes for living are not to be replaced by our whims of selfishness. I "need" to be happy seems to be the new goal for many—young and old. I "need" to feel... I "need" to... I "need"... I!

As I have shared already, I grew up with lots of rules, many of which I fought against. Rules of dress, rules of church attendance, rules of Sunday behavior (i.e. no playing hockey Sunday), rules of driving (how many tickets did I get?) Lots of rules! However, I now look back and realize just how very important those rules were in protecting me from dangers, shaping my values, and assisting me in making the best choices.

I realize that my children and grandchildren live in a world so much more permissive, and one far removed from what I experienced in my youth, but there still remains the need within man for direction and codes of behavior.

The new "gray" seeks to blend the black and white of God's sovereign rules in order to appease man's desire to be free of the consequences of steering off the narrow path or piloting outside the channels to drift around in the shallows.

Part of my daily prayers for my descendants is that their eyes would always stay focused on where my God is leading them, directing their steps, plotting their life courses; that His rules given in the greatest measure of love would always guide their decisions.

Proverbs 3:5-6, 11, 12 (NLT),

> *"Trust in the Lord with all your heart; do not depend on your own understanding. Seek His will in all you do, and He will show you which path to take. My child, don't reject the Lord's discipline, and don't be upset when He corrects you, For the Lord corrects those He loves just as a father corrects a child in whom he delights."*

Now, back to boating!

It seems that I have always been drawn to water.

Rock Lake, Echo Lake, Trent Severn Canal, Lake Simcoe, Lake Ontario, Niagara River, Erie Canal up till now. The list would later be expanded to include Detroit River, Lake St, Clair, St. Clair River, Missouri River, Tampa Bay, Gulf of Mexico, Atlantic and Pacific Oceans, as well as oceans of the Caribbean.

Each with its own attraction of force, rhythm, movement. There is probably a life lesson here somewhere. I will leave that for future analysis!

Over the next years as residents of Greater Buffalo, our family delighted in the freedom of tackling those rapidly flowing waters right outside our marina's entrance and embracing the wind while racing along the shores of New York and Ontario. The boat became our escape from whatever we had endured the week before. Our chance to separate ourselves, if only for brief hours or an extended weekend, from the unspoken anxieties coupled with the weariness of cancer and radiation treatments. Just to have moments where we could laugh together, share picnic meals, awake to misty mornings along the banks of the Erie Canal, or learn the mechanics of maneuvering through boat locks. Sometimes we just lazed aboard the boat as she rested in our riverside slip. It was enough to just be together! There was always fishing off the dock and somehow food always tasted so

IT WAS ENOUGH TO JUST BE TOGETHER!

much better on the boat! Especially Jane's famous chicken salad which accompanied us on most of our boating excursions.

Of course, some of my memories of our boating experiences may differ somewhat from the rest of the family. Jokingly, Cindy reminds me that she remembers the times of heated "discussions" her parents had occasionally as I, Captain of my Ship, was piloting our vessel at full bore speed while First Mate Jane was reading the navigational charts for water depths. I could visually see where I wanted us to go while she could see where we should not be going and was expressing her concerns. Our boat was equipped with a depth finder which sounded a loud warning when we had entered dangerously shallow waters, but what man listens to that?

Now, that same man would listen to his wife's loud warning if he was smart, and I learned that very quickly. It was easy to ignore the boat's danger alarms, but never advisable to do the same with your wife's verbal soundings! She had the charts after all!

I just had desire for speed!

Poor Cindy has the memory!

Let it be noted that my wife and I never argued. Ours were always "discussions." At least that is what we pointed out to our children. There is a difference! And I might add that this reasoning is still practiced to this very day!

With a chuckle here, I remember our first trip up the Erie Canal, a masterfully designed water "road" built in 1825 which was the major commercial canal system connecting the Great Lakes to the Atlantic Ocean. Its history is amazing as it cut through farmer's fields, towns and cities, and under bridges to create a new way to move bulk goods from the East Coast of US and the western interior and the reverse route. Years later, with the emergence of more advanced means of transporting products and cargo, it found a new life as a recreational route for pleasure crafts. What a unique experience for pilots and crew as they learned to maneuver the challenges of canal boating. "No Wake Zones" were strictly enforced. Narrow sections of passage required alert steering. Port and starboard passing was done with politeness and care, so everyone remained safe. And those locks!

Wow! What a challenge as there were strict rules to follow entering and exiting. One did not just drive one's vessel into the tightly walled structure designed to raise or lower boats from one elevation to another. It required skill to not scrape boat sides along slimy, rocky walls while threading rope lines through permanently secured side support metal bars thus allowing a boat to move up or down as rushing water filled or emptied the canal. Sounds confusing and a bit scary? Well, it was! Took some doing, but my crew (my wife!) and I figured it out as we devised a plan using only one long line attached to stern and aft boat cleats. It was a sense of accomplishment.

Our canal trips were always an adventure, but one definitely stands out far above the rest for excitement and embarrassment all in one. Jane and I made plans to do an overnight stay at The Basket Factory located along the Canal route. The restaurant rented marine slips along the river outside their facility, so it was a great arrangement—tie up in a nice spot and eat at a great restaurant. It was one of the few times we left the children with friends and boated alone. The current buzz word would be "date night" I guess.

The trip was progressing smoothly, and we were enjoying the leisurely pace through farms and small communities bordering our water route. Other boaters had cautioned us to be on the alert for floating objects in the water as the Canal was famous for objects like logs and tree branches which were often below the surface. Well, we did just fine avoiding the visible dangers, but it was the invisible which was our undoing in spite of my First Mate's sharp lookout.

Sure enough, one such hidden car seat hit our engine prop and we were rudderless, drifting along without any control of this very expensive toy (in the opinion of our fledgling budget), and no other boaters insight to come to our rescue. Good news was that we were right under a highway bridge and could tie off at a small-town park dock. Now, what to do?

Through a visual closeup of the engine prop, I determined that it was none functional and would need to be replaced.

Leaving my First Mate on board and in charge, I hitch hiked into Rochester, New York to the closest marine dealer who was more than happy to exchange my $125 for a shiny new prop and instructions on how to replace it. Back I hitched to the docked boat, donned my swim trunks and a life jacket to enter the water intent on properly replacing damaged prop.

It looked fairly straightforward, and the task was soon finished. We were back on our adventure with wiser eyes watching for the dreaded debris. All passed smoothly with our vessel once again leisurely gliding along.

Imagine our surprise when all of a sudden, my ability to steer a straight path abruptly ended and the boat just went in tight, slow circles—around and around and around. Now what had happened?

This time we were able to paddle to a rather dilapidated private dock along the shore and I once again went into the murky water to discover that we did not even have a prop.

Gone!

Vanished!

Sunk in the canal!

It seems my skill of replacing the prop was in need of a refresher course as I had not properly tightened the lock down clips.

Yes, I once again made the hitch-hiking trip into same Rochester Marine store to purchase my second prop in five hours! It was a humbling experience! And an expensive one as it wasn't a "2 for 1" sale day! The shop owner made his sale's quota that day off one customer. Me!

So it was back to the boat, swallowed my pride, carefully read the instructions, got back into the water, tightened the clips properly, and continued on down the river a great deal smarter for the experience.

Later, we had a good chuckle over this learning moment!

Much later!

It was a blessing that my family really enjoyed boating together and we were becoming comfortable with the rigors of boat ownership—washing and waxing exterior surfaces, vacuuming interior carpets, polishing chrome, bleaching or sealing teakwood, scrubbing canvases and bumpers, or assisting in docking tie ups. There was a lot of work maintaining the boat, but the pleasure came when we could invite friends and family to join us as on our voyaging.

What followed soon after our first months of boating life was the development of a strange (but common) condition within me as a sportsman. Jane aptly named it, Foot Fever—a phenomenon or malady which overtakes a man to the extent that he secretly reads and researches material pertaining to the next boat he will be purchasing, one which is longer, wider, bigger, and faster than his present vessel. Such a boat was on my radar and, after much discussion with my current marina manager for his assistance on a trade in, I was soon the proud owner of a beautiful thirty-foot Sea Ray Sundancer, a dream of a boat in creamy white with blue trim.

Now to introduce our new boat to the rest of the family who were totally unaware of my executive decision to improve our boating experience. Of course, I could have just reminded my wife of her "reworking" of the backyard pool idea, but that would have not been too healthy. So, I came up with a great plan which actually worked! The kids were thrilled with more sleeping space while my wife was impressed with the special name I had scrolled in a fancy decal across the aft section. For as long as this boat was ours, she would be called,

"SEA JANE RUN!"

Brilliant move on my part.

She loved the idea, and I was forgiven for making such a big decision without her input. I think at this point in our marriage we did come to an agreement that any purchases over one hundred dollars needed to be discussed by both parties.

Did not always happen, but at least we tried.

Actually, there was another incident of a major surprise purchase made and this time it was not by me! I have mentioned before that my chemotherapy regiment was extremely difficult and I was often nauseous. To combat this side effect, I was allowed to take a drug called Ativan which did its job well to curb my vomiting, but it also resulted in short term memory loss. Sometimes this was forgotten in our daily life decisions.

I need to go backwards here for a small detail which plays a part in this story. As I have previously explained, two years after we were married, our budget improved somewhat so we could purchase a real Maplewood dining room table with four chairs to replace a steel legged and Formica topped beat up beauty as old as we were! It may still be in the old trailer in Spring Arbor! The new dining set traveled with us in our next seven moves and held up remarkably well.

Well, now our new Buffalo home had a real spacious dining room which just begged for a larger, nicer table and chairs to accommodate all the company we enjoyed. A china hutch would be nice and maybe even one with a felt lined silverware drawer.

My wife was now the one doing the secret research for a desired upgrade.

It worked out great that one weekend when her parents were visiting, she enlisted her mother's assistance in furniture shopping while I was relaxing at home. Much to their delight, they located a beautifully elegant solid cherry wood table, six upholstered chairs, and a two-piece hutch with clear glass shelves bathed in an accent light. There was even a big felt- silverware drawer! The complete package!

All on sale! The Jackpot!

All Jane had to do was complete the paperwork and arrange for delivery. Small glitch here—her private school salary was not enough to allow her to qualify for financial services, so my credit and salary information was required. She was bummed, but not deterred. I signed the paperwork which allowed for a completed transaction and a two-week date was set for delivery of our new furniture.

Imagine the delivery crew's surprise when, upon their attempt to deliver said furniture, I greeted them at the door with a shocked response explaining that we had NOT made such a large purchase. They must have the wrong house! Imagine my shock when their orders clearly showed we HAD made the purchase and there in bold, black ink was my signature.

My dear wife to this day still insists there was no deception involved here! I did not remember signing the form nor even our discussion of the purchase.

In retrospect, the furniture was put to good use over the years as it survived five more major moves. It could tell many a story of times shared with family and friends.

Keeping with this thought of times spent together with others in various activities, I am reminded of the hours over the years I have had the privilege of playing high school football, college soccer, and the hockey in Michigan. God bless the country of my birth, Canada, for refining hockey in the early nineteenth century! I have shared the ice with many amazing young and old men who eagerly strapped on sharpened skates to skim across the surface of the frozen water in the hot pursuit of that elusive black puck. Win or not, we all enjoyed the camaraderie of sweat, aching muscles, full on body checking, good natured ribbings, and the friendly banter in the locker rooms. In seven of the places we called home, I was part of a hockey team. In Buffalo, the stress of my previous week was always relieved when I stepped onto the ice and took my place as a right winger ready to score, or at least try.

That said, it was with the sense of a great loss when, because of my cancer treatments and their ravaging side effects, I had to hang up my skates and relegate all my equipment to the basement or attic. I was only thirty-six years old and had played this revered sport for over thirty years. To say I had dreaded this moment would come as an understatement. One of the last games I played in Buffalo holds a bit of a scary moment for my kids and confirmed my suspicions that this part of my life was soon to be relegated to memories.

IT WAS WITH A SENSE OF GREAT LOSS WHEN, BECAUSE OF MY CANCER TREATMENTS, I HAD TO HANG UP MY SKATES

During my shift on the ice, I was streaking along in full speed mode when an opponent decided to halt my progress by shoving my face into the side protective plexiglass boards. This violent check occurred right in front of Matt and Cindy as they pressed their little faces to the glass and were loudly cheering for their dad. Yikes! Lots of blood smeared the glass as my face was cut. Our family then spent the next couple of hours in an Urgent Care getting me patched up. Thus, the end of hockey for me as a player. It was a very sad time for sure!

I have spent a great deal of time describing the sporting and spiritual sides of our passage through New York State. But in case someone thinks all our life consisted of was chemotherapy, radiation, church, and sports, I was still gainfully employed by Ford Credit and kept myself to a very tight work schedule with the intent of keeping some stability in my life. Monday through Friday and even some weekends found me behind my desk sorting through challenging paperwork, writing reports headed to Corporate Office in Dearborn, facilitating dealer meetings, and keeping my finger on the pulse of the office staff as they concentrated on reaching successful performance goals.

I should mention here that my various positions of leadership with Ford over the years had not been without its benefits in the area of transportation provided for my use. Company cars became standard issues, and I was privileged to drive many a fine vehicle. I fondly remember a stunning silver Thunderbird with red interior, an older gentleman's style Crown Victoria, a sleek black and gold Lincoln Mark 7. Each year a new model was available for my use, so we leased Jane and the kids a car which suited their daily adventures. Strange as it may seem, from 1976 to 2005 we did not personally own a car. Executive leases were at our disposal. It made for an interesting moment when many years later, our kids had to buy their own vehicles plus insurance to cover damages or maintenance. Reality check!

I almost forgot to mention that we even "drove" a snowblower which had the famous Ford blue oval on it! A vital purchase in the middle of our first raging snowstorm during our inaugural wild Buffalo winter while I was in the throes of that first wretched regiment of chemotherapy. After watching almost fifty inches of snow fall in forty-eight hours, I determined that my wife's slim aluminum shovel was no match for what blanketed our house and entire neighborhood. We soon became owners of a huge self-propelled, walk behind, rumbling machine which did boast of its maker as Ford Motor Company. What did you expect? Only another Ford product would fit the bill and be allowed in the garage!

Harkening back to her farm heritage with its tractors and machinery, my wife thoroughly enjoyed firing up the beast and attacking the snowy adversary over the next years. As they got older, even the kids did not complain when it became their responsibility to clear our drives and sidewalks.

As Branch Manager, I was keenly aware of my responsibilities and will always be grateful for the professional staff under my direction. They were extremely supportive of me during the days after treatment when I was not physically in the office or maybe not at my best. It was not my goal to present an "Everything is fine" face at work nor did I want to be a complainer who used my disease as a tool to slack off or over delegate my work tasks to others. Personally, I was a challenge for God as my human pride wanted to NOT be known as the guy with cancer. That was not the legacy I wanted to leave with anyone. But in love, God gave me the strength to push aside that temptation to isolate that part of my life. I was a cancer victim, but not a defeated one!

Credit too must go to my employers. When one is faced with a catastrophic illness, there is always the underlying fear that your job could be in jeopardy. I will not deny that I was worried about the reality for future advancements with the company as I believed that, behind closed doors, upper management was probably in discussions as to my work capabilities or even my future.

It is with a loud and firm voice I report here that never once at that time was, I ever made to feel that my job was in danger. In fact, just the opposite occurred when, after four years, I was promoted to the home of the "Glass House," world headquarters for Ford Motor Company and Ford Credit in Dearborn, Michigan.

The Move of a Lifetime!

The Big House!

The home of the automobile company under which my Grandfather Revell had opened his dealership in that little village beside the lake in Ontario, Canada in 1936!

The Mecca of my dreams as a fledgling employee fifteen years in the rear-view mirror.

I could hardly believe this confirmation of the company's loyalty to me and their affirmation of my skills. It appeared that, in spite of my precarious health history, Senior Management was still committed to advancing me. This was a direct and clear example to me that my God was still working in my life. He had not abandoned me to the darkness of a wretched disease which at any moment could completely wreck my very life. I had already endured rigorous chemotherapy and extended radiation regiments designed to destroy those original cancer tumors.

Unfortunately, the battle was to continue as I began to experience bone pain in my left hip which then required additional chemotherapy, orally and infused. The job offer came at just the moment I was once again riding a bumpy trail.

Without a moment's hesitation, I accepted the promotion and then set in motion the relocation process with the family. This was going to be another very big move for us as we were all firmly entrenched in our beloved church and school.

Emotionally, this was without question the deepest we had allowed our roots to grow. Our lives had been deeply entwined with others through the sharing of emotional lows or highs, moments of raw anxieties, and the joy of victories both physically and spiritually. One of the blessings of suffering, odd as it may seem, is the connection which occurs between people who are willing to open themselves in honesty. Unconsciously, each of us had been thrown into the battle waging between my Creator and the evil forces roaming the Earth to destroy anything good, including me! God had orchestrated for us unbelievable opportunities of trusting His timing and provisions. Matt and Cindy had come to Buffalo as very young children blessedly oblivious to the cost for each family member in a cancer diagnosis to a loved one. They would now be carrying with them a new reality and better perspective, albeit forced upon them, of suffering, disappointment, and compassion.

In spite of the darkness which had encircled us many times, these had been amazing years in Buffalo. Never would we have imagined that we would carry with us such wonderful friends and memories.

So once again, I packed up the contents of my desk and removed my personal belongings from the branch office to make way for my replacement. It had been nineteen years since I had, as a young Canadian lad with adventure in his vision, pointed a car in the direction of Michigan to begin a new chapter of life. This time I would be carrying a whole distinctive cargo of new personal experiences and career expectations.

I was less confident in my future, but more confident in my God's faithfulness regardless of the view from my front windshield.

I shall now attempt to present my second Executive Summary of work experience over the next twenty-four years. It will shorten the printed word considerably which may not meet my detail-focused writing partner's desire to tell "the rest of the story!" (Paul Harvey)

- DETROIT WORLD HEADQUARTERS—1988 to 1993

- RESOURCES MANAGEMENT MANAGER—study processes and allocate time/headcount for branch operations

- CUSTOMER RELATIONS MANAGER—manage all customer complaints directed to the Senior Executive Management officers one of which was Edsel Ford—great grandson of Henry Ford, the founder of Ford Motor Company.

- OMAHA, NEBRASKA—1993 to 2005

- CUSTOMER SERVICE CALL CENTER MANAGER—handle all companywide customer, dealer, and Executive complaints. Responsible for all customers written and telephone contacts regarding financial service accounts (loans and leases).

- DIRECTOR OF CUSTOMER SERVICES FOR NORTH AMERICAN OPERATIONS—manage all customer contact centers in Nashville, Omaha, Costa Rica, Ottawa, Ontario, Canada, and Edmonton, Alberta, Canada.

- TAMPA, FLORIDA—2005 to 2008

- SYKES ENTERPRISES—DIRECTOR OF CLIENT SERVICES—manage client/customer contacts in Costa Rica and El Salvador for clients in North America.

There you have it! Executive summary! Clear and concise!

Once again, my co-author gently reminded me that my life journey portrait could not be painted in just two colors—black and white. It must be told through the vibrant colors of God's faithfulness, His relentless care, His gift of Jesus as my Redeemer. Brush strokes of suffering, joys, sorrows, disappointments, and victories sweeping across a blank canvas to create an amazing picture of love. One which my children, their children, and their children could be reminded of as they face their own struggles.

In Psalm 145:1-6 (MSG), Hebrew King David expressed this perfectly when he declared over two thousand years ago:

"I will lift You high in praise! my God, O my King! And I'll bless Your name into eternity. I'll bless You every day and keep it up from now to eternity. God is magnificent; He can never be praised enough. There are no boundaries for His greatness. Generation after generation stands in awe of Your work; each one tells stories of Your mighty acts. Your beauty and splendor have everyone talking; I compose songs on Your wonders. Your marvelous doings are headline news; I could write a book full of the details of Your greatness."

2017 JEEP SAHARA

DETROIT, MICHIGAN

A city of extremes whose history is as colorful as a new box of Crayons. Its maze of streets has known every people group and been witness to every possible human experience from poverty to wealth, greed to sacrifice, laziness to ambition, dreams to reality, and simplicity to complexity. It can boast of inventions beyond man's wildest dreams, but also decry the tragedies of man's nightmares. Its nicknames are as diverse as its occupants: Motown, Hockeytown, The Motor City, Tiger Town to name a few.

I am not planning to digress into its earliest days here but will just mention that this Midwest city has had an intense history from wandering fur traders to brilliant inventors. Its majestic estates built by wealthy auto barons brush up next to cardboard huts of the homeless. Names like Dodge, Chapin, Joy, Alger, and of course, Ford left their marks through their wonderful vehicles of transportation, right alongside history's recording of many dark days under serious civil unrest and discord. Not to miss mentioning the wonderful creativity birthed here through music from all venues of sound. What an amazing story!

My earliest exposure to this city of extremes had come when, as a young Toronto Maple Leaf's hockey fan as well as a secret admirer of the Detroit Wings with their super star, Gordie Howe, I had listened in on their fiercely fought games over the radio through the voice of Hockey Night in Canada. Every Saturday night throughout my childhood, Foster Hewitt announced each game—the intensity of excitement in his voice drawing a visual picture in my mind of the action unfolding on the ice. Eventually, radio was replaced by television and the hearing became seeing which only increased my enthusiasm. To say then that having to cease playing hockey was a great disappointment to me is truly an understatement.

But life changes things and we move on.

In my case, boating and golf filled that sport void left by hockey's departure. Not the same level of physical exertion, but exercise none the less and a chance to build relationships with other fellows. Even to the point of forming a golfing group called The Golfing for God Guys in Omaha, Nebraska.

Oh wait, that story belongs in the next chapter, so back to Detroit.

So once again, a hotel (a much nicer one this time), became my abode for several months while Jane and the kids remained back in Buffalo to finish the school year, keep the house in tip top shape for open houses in the process of selling, arrange for a moving company, and begin the task of filtering out all the accumulated household possessions which did not need to be dragged to the new house. Now that created some interesting discussions between my children and their mum as this was the first move for Cindy and Matt within which they could voice their opinions on what was valuable and warranted a box labeled, "Keep," or what was considered unnecessary and deserved to be left behind.

Thankfully, this was another company move fully funded by Ford Credit, so everyone's prized and valued treasures were included in the weight count for the transport. Even my old leather hockey helmet from my youth and the Goat Island lobster trap avoided the cut! Priorities here!

Thus, it was that, with the job of selling the house and wrapping up our astonishingly sweet yet decidedly bitter years in Buffalo resting in my wife's experienced hands, I pulled up to the front doors of the Dearborn office of Ford Credit World Headquarters to begin the process of acclimation to a whole new set of skills in the field of Automotive Finance and Customer Service. This was a dream come true and I was up for the challenge.

It did not escape my notice that my new office was one of many, many office spaces encased in the one-story structure. I was, for the present time, a small fish in a big pond which would require some adjustments from my previous roles as the big fish in a small pond. I was still considered upper management, but just not at a separate location.

Of course, it will surprise none of the readers of this journey who know me well that one of the very first projects on my work calendar was to arrange my new office to suit my style of work environment. Some (including my sisters, my wife, my children, my grandchildren, my neighbors, my closest friends, and my fellow work comrades) believe that I have a type A personality which supports a significantly obvious commitment to order and a symmetrical approach to all details in my life.

MY PERSONALITY SUPPORTS A SIGNIFICANTLY OBVIOUS COMMITMENT TO ORDER AND A SYMMETRICAL APPROACH TO DETAILS IN MY LIFE

Clothes hanging in my closet are arranged by function and style. Contents of my bathroom drawer are arranged in a non haphazard line while framed pictures or mementos symmetrically are arranged in my office. Desk top contents are positioned as to their level of importance in the tasks of each day. Even my garage does not escape the critic's eye of my desire to organize, reorganize, and further organize as much of life as possible.

Because of this ingrained sense of order and structure, I naturally brought to work that first week on the new job, a generous supply of picture nails, a small hammer, and several valued mementos to be displayed on the walls of my personal space. It was only when the first tapping of my hammer came to the attention of a fellow worker that I learned just how different this office setting was from what I had previously experienced. It seems that hanging pictures was a union covered task which could only be performed by a unionized person from the physical building management staff.

My hammer was silenced, and I filled out the appropriate requisition for a picture hanger. Walls were marked with tape where hangings were to be placed. Lesson learned and quickly.

Another interesting detail and not at all as embarrassing as the above moment, was the realization that as an upper management person, I was entitled to a company car which would be serviced and maintained at a unique onsite service center. There was even a car wash and gas bar totally at my disposal for use with the company cars and of course, manned by union fellows who performed the necessary services to keep my vehicle performing well. Over the next five years, I may have earned the unofficial title of the "Most Loyal Patron" as awarded by the car wash staff. That should come as no surprise to anyone. Everyone knows a clean car rides better as well as getting better gas mileage. It is just a fact!

Not only was I fortunate to have access to the service center on site, I was also privileged to have admittance to a very unique floor in the adjoining tall World Headquarters building. Fondly named the "Glass House," it housed the offices of the very highest level of Ford Executives. Upon a certain floor was the Executive Dining Room with its own kitchen, chefs, and wait staff. It was like dining in a very nice restaurant, so business dress was the accepted and expected attire if one was to dine there.

In fact, at that time we were all expected to be dressed in business attire—suits, ties, dress shirts, polished shoes for men while the female employees were always to wear modest dresses, business suits with skirts or tailored pants, and appropriate shoes. It was not until business casual was introduced that we were allowed more casual clothing albeit restrictions in place to permit only the wearing of jeans on Fridays.

I enjoyed the special dining room and even took my wife there once to have the experience. But as time would have it, things changed, and the dining room was fazed out. A tradition of history which had seen its day. A nice memory, nonetheless.

Throughout my story, I have included the role the automobile has played in my life. Cars have always been very important to me even as a small boy. Proceeds from car sales fed my Verona family, paid for my college education, allowed me to marry at a young age, and drove the engine of my career with Ford Credit. Vehicles transported myself and my loved ones through every scenario we experienced. It is not possible for me to include drawings of every car I have owned or had the privilege to drive so I have chosen some of the standout ones. If I counted on my skill to draw said vehicles, the results would be like Lego toys fashioned by a toddler. To the rescue here has come my granddaughter, Lauren

Washburn Evans, whom God has gifted with an amazing artistic expertise which she was willing to use in the illustrations I wanted to include.

Of course, cars were not the only means of transportation I have enjoyed over the years. I have been privileged to own some pretty cool motorcycles and have included them through drawings done by William John Washburn, our 12-year-old grandson who, like his sister, has also been gifted with artistic talent. I thank them both for adding such a special touch.

Keeping up the theme of traveling down a road, I followed the next sign in front which directed me to "Merge" into the traffic ahead of my steps. It did not take me long to settle into the responsibilities of my new position and I can truthfully say that I enjoyed nearly every day I was privileged to walk into my office.

Yes, I did say "nearly" as there were moments over the next six years when maybe my enthusiasm was a bit tempered. This was not the result of poor performances on my part nor those of staff or fellow workers. These bumps in the road, so to speak, were the results of being the brunt of persons who were not comfortable with themselves nor happy with how their lives were personally unfolding. I mention this not to perform character assassination on anyone, but to share the valuable lessons God taught me about honesty, staying focused on preserving my character, displaying job performances which reflected integrity, and treating others with respect in spite of what is handed back.

I was not responsible for the choices made by others, only my response as it showcased my personal walk with Christ and my commitment to respectfully working with all types of personalities in any situation. My loyalty was to my Savior, my family, and my self. In that exact order.

Matthew 5:44b (MSG),

> *"Let them bring out the best in you, not the worst. When someone gives you a hard time, respond with the supple moves of prayer, for then you are working out of your true selves, your God-created selves."*

Having established myself in the new work environment, I now once again needed to begin the house hunting process. For the seventh time since 1972, I spent my weekends and evenings on the sometimes-grueling task of researching communities and visiting homes for sale in the suburbs around Detroit. Not only was I armed with the experiences of past house purchases, but I also had as my search partner, my dear wife and her in-depth research of Michigan schools—public and private—as well as churches best suited for our family. Purchasing a home is such a huge undertaking that it is great when experience can streamline the process.

It was very helpful also that the relocation package Ford provided allowed Jane to fly in for a weekend of house hunting as by then I had zeroed in on several areas of interest and one house in particular.

Once again, God was so faithful in leading us to the precise house in the exact neighborhood He had chosen for us knowing what we did not—just how vitally important our neighbors would be in our lives over the next six years.

Proverbs 20:24 (MSG),

> *"The very steps we take come from God; otherwise, how would we know where we're going?"*

The residence He led us to, was a rather plain brick two story with side load garage positioned on the front corner of a cul-de-sac at the back of a beautiful area in Farmington Hills, a Northern suburb twenty miles from my office. It was not a pretty house as it had sat empty for over one year with no one interested in adopting it. The large front lawn was overgrown with burnt grass and much of the landscape needed haircuts. The entire structure was desperately crying out for a paint job.

Jane said it looked sad—very sad!

But wait!

It had a pool, a cement pool with diving board which pretty much filled the entire back yard. Two tiers of wooden decking edged alongside and just yelled, "Entertain here!" It had good bones and just needed some tender loving care both inside and out.

Speaking of the interior, it was unusual for us in that directly off the inside garage door was a vaulted bonus room with built in bookshelves, all the countertops were very low (just how short were the previous owners?), basement stairs were open, the dining room walls were wallpapered in expensive grass cloth, and the kitchen was carpeted in colors of beige, orange, and brown. Ask Cindy how much she hated that carpet!

And that pool!

"Oh, my stars!" to quote my wife.

What a mess! That once pristine, custom designed pool was currently half full of brackish winter water due to the partially submerged tarp cover. The visible walls were slimy and deeply stained. Weeds wildly spread their ugliness next to the low clapboard fence which had once been a crisp, colonial gray color, but was now just weathered and unattractive. Privacy evergreens and bushes joined their front lawn counterparts in untrimmed conditions.

The entire property was a bit of an eye sore in the pleasant neighborhood, yet it just seemed to plead in soft whispers, "Please see my potential and take a chance on me!"

So, in spite of misgivings, we were drawn to this house and proceeded to make a very low offer which did not sit well with the listing agent. She was adamant that the company now owning the home would not accept such an offer. Maybe she was a little hesitant to submit our conditional offer which requested that the pool be serviced to return it to its original operating condition. This would be a very expensive undertaking, but one we required if they wanted to get this property off their books. By now, we were not greenhorns at house buying or negotiating. (Funny side note here is that the company was the Anheuser-Busch Beer Company.)

The offer was reluctantly submitted and to the amazement of the agent, it was accepted! The house was ours and at an excellent low price. Pool renovations started immediately under my close supervision and results were amazing! Within a month's time, the upgraded pool pump was circulating sparkling water around freshly painted cement walls of soft blue and the decking had been power washed to perfection. We were once again the owners of a beautiful pool just waiting for enthusiastic swimmers both young and old to swim, dive, or just float within its coolness. Many a game of "Marco Polo" would resound throughout the neighborhood as our backyard became the gathering place for fun, frolics, and fellowship.

Not only did we have a potentially comfortable home, but there would be such community blessings for our family. Once again, our God was quietly directing our journey. Could there have been other houses in other areas we would have been satisfied with? Yes. But this was to become a unique home surrounded by special people for a special time in our lives.

So armed with our new mailing address and a mind fully engaged in furniture placement and redecorating, Jane returned to Buffalo to resume her final weeks of teaching as well as setting in motion the actual house packing process with a Ford arranged moving company.

In retrospect, I should have warned the movers that this was not our first move so as to have saved them from several moments of repacking boxes slightly different than their usual manner. My Pit Bull was in full command of just HOW she wanted certain items packed. She had learned that drapes folded and layered in a deep wardrobe box would always result in drapes pressed with every permanent angle of creasing. The use of heavy duty padded hangers for all drapes solved the problem. It was also a fact that knickknacks shoved in and around lamp shades guaranteed dents and tears in fragile material. Thus, to their consternation, every loose item of the extra specially prized bric-a-brac every family possesses, as well as various sizes of our artwork, was collected on the dining room table waiting for boxes marked with a bold "Fragile" sign.

All audio equipment cords and controllers were to be individually stored in zip lock bags labeled as to their uses. Zip ties did the trick of bundling stray cords before being boxed in clearly marked containers. This saved a lot of frustration at the unpacking and setting up of televisions and the like.

Don't tell my wife this, but I was always very thankful to miss out on all the fine details of the actual packing of our household possessions as there was ONE chief and ONE only! The rest of us Indians just needed to follow directions and stay quiet! Of course, my job responsibilities demanded that I not be present until the last days when the truck was to be loaded, so by then all the decisions for packing had been made. Only one time did I have a very strong opinion on the moving of an item, but that is a story for Omaha to Florida and involved a motorcycle!!

Finally, the time came for my family to bid goodbye to their friends and join me in Farmington Hills, Michigan for the next leg of our adventure on the winding roads of my life journey. It was a very emotional time for each of us as we had nurtured deep, deep roots both physically and spiritually while in Buffalo and the pain of pulling away was intense. Several years later, a very wise friend of ours compared the emotions of moving to those of experiencing the loss of someone special.

In order for the new place to become acceptable and even welcomed, the grieving person needed to accept what had happened and not be afraid to put out new roots—roots of trust that God was going to lessen the sorrow while still

IT WAS BEST TO TRAVEL WITH THE ADVICE OF THE "NO U-TURN" POSTING.

preserving the good things which memories can become. Someone who never did the moving-on would always harbor the thought that this new place was only temporary. It was best to travel with the advice of the "No U-Turn" posting.

Soon summer was upon us, and we were more than ready to break in the newly refurbished pool. But first, moving boxes were all emptied, artwork hung, all that bric-a-brac was displayed, kids' rooms reflected their own style, and a new lawn mower was unleashed upon that wild front lawn. Several trips to Home Depot resulted in gallons of paint cans, multiple paint brushes, a scraper or two, drop sheets, and all the additional items we would need to freshen up that unsightly fence. While I continued to depart each morning for the 20-mile trip south to the office and the perpetual traffic struggles, my children attacked the lawn, fence, and deck under the firm direction of their mother who was keen on restoring our new home to its place as an acceptable member of the HOA.

Now, I would love to say they always jumped right out of bed each summer morning to enthusiastically plunge into the jobs as assigned, but they were normal kids who had a greater interest in plunging into that cool pool instead. They soon learned certain things were expected by their parental figures who believed in the infamous adages they themselves had been raised under in the dark ages of old!

"Work time comes before play time" or this one "As long as you put your feet under our table ..."

Don't feel sorry for them! There was lots of free time and fun in the sun when the weather got too hot, or the work was finished.

Having previously mentioned how humor has often been interjected into our lives, I would like to insert here a pretty funny incident involving the pool, the kids, and a big rodent! Several days after the moving van left and unpacking was in full swing, there was a loud shout which drew our attention to the window facing the pool.

"Mum, there is a big rat on the deck!"

Sure enough, reclining like the Prince of Egypt on a chaise, soaking up the warm summer sunshine, and enjoying his wooden domain which had been undisturbed for nearly a year, was a very large, hairy animal. Upon closer observation, it was discovered that it was NOT a rat but rather a plump and contented ground hog who had taken up residence under the deck!

One can only imagine his extreme shock when the patio door slowly opened and a loud, firm, commanding voice bellowed, "Hey, what do you think you are doing?"

With eyes bulging from sudden fear, the poor fat fellow sprang to his feet, vaulted off that deck, under the fence, and as far as we can tell, he is still running across the fields of Farmington Hills! We all had a bucket of laughter over that one.

Speaking of fun, we had decided before leaving Buffalo that the boat would accompany us to Detroit and fortunately, it was considered to be part of our household contents so the company would cover the cost of transporting such a large item. Good news for us!

We then had to locate a new marina in Detroit area within which to moor the vessel. Another extensive search for me as there were many marinas to choose from. Imagine how excited we were that boating on the immense expanse of waterways which flow from its point of origin at Chicago's shores, into Lake Michigan, swiftly passing under the Mackinaw Bridge, rushing through Lake Huron, flowing into Lake St. Clair, filling the Detroit River and Lake Erie, coursing over the falls of Niagara, and into Lake Ontario to eventually connect via the Saint Lawrence Seaway with the Atlantic Ocean. It boasts of a never-ending water flow from Chicago to the Strait of Honguedo, north of New Brunswick, Canada. A very long distance for sure!

Trust me!

We did not traverse all those water trails as Lake St. Clair east of downtown Detroit became our port of relaxation. It was nice to have a well maintained, gated marina with a country club like atmosphere. Even though we did not utilize all the amenities available to us, we did enjoy the security of knowing our boat was always safe and secure whenever we chose to use it. And use it, we did. Over the next six years we took the boat out on the water many times to cruise around observing the grand estates on the Michigan coastline as well as the interesting places boarding on the Canadian coastline.

One special excursion took us into the cove right outside the beautiful estate home of Edsel Ford, son of original Henry Ford. It was a stately home with magnificent grounds open to the public. We were able to anchor the boat and enjoy the serene surroundings from the water side.

Our walking tour of the place would occur later when we had the chance to view it from the inside. It was as if the family had just left for the day with plans to return later. A very homey place even as a domain of the wealthy. The appeal of touring this estate could be credited with it belonging to the Ford Family whose historically creative minds enabled me to pay the mortgage on my house. Or could it have been my wife's keen interest in history?

It may come across as extravagant to have brought the boat with us to Michigan and I will admit it was expensive to maintain the slip in the marina as well as the boat itself. But over the time we were there, that boat and our family's time on it became a refuge for my loved ones as life sometimes pressed in on us to discourage us and steal our joy. Many a weekend was spent cruising around shallow Lake St. Clair just enjoying each other or drifting along lazily swimming. Also included in these moments were friends of the kids, family, and relatives invited to share good times together. Many a chicken salad was served as well as more Vernors Ginger Ale! Even my mum would approve of that liquid of choice.

Speaking of friends, our new neighbors were very friendly and within the first week of settling into the house on Country Ridge Blvd, we were warmly welcomed by everyone. And I mean everyone!

Our corner of the community was literally teeming with young children of every age from infant to preteen. Just in our cul-de-sac alone there lived 12 kids! Our own two were thrilled to discover that the family whose front yard overlooked our backyard had two boys the same age and a younger daughter. Bill and Diana Stella with Tony, Gino and Arianna joined our list of dear friends who laughed and cried with us through many rough and smooth stretches of our life's journey as a family.

From the very first months of our settling in, we experienced their sincere friendship and caring for us. They were unselfish, sensitive, compassionate, and funny all rolled into the best type of neighbor/friends possible. Once again, our God had maneuvered our steps to the front doors of caring people who would fill the friendship space left vacant by our moving from each place we had lived since 1970! He always did!

In retrospect, I have made a brilliant discovery that there seems to be a distinct behavior pattern present in my life which should be included in this legacy story. With each job relocation, an interesting process had taken place—accept promotion, find new community, pack up household possessions, obtain all medical records, move lock stock and barrel, identify a church, choose a school, re-establish medical connections, and begin the forming of friendships. It became a grand adventure for the four of us and one which we accepted as part of living in the corporate world.

It all usually came together through a transport full of hard work, a truck load of organizational skills, a van crammed with good humor, and a caravan of acceptance of changes—small and great. I have been richly blessed by my wife and children's enthusiastic co-operation in the whole maze of changes we have had to motor in and through the entire expanse of my career with Ford. They were (and are) the very best bonus God has gifted me within my entire life.

Having mentioned church and school as to their extreme importance for us whenever we settled into our new locality, I can relate that God continued to turn our eyes toward that same road sign in our path, "No U-Turn." Buffalo was behind us.

Once again, my wife's investigative mind shifted into high gear as she researched all the private schools within the greater Detroit area with our full intent of continuing the kids' education in a setting which reinforced the moral truths we were teaching at home. An added bonus would be if said school was affiliated with a strongly conservative church and had an excellent academic curriculum.

As a result of her hard work and reliance on God to pave the way for clarity, we made the choice to enroll Matt and Cindy in Southfield Christian School housed on the campus of Highland Park Baptist Church in Southfield, a suburb within ten miles of our home. It met all of our requirements as Matt and Cindy entered fourth and sixth grades—those precariously crazy preteen time zones during which parents wonder if they have entered an endless game of bumper cars or a roundabout with no exit lanes. Would we all come out the other side in one piece?

I can in all honesty declare that we had been abundantly blessed in the character and personalities of our two children. Very seldom was there any need to exact upon them severe punishments for wrong choices or banish their faces from our presence due to attitudes projecting disrespect. For the most part, the exterior of our family "vehicle" remained unscathed and intact, not subjected to disfiguring dents or scrapes. What I am trying to say is that they were normal with the usual squabbles and mild discords, but they never caused us permanent heartache.

Even to this day, they both exemplify a strong, daily walk with their Lord which is very evident in lives centered on the Truths of Scripture, dedicated to moral integrity at work and at home, Holy Spirit led wisdom in parenting, and love for family and friends. It is very obvious to see who drives their personal vehicles—their Savior, Jesus Christ.

Over the next five years, SCS (Southfield Christian School) and HPB (Highland Park Baptist Church) became our center for schooling, sports, drama, music, social gatherings, and most importantly, spiritual nurturing. Just as at The Chapel and CCA in Buffalo, God had created for us at such a time as this the very best place for replanting our roots where they would be strengthened, protected, and encouraged to mature.

I will always be amazed when I look back at the roads laid out for me to travel upon that my precious God, my Savior, Jesus Christ, and ever-present Holy Spirit supplied with every detail covered and every need met. When we had the drive to run full speed ahead, they quietly but firmly governed us. When we experienced flat tires of emotions or physical strength, they supplied fresh wheels through the unending circle of friends and family offering companionship. When our spiritual gas tanks were on empty, they refueled us through wise teachers, retreats, Bible studies, home teams, and pastors. We never were abandoned, rejected, or isolated to blindly drive through the foggy stretches of life. Even in the darkest moments of sickness, disappointment, or discouragement, there is always a sign to follow, "KEEP RIGHT." This is best described through the words of King Solomon penned thousands of years ago but still relevant for today.

Proverbs 3:5-6 (MSG),

> *"Trust God from the bottom of your heart; don't try to figure out everything on your own. Listen for God's voice in everything you do, everywhere you go; He's the one who will keep you on track."*

Now that the kids had been enrolled in school, we turned our attention to checking out the church associated with it. Seemed like a logical place to worship, and after several Sundays of observing both main service and the youth program, we all agreed this would be a good fit for our family. Time would definitely prove that this was the very exact place we were to park our spiritual vehicle for the duration of our journey through Michigan. Regardless of lacking a Senior Pastor for the next three years, the church community continued to grow and fulfill its mission of caring for each person who walked through its doors. We were to be on the receiving end of incredible love sooner than we could have imagined.

Twelve

ROAD WORK AHEAD

My GPS now must record for you the next stretches of the almost unbelievable course I had traveled upon since October of 1984. Using the word "must" here may seem odd so let me explain. Looking in my rearview mirror while driving is an absolute necessity to safely operating any type of vehicle. That mirror gives me an instant reminder of what I have passed as well as what has been left behind, a distant memory. In walking you through the next 5 years, I will be required to dig deeply into memories which may be uncomfortable for me, but I am determined to show you just how faithful my God has been—even in the darkest part. He can be the same for you!

Moving to Michigan gave me a chance to glance back at my health struggles in the mirror of my mind and then fully focus my eyes on the future, hoping that never again would I be faced with new cancers requiring additional grim treatments. I was happy to leave the painful cancer experience behind as if my memory mirror was all fogged over.

Each month in our new community put space between my backward glances and the promising future ahead.

As I saw it, the persistent bone pain in my hip was being successfully monitored by an elderly doctor who was a medical school friend of my Buffalo oncologist. Doctor L. was from the old days of cancer care when caution and conservative practices were the routine. He was practical and reserved in his methods as he treated me from his office associated with a small suburban regional hospital. My new regiment consisted of one low dose chemo pill taken each day for what would be the duration of at least one year. No infusions. No radiation. No new CT scans. No new X-rays. No extensive blood count workups. Just a wait and see for now. Piece of cake as I saw it. This I could handle. What was a little discomfort with all I had previously undergone?

Work and family time filled my days and nights. It was my practice to ignore pain and discomfort in order to live a more normal life under the dangerous practice of my extremely high pain tolerance. Many times, I think my spouse heard that little noise I made at night when the pain was strong, but I may have ignored her concern.

However, she was one person who had willingly traveled with me over every bump, every smooth stretch, every hill and valley for nearly twenty-one years, and was unsettled in her mind that something was just not right with my medical care. Quietly, my wife began to seek God's direction and leading in seeking a second oncological opinion for me. The expanse of the Greater Detroit area presented hundreds of doctor options, but how could she know who or where to turn to for the best care?

Well, the answer was no farther away than our back fence! You see Bill Stella, our new neighbor whose house we saw every day from our windows, had a brother who was an Oncology Specialist in Ypsilanti.

It just happened that Jane mentioned one day to his wife of the quest to find another doctor. Diane made a call to her brother-in-law and within a short time, had the name and phone number for someone he recommended us to contact. My God was paving a new course, a new road for us to quickly follow. Little did we know just how much of a blessing and miracle that recommendation would be for our family.

Wasting no time, my resourceful wife placed that one call to the office of Dr. Chatchada Karanes, M.D., Hematology Specialist at Harper Hospital in downtown Detroit. It was pretty amazing that Jane was able to speak directly with Doctor Karanes after just a few short rings of the phone. Definitely a divine working as usually a physician's staff monitors all calls. Immediately there was an interest in my situation followed by the setting of an appointment two days later! This was one of those resoundingly loud, "Yes! Right now!" answers to a prayer. Remember my little boy's candle story from the Buffalo days?

There was a revived hope in our home that possibly with a new oncologist reviewing my case history, we might have a chance to add more years to my life. I reference here the moment back in Buffalo when I was made to realize throughout the doctor's point-blank assessment of my advanced stage cancer condition that time was not in my favor. In my anxiety, I asked God to grant me enough extra time for me to see my kids graduate from high school. In His lovingkindness, I have actually attended those graduation ceremonies, been proudly present at their weddings, joyously welcomed their children and even great grandchildren! I have been allowed to assist in their relocations, been entertained royally in their homes, and continue to this very day to be a part of their lives as responsible adults, amateur sports coaches, a businessman with integrity, a supportive Army wife, and strong followers of Christ. Repeatedly over the length of my extended years, I have heard my Father's voice reminding me of His amazing grace.

I have been truly blessed!

So, with that said, should I end this manuscript here and wrap up my life ride with a verse or two?

Hardly, as there is much more to share in this amazing adventure the young lad from Verona has been allowed to experience. This quote by Steve Saint, son of martyred missionary Nate Saint, best expresses my desire to continue sharing my story.

"Your story is the greatest legacy that you will leave to friends. It's the longest-lasting legacy you will leave to your heirs."[1]

Thus, with this purpose in my front vision, I am firing up the writing engine and continuing to accelerate down the road ahead.

Thanks to my wife's personal need for details beyond executive summaries and coupled with her God-given satisfaction in organizational results, we carried with us to our first new oncologist appointment files full of medical records. This was another of those lessons we had learned since 1984 that would prove to be immensely valuable over the entire span of my health needs and physical history. Those files contained previous diagnostic testing reports, blood counts, X-rays, medicine doses, and doctor referral letters. What seemed to be an obsession for perfectionism on our part actually was a valuable personality trait I was born with, and Jane acquired. She may debate that, but I know it to be a fact!

Immediately at that very first consultation with this new oncology team, we were dumbfounded at how much had been missing from my previous care regiment under the older doctor in the suburbs. With firmness and a clarity of my needs, Dr. Karanes ordered a CT scan, blood work, and my first bone marrow biopsy. She was a calm, highly respected, superiorly intelligent physician who utilized a quiet and caring bedside manner.

The arrogance I had previously observed in other doctors was totally non-existent in the team she expertly led. Their lives were dedicated to pursuing every new avenue of treatment for their patients. They had left behind the usual "wait and see" methods in favor of aggressive treatments centered on in-depth research. I was to benefit from their relentless pursuit of a cancer cure for my specific disease. I was not just a number on a patient file.

I WAS TO BENEFIT FROM THEIR RELENTLESS PURSUIT OF A CANCER CURE ...

Here could be erected another milestone marker my family and I passed by on our ride along the highway we were being forced to traverse. This marker stands as a sign noting the rapidly developing cellular battle occurring within my body which would soon propel our vehicle unto another section of deeply rutted lanes full of twists and turns. We had passed the "Scenic Lookout" sign and needed to tighten our seatbelts for sure.

Now, you may be asking just what is so important about bone marrow that it needs to be included here. It is the soft, spongy tissue found in the center of the large bones in the body (such as hip, breastbone, and pelvis) where blood vessels and stem cells live. It helps produce red blood cells, white blood cells, platelets, fat, cartilage, and bone. In essence, it holds the key to human existence by being the seed bed for all human cells. By using a needle extraction process to remove some marrow for study, an oncologist can determine cancer type, stage of cancer, levels of iron, and state of the cells. That is a pretty basic description but does give you some idea as to the importance of bone marrow.

I have mentioned the various testing procedures which had been ordered for me as a precursor for my care. Well, let me tell you that, even though I was very willing to receive the best results from these tests, I was totally unprepared for the gruesomeness of the bone marrow biopsy. Sugar coating will not be done here when I share how painful it was. In order for bone marrow health to be evaluated under the microscope, it was first extracted from the largest flat place in the body that being my hip bone. An incision allows the passing of a hollow needle into the ridge bone to extract red marrow.

The process for me was to be repeated many times over the next several years as a vital part of disease evaluation and future treatment regiments were determined to be necessary. This was without a doubt the one test I quickly grew to hate. That was followed by the eventually difficult process of blood draws from my veins which soon developed attitudes of their own in rebellion to invasion.

Because a cancer diagnosis is always the prescription for advanced testing and repeated medical procedures which carry with them various levels of pain or discomfort, I realized that this new regiment was going to be a regular rough ride for me. I shared this with Jane on the way home from a difficult extraction session and she lovingly expressed her love for me by stating that she wished it was her going through all of this. I expressed my true thoughts by responding, "I wish it was you too!" In all honesty, that is probably exactly how I felt!

We have laughed about this over the years! Got to keep that Revell humor active!

After that first harrowing biopsy experience, I quickly learned to ask for pretesting administration of that short term memory drug, Ativan, which had allowed for our new dining table set purchase in Buffalo. This time, no new furniture was purchased! Lessons learned. Another Buffalo story to remember!

How does one find blessings in all this painfulness? I think at this point my family and I began to understand just how wonderfully creative the Trinity of God the Father, Jesus His son, and Holy Spirit were when they designed the human body! Takes my mind back to my analogy of the car designer. Each and every part of our bodies works in a divinely orchestrated manner to ensure the successful functioning of the entire unit. Each part has its own purpose, and a diagnostic evaluation will show the exact reason for operational failure of some companion part. If the gas in a car is bad, its engine will sputter and eventually seize up resulting in no further advancement along a journey. Works the same in the human body. Faulty parts caused damage. My cells were definitely in need of a maintenance recheck and we were in the right body shop for sure. God confirmed it for us right from the start.

Once more, I can tell you it was frightening on one hand, but so encouraging on the other as test results rolled in and upon my next consult, a new plan for chemotherapy was in place. We moved into a higher gear of operation to more aggressively attack that large mountain of cancer looming on the horizon. The wait and see time was over.

Walking through the doors of Harper Hospital on our way to the Cancer Clinic floor was certainly an eye opener for us. It was the largest medical facility we had encountered with much hustle and bustle occurring in each corner and on every hallway. At that time, we could have never imagined how much our lives would be affected over the next six years within the walls of this place.

Interestingly, it would become both a source of extreme pain as well as an oasis of healing. Faith in God would be tested. He would prove that He would always be relentless in gently caring for our emotions as patient, spouse, and children. This was to be our family's next battleground for my very existence.

Because I had received my Buffalo chemotherapy infusions in the private office of the attending physician, I was not prepared for the totally different setup at the new cancer clinic. On my first treatment day, I was ushered into a very large, softly lit room with no windows and walls completely encircled by tan colored vinyl recliners. I don't even think there were curtains to separate each patient from the next. It seemed a bit stark and impersonal for people struggling physically and mentally to handle what was to transpire every time they entered the doors.

After blood work was done and hustled off to the labs for scrutiny to determine acceptable treatment levels, each person received their individualized chemotherapy through previously inserted vein catheter lines. The staff worked very hard to meet our needs, but their main focus was to order the required drugs and get the process underway as quickly as possible. They kept a close eye for immediate physical effects throughout the sessions and were quick to administer anti-nausea meds, cold packs, blankets, liquid refreshment (no booze of course!), or light food items as tolerated.

At this point in my cancer battle, I had developed, without even realizing it, the habit of shutting the door of my consciousness when it came to treatments. It was as if I was standing behind a glass wall observing what was happening around me without actually being emotionally involved in the experience. I did not talk to anyone else in the room nor did I interact much with the staff. It is very fortunate for me that my companion through all of these stressful times was a communicator who actively engaged everyone around us as I underwent each sometimes-painful session. Oftentimes, I was in a self-induced fog as soon as we entered the room and was not released from it until we were on the way home. Once again, I am thankful for my wife's outgoing personality as she kept us connected with staff and fellow patients. Her inquisitive mind stayed tuned to whatever was happening with me and she would share details later which had escaped my notice. I just wanted to get chemo and leave! Sometimes I felt very alone even in the busyness of the clinic room. This was repeated over and over and over many times!

But God had not turned His back on me nor my family!

A large part of His measureless caring came to us in the shape of family members who completely encircled us with compassion. I don't wish to ignore all the efforts people made to help us so here is my apology if I leave someone out. The list is very long of the unselfish people who carried us through each battlefield. It reminded me of pictures I have seen of a soldier carrying his wounded mate slung across his shoulders over extreme terrain with the sole intent of reaching safety.

Once it had been established that this cancer battle would be a complex one, we were blessed over and over by the presence of my parents whenever they were able to be with us. Thousands of miles were recorded by their car tire treads as they covered the distance from Verona to Detroit. I am convinced there are volumes of their prayers for my family filed in Heaven's archives.

Each time in their absence, my sisters unselfishly picked up the operational burden of Mum's dress shop. Never did they ever make me feel that I was depriving them of their parents or adding to their work responsibilities. They have been the most amazingly loving siblings.

Several times, Jane's sister Mary generously gave of her time to be with the children in our home during times I was hospitalized. She drove down from the "Thumb" of the state and stepped in as the major chef and housekeeper. Her assistance extended to the boat maintenance when she once made the trip, even after being the victim of a car accident that very morning, to help my first mate wax and clean the boat before spring launch. Sisters bonding at its best. Wax on! Wax off! Sore muscles for sure, but lots of laughter!

In addition, Mum and Dad became the chauffeurs to school and sports practices as we felt the importance of keeping a normal routine as best, we could for the kids. Jane's parents stepped in also to relieve some of those daily responsibilities. I like to believe the kids had somewhat of a normal childhood in spite of my health problems. They certainly had lots of cheering spectators at their games. And the occasional vocal sideline coaching parent much to their chagrin!

And then there were all the prayers ascending to the Father on my behalf! Sincere voices collectively asking for my healing, wisdom for medical teams, favorable test results, strength for my caregivers, physical rest, and peace in my spirit! I can honestly say that there were hundreds of people around the world praying. I was to discover that one of the unusual blessings of moving my family to so many different places was the lifelong connection with legions of faithful believers.

THERE WERE HUNDREDS OF PEOPLE AROUND THE WORLD PRAYING

Here is a picture of a remarkable group united in powerful prayers after Jesus departed to Heaven as recorded in Acts 1:13-14 (TPT),

> *"Arriving there, they went into a large second floor room to pray. Peter, John, Jacob, Andrew, Phillip, Thomas, Bartholomew, Matthew, Jacob (the son of Alpheus), Simon (the zealot), and Judas (the son of Jacob), and a number of women, including Mary, Jesus' mother. His brothers were there as well. All of them were united in prayer, gripped with one passion, interceding night and day."*

What an amazing group of praying souls united just as many were for me. From all walks of life! My words of gratitude are endless and heartfelt.

That was just a little side trip I took in sharing my story, but you probably have realized that my writing co-pilot does like to do the occasional off roading to add a bit of wisdom we have learned along this journey. That is the beauty of fifty plus years of marriage based on a partnership of love.

Now let's drive on!

Volleyball was Cindy's sport of choice while Matt found his interest lay in soccer. At an early age, they each displayed a naturally strong ability in their sport, and it was a huge bonus for us as parents to see them excel through dedicated practice under each coaching style they experienced. At one point, my wife and our neighbor Diana even had to coach Matt's first season of indoor soccer when none of the other parents would step forward. What an experience for the coaches, the players, and the referees! The mums even enjoyed it and the team won the indoor trophy that season for their age group!

It was also during this timeframe that Jane was able to coach Cindy's first volleyball team at school. Another God ordained opportunity to be involved in their young lives at just the right time.

Both kids excelled in their sport to the point that they were chosen to be part of select teams. This required extra funds and time commitments for us, but we were thrilled that they had such wonderful opportunities for future skill development and team camaraderie.

There was even a lengthy time when I was unable to attend Matt's indoor soccer matches due to an extended stay in the hospital so, Steve and Julie Vanker videotaped each game. Thanks to their thoughtfulness, I did not miss any of the action.

Believe me when I say that helping people doesn't have to be in some big Hollywood style way, but it is the little services to others that can make the difference and smooth out a stretch of highway on a bumpy "life" ride. I am hoping you have begun to see the many ways my God used (and continues to use) people to encourage me, comfort me, and renew my faith in His amazing grace. Each person who cooked a meal, sent a card, made a phone call, sat by my hospital bed, chauffeured the kids, made a house visit, mowed my lawn, shoveled my drive of snow, and prayed for me was helping carry a heavy burden which at times seemed starkly surreal.

What WASN'T unbearable but pretty amazing was the fact that all through those first years at Ford Credit in my new positions, I was able to successfully perform my work responsibilities. Even when a new cycle of chemotherapy was thrust upon my body resulting in exhaustion, I was able to receive infusions and still go to work week after week. My determination to not be a victim nor a whiner thus collapsing into a mindset of misery or self-pity became my personal objective.

Sometimes this resulted in a personal drive to stay on point as an executive instead of staying home to rest and heal.

Each morning that I could shave, shower, dress in my business attire with those freshly polished shoes, and head to the Glass House was the "Through Traffic" sign I set my sights upon. As long as I could keep up with the daily traffic even if only at a reduced speed, I was appeased. Unless they closely worked with me, many of my fellow Ford colleagues were probably unaware of the extent of my health struggles and that was fine with me for the time being.

Much to my satisfaction, the areas of my work assignments occasionally required that I made Ford Credit Branch Office visits for consults with their staff to introduce best practices in financial business. This included international travel as well as in the contiguous United States and Canada.

These were welcomed breaks which satisfied my need for normalcy in the midst of cancer craziness.

My employers are to be commended for how they stood by me at each sharp turn, rough patch, and bumpy road upon which I was forced to drive. This was also new territory for them in dealing with a serious medical diagnosis for one of their employees. We were all poised to enter uncharted territory as there were discoveries in cancer research which would be very expensive and harbored no definite guarantees that monies spent would result in big returns. The bottom line for any company is money and profits and I was well aware of that reality.

This brings me to the next stretch of my life which was to become a most intense, challenging, and expensive route for me to travel. Under Dr. Karanes's careful supervision, I had been quietly motoring along on the receiving end of chemotherapy regiments which were treating whatever cancer cells were wandering around my body. I tolerated them better than before thanks to new anti-nausea meds. Whenever a new problem popped up, treatment was altered with the hope of disease destruction.

Like driving on a soft tire, I knew my hip pain was an issue but was totally unprepared for just how big of an issue it would become until one night in January of 1991. Our treasured friends, the Stellas, graciously invited us to accompany their family to the inaugural event for a new professional indoor soccer team at Joe Lewis Arena in downtown Detroit. They hosted us in a very nice private box, and it was loads of fun for almost the entire evening. I say almost because this was to be one of those milestones moments in my life which would again alter many things in our family.

While watching the game, I began to be aware that I was experiencing a rapid rise in body temperature accompanied by a severe pain in my "bad" hip. I could not stand. It was as if my hip was frozen in place. Not wanting to spoil the evening's fun and speaking only to Jane, I let her know something was wrong. Of course in her usual emergency response fashion, my Pit Bull immediately sounded the alarm for assistance from the facility's onsite emergency nurse, and before I knew it, I was in a wheelchair being pushed to a team entrance only side door and loaded into our car for a mad dash to the Emergency Department of Harper Hospital. It had begun to snow heavily which only added to our anxiety as my physical condition was deteriorating quickly and we were at a loss as to why.

The next five hours were a nightmare as we were forced to remain in the ER waiting area due to a breakdown in communication between the attending staff and us. Being a trauma center in a large city infamous for crime, this facility was extremely busy with processing and treating victims. We were relegated to a corner and told repeatedly that our "number" would be called. One can only imagine how frustrated Jane became as she watched me slipping farther into unconsciousness as my fever raged. Her repeated pleas through the little round speaker imbedded in the reception window just bounced off of seemingly uncaring ears. There was an order to their service, and it would not be altered. Sit and wait!

Unfortunately, the car phone was just that—connected to the car, so unavailable for us to contact my medical team—even though their offices where a few stories above us in the same building.

Finally, after repeated attempts using the pay phone, Jane was able to reach my doctor who notified the ER staff that I needed to be seen immediately. Those barred doors flew open, and I was hurriedly ushered into a stark, white examination area where it was quickly determined I was in an extremely dangerous condition. My fever had escalated to a life-ending level. My cognitive responses were at a standstill. In fact, in mechanical terms, my tires were all flat, my gas tank was registering empty, and my engine light was brightly flashing. I was dead stop in the middle of the busy expressway. (No pun intended here!)

MY FEVER HAD ESCALATED TO A LIFE-ENDING LEVEL

In this perilous condition, I was moved upstairs where measures were rapidly in place to literally save my life. After several more hours of intensive medical scrutiny, it was determined that I was suffering from a Group B Streptococcus left hip infection which was manifesting itself in corrupt fluid retention within the hip. Imagine having a massive strep throat infection but just not in the throat. That weakened hip had become the host site for something intensely virulent which needed to be drained.

By now, Jane had alerted my Florida Snowbird parents and they all determined it would be good for them to be with us during this precarious time. The children had been looked after by the Stellas as their mum had not left my side during all of this. She only left me to make a mad dash to the airport through one of those wild Michigan snow squalls to pick my parents up and bring them back to hospital for a short visit with me. They needed that as much as I needed to feel them close by. It must have been so hard for them to see their son in such a serious health crisis. Their prayers and loving touches were so valuable to me. It was a very stressful moment for us all.

By now, my medical team had made the decision that I needed to be moved to another hospital just up the street to be under the care of a new physician who specialized in damaged joints. What a blessing for us that six months before this critical moment in my health, Dr. Robert Fitzgerald had arrived in Detroit to take charge of the Orthopedic Unit at Hutzel Hospital as their Chief of Orthopedic surgery. To put it simply, he was the head mechanic who repaired hips.

He was "the Boss", the top of the pecking order, the man in charge. It is no accident that he was in place at this specific place because I truly needed an expert to repair my severely damaged hip and help me regain my mobility. Once again, God had positioned me in the place of the right connections for my good.

Surgery confirmed the extent of the bone damage caused by the infection and I was placed on very strong antibiotics to destroy unfavorable bacteria as well as being placed in isolation status. The nursing staff closely monitored me but not nearly as closely as my personal Pit Bull who spent many nights next to my bed sleeping on an army cot upon which a large elephant had recently rested! At least that is how Jane described the collapsible cot with its sagging middle.

Like a mother tiger, she protectively watched over me. This proved helpful as on one late night a nurse entered the room to perform a drainage procedure on my fluid collection bag, but she did not wash her hands nor put on protective gloves. This did not set well with my guardian, so she strongly expressed her opinion the next day to the nursing Supervisor. It wasn't long before Dr. Fitzgerald stormed onto the floor to loudly re-educate the nursing staff that this was totally unacceptable!!

The Boss was not happy, and everyone knew it! We were reassured by the man himself, who made his rounds very late into the night for some reason, that the behavior had been corrected and would never happen again under his watch.

Through close monitoring and with the strong antibiotics coursing through my veins, I began to heal. Mum, Dad, and Jane juggled the kid duties with the help of friends from church or school while I was put through the paces of some moderate rehab once I was strong enough to stand. It was so good to finally be well enough receive visits from the kids. They needed this time with their dad as much as he needed their youthful banters and details of their preteen lives.

By now my wife could almost just point the car in the direction of downtown Detroit and it would steer itself into the hospital parking lot. The parking attendants and security staff recognized her and often walked her to car after her late-night visits as the surrounding area was dangerous. Everyone was kind and on the lookout for whatever our family needed. I looked forward to every visitor who took the time to encourage me, and it was interesting to witness their reactions to whatever was taking place outside my room windows.

This section of Detroit had been the location of many majestic homes built by the wealthy in late eighteen, early nineteen hundreds and were elaborately gabled in architectural details. This had been the home base for many of the upper crust of high society. Beautiful three and four storied houses with sweeping driveways and carriage houses. Impressive and palatial!

But as happens over time with the altering of personal fortunes and the eventual attraction of suburbia living, these homes were abandoned to sit in disrepair and emptiness. They became burned out shells, painted with graffiti, and in general abandonment to the elements. The homeless found shelter within their scarred walls as well as drug users and those with little hope of a better life. It was sad to observe, but also a valuable education for my family as residents of the middle-class social bubble out in the burbs. None of us, including my parents, had ever seen drug dealers making their living or ladies of the night "working" the corners just to survive from day to day.

It may seem odd for me to include this short "Look Out" point here, but I believe God uses EVERY experience of our lives as teaching moments. Compassion for others less fortunate is hard to develop unless one actually sees the needs. It is easy to condemn when one is not affected.

After nineteen boring days in the hospital, I was extremely anxious to go home. Determined to return to life outside the four walls I felt trapped in, I had doubled down on my physical therapy sessions with renewed vigor. The strong drugs pushing my body to heal were doing their job with amazing speed, so I verbally presented my business plan to Dr. Fitzgerald. Every extra day confined to this place was creating more anxiety than was healthy for me and detrimental to my overall state of mind.

Chuckling out loud, his response was an interesting one. For the next month, if my wife would to be willing to be trained in at home administration of the drug, Gentamicin, the highly toxic broad-spectrum antibiotic which was destroying the evil bacteria hiding within me, then he would release me. This would require IV infusion every four hours around the clock for 30 days. Every four hours with no stopping! Day and night! It was all up to her decision!

Can you imagine the pleading in my voice when this tentative plan was presented? I was desperate to be in my own bed in my own house! I may have even promised her a cruise or two if we could just spring out of this sterile environment.

Obviously, I can report that she readily agreed and proceeded to receive the short but intensive training on the mechanics of infusion and care of a Hickman heart catheter with its lines and caps. Finally, I was able to climb into our car to be chauffeured home with well wishes from medical staff, a whole file full of care instructions, and the hope that this dark chapter of my life could be left in the dust! I was one happy camper for sure!

It was good to be home! Even nicer when, during my absence, my folks had purchased a very nice La-Z-Boy recliner for me to use as I healed. What a pleasure to sink into its cushioning frame from which I could view the daily happenings of my family. We were soon on a pretty tight schedule of home-care nurse visits, weekly deliveries of the infusion supply as well as the all-important bags of drugs which needed to be stored in the refrigerator. The vegetable drawer became a mini pharmacy for one month.

True to her promise, Jane took over the process of hanging the drug bag and hooking my catheter up to receive the healing liquid on a regulated drip line. Every four hours around the clock for 30 days! Now, just imagine you are receiving cold liquid coursing through a plastic line directly into your heart to begin its slow routing throughout your body. Brrrrr! First time this occurred I informed my resident nurse that I could feel every cold drop and it was not comfortable! Her practical solution? By transferring some of her own body heat around the bag for a short period of time before introducing its contents into me, she warmed it all up. And the warmest place was between under her arm pit! Well, she was creative for sure, and it worked! Once again, a dose of humor carried us along like an injection of gas additive into a sluggish engine!

Usually, it was a slow infusion process except for the one time my technician attempted to speed up the 4:00 a.m. drip action thus reducing the time she had to monitor in order to not allow the line to run dry resulting in my demise. I immediately was awakened by a rush of fluid flowing into my heart and lungs. My relief driver had been flagged in the act of passing in a "No Pass" zone. Pressing on the bag had indeed increased the force of infusion. I immediately felt the rush! Action was corrected and lesson learned. "Reduced Speed" sign was posted!

Eventually, we settled into somewhat of an operational pattern for the next 2 months as I pushed myself to regain strength in walking and overall health improvement. It was a good time to be house bound as the winter weather conditions reduced outside activities. Along with home health care nurses, a physical therapist made weekly visits to assist my range of motion. Basically, my primary and urgent goal was to return to work as soon as possible. Enough of this sitting around!

Remember my nickname is "Rev" and not for a pastoral calling!

My employer was so supportive through all of this, and they also were ready for my return. However, standing in my way holding a big "STOP" sign was a company nurse who would be signing my clearance forms after reviewing all medical records. My carefully honed skill at managing the Pit Bull I was married to did not prepare me for the fierce Rottweiler facing me in the medical office at Ford Credit. After nineteen days in hospital and six weeks of homebound recovery, my personal opinion was that I was ready to sit behind my desk, travel on business, and pick up my responsibilities once again. This company nurse was not having any of this and stamped my papers as unfit to return.

Well, this was not happening in my mind, so I promptly requested that my attending physician write a clear and concisely worded letter that I WAS fit to return to previous duties as all infusions had ended.

Bingo! That did the trick, and the roadblock was quickly removed for my return. What a day of celebration when I could back the car out of the drive, wave goodbye to my family, and once again merge into the traffic heading into Dearborn. Across my lips would never again come a word of complaint over traffic conditions as I was in motion again!

My relief at the new freedom was not immediately shared by my caregiver who suddenly realized that she was not able to closely monitor my temperature, healthy diet, and pain level. It was required of her to hand over to me, the guy with the dangerously high pain tolerance and male bent to ignore signs of stress, total control of everything associated with my recovery while at work. That wasn't part of the Instructions for Home Care handed out at the hospital. Caregivers have such great responsibilities and can develop a heightened sense of protectiveness for their charge.

It is staggering how much we all learned over the years about traveling through serious health issues. Maybe we should have written a book. Joke intended!

Once Jane was assured through many daily phone calls that I was using my crutches, drinking lots of water, and taking my pain meds as ordered, she relaxed somewhat. In fact, I was doing so well that she began a serious part-time job search to fill the empty caregiving hours. It came in the form of a Children's Librarian position at our large community library not far from home. She was thrilled to convert all that caregiving energy into creative activity planning for children's programs while surrounded by excellent coworkers. And as we were being reminded over and over again through every leg of my life travels, God's intent here was to supply us with a super supportive group of people just when we would need them the most.

The next eight months in our household were jam packed with many school activities, club team soccer and volleyball practices or games stretching from one side of the metroplex to the other, library and Ford work schedules, church gatherings, boating trips, pool parties or holidays with family or friends, and whatever else we could pack into every moment! My crutches were soon relegated to the front hall closet as I was under full power with just an elongated hip scar to remind me of the ordeal I had been through. It was tremendously good to be once more driving my family down a straight road with no ruts or gravel.

Psalm 3:3-5 (MSG) came alive for us.

"But you, God, shield me on all sides;
You ground my feet, You lift my head high;
With all my might I shout up to God,
His answers thunder from the holy mountain.
I stretch myself out. I sleep."

Having passed through a life-threatening storm, the new view out our front windshield looked clear and promising for the first time in several years. My managerial position at Ford was rewarding and challenging which suited me just fine. With renewed physical strength and personal drive, I had eagerly resumed business travels to various areas around North America.

Over and over, as I met with Ford Credit staff, I was warmly greeted with well wishes for my renewed health. It was such an encouragement to hear that many people who barely knew me had been praying for my recovery. By adding those prayers to the reminders of the intense intercessory ones lifted up to Heaven by family and friends, I was overwhelmed by the wonder of it all. Here I stood, having been forced off the road into the foreboding darkness of deep woods void of any sunshine breaking through to illuminate the precariously narrow byway any disease can force one to navigate.

God was (and is) so amazingly good and consistently faithful! He had supplied me with a prayer covering totally beyond what I could imagine. I thanked Him over and over for the faithfulness of praying people.

Once again harkening back to the tender story of my little boy's candle experience with its lesson of the many responses God will choose when answering our sincere requests, I can see that for this time in my life, He chose to say, "Yes!" It was a moment to celebrate what had taken place.

Included in that multitude of praying folks was our wonderful home team Bible study group from our church. They were a mixed age group of couples with the deeply rooted desire of supporting each other wherever and whenever there was a need! What supportive allies they became as our home was flooded with delicious meals, encouraging phone calls, personal visits, and just plain love! The group sprang from the large Sunday School class which also embraced us with every possible example of Good Samaritan type caring. Just like the people at our beloved Chapel in Buffalo, these fellow believers fully portrayed the beauty of true Christ following! Because their names are too numerous to mention, I always fear I will leave someone out who ministered to us but they each know our family was (and is) grateful for all they did to help us.

I need to push down on the accelerator a bit here to move along in my story telling or this narrative will be longer than the novel, *War and Peace* with its 365 chapters containing 1,500 pages!

The Michigan fall season of that same year was resplendent in its almost unbelievable colors of foliage when I boarded a plane to embark on a two-week business trip to Europe. It was to be a very action-packed journey covering several different countries through numerous plane and train connection. I was looking so forward to meeting our Ford counterparts in the European vehicle markets to exchange best practices and interact with their methods of operation. I knew it would be a bit hectic but relished the idea of expanding my expertise and adding to my business resume the experience of different market perspectives. It was time to spread my wings a little more. However, little did I realize how this trip would do everything BUT spread my wings.

As my fellow Ford traveling companion and I began to make our way around the prearranged destinations in England, Germany, and Switzerland, I was nagged by a persistent ache in my recently infected hip. The pain was dull at first, so I did what most men usually do—ignored it! Must have been caused by the long flight from Detroit to London or so I reasoned in my desire to not allow this trip to be altered in any way.

This decision worked for a couple of days, but it soon became obvious to me that this message from the pain receptors in my body was becoming louder and louder. It was like the sound a car tire makes when it is slowly loses air in the throes of deflating before registering a complete blow out!

By the end of the first week, I knew that this weakened hip was failing me as the intensity of the pain accelerated and my walking stride reflected the strain of trying not to limp. Ice packs became my companions whenever they were available.

Now, you may be wondering what the Pit Bull thought of this development and I can assure you, she did not have an opinion as I had not shared my present situation with her. Probably not a good choice as became evident upon my return flight home to be greeted by a shocked and dismayed wife who had been quickly warned by my traveling colleague that I was not in the best of shape. Trust me when I say honesty is always the best policy, especially when one is married.

It was very obvious that I needed urgent medical attention and we were soon in the presence of my orthopedic surgeon who, after studying the new X-rays, announced that the hip was fractured and would require replacing. It needed to be done now!

All options were off the table and it became necessary for me to arrange my work schedule for an extended sabbatical, or in car terms, a detailed restoration of the hip joint and socket as well as reinforcement of the femur bone above the knee. Oh boy, this was not going to be an easy repair nor one I had planned on. My high pain tolerance had finally caught up with me. No amount of Advil or Tylenol would banish the pain.

Let me speak a word or two here as uttered with the voice of deeply lived personal life experiences born out of suffering. I do not claim to be a book-trained theologian with extensive studies in the Bible's doctrine nor one who possesses the ability to see visions or interpret dreams. I have no boast of immense religious insights. But I can speak with authority to the importance of pain in our human lives. It is the blessing God has given us for sure, though often we don't view it as such.

For years, I had put into practice a behavioral pattern of pain denial which was not healthy. Now don't interpret this comment as a license to be a hypochondriac and bemoan all aches nor overmedicate one's self. Not my intent at all. But there is a danger in ignoring the Creator's perfect master plan in equipping man with an internal mechanism which sounds an alert to our body's need for attention and repair. Pain is our inner voice speaking to us that something is wrong. Thankfully, we have at our disposal amazingly gifted medical experts who can assist us in the best avenues of pain treatment or management. God has designed their creative minds to pursue problem solving which will benefit all humanity.

Over the years I had cursed my pain experiences and figuratively shoved them into the trunk of my traveling vehicle along with the seldom used spare tire. There but not visible!

That plan worked until I realized just how valuable pain recognition is and how managing it on a regular basis allows the body to heal. One of my oncologists wisely instructed me to not allow my pain to rise and fall in extremes thus taxing my body.

Having taken a moment to sit along the roadside and ponder the issue of pain, I will once again steer my "life" car back into the swiftly moving traffic of memory sharing.

December found me scheduled to enter Hutzel Hospital for my hip revision which we understood to be a long and complicated procedure. Part of me was dreading the whole process as well as the long recovery, but the pain I was experiencing kept me focused on finding relief as quickly as possible. Unfortunately, the surgery was scheduled for the same week as my wife's birthday. She never complained as we have always managed crisis situations as a team centered on the best results for the greater good.

True to their love for family, my folks came to help out. They were always willing to take charge of whatever was needed by Jane, the kids, or me. If they were not manning the school carpool, cooking meals, cleaning the house, chauffeuring to sports events, or anything else posted on the family calendar, they were tag teaming Jane at my bedside. I have been blessed over and over by each person who has stood by my side, but Mum and Dad are at the top of the list for their love expressed when I am sure their hearts were heavy with worry.

My employers once again graciously worked with me to adjust my responsibilities for the six weeks of the temporary disability time frame I would need for rehab and healing. Over and over, I have been reminded of just how very accommodating they were through every health crisis I presented them. Never once was I made to feel a burden to the Ford Credit organization. With upper management's reassurances that my job would still be in place, my mind was at rest.

Surgery day arrived and it was as predicted, a long, grueling procedure which lasted more than nine hours under a pretty tight infection control setting. I will spare you the details except for mentioning the size of the tools the surgeon used to extract the hip joint! Last thing I remember was commenting about that to the operating staff who promptly sent me off into the twilight zone.

When it was over and I had awakened from my induced slumber, I was overwhelmed with emotions to realize the excruciating pain I had been living with was gone! In its place was a new joint and a railroad track of staples closing a pretty extensive wound. I would be left with a permanent reminder of the wonder of modern medicine, the skill of my surgeon, and the amazing ability of the human body to heal. Not only was the pain gone but I was able to stand and walk less than 24 hours after the operation. Of course, a physical therapist was right by my side to supervise my first hesitant steps until that glorious day I could go home where the rest of the family would continue the watchful eye of supervision.

The blessed day arrived and once again, I left a Detroit hospital with a pair of crutches tucked under my arms, many well wishes from my medical team, and a fist full of instructions for living with a refurbished hip. The very first caution to be followed for several weeks was the importance of NOT bending over to pick up anything. I had actually been given a hand tool with a grip mechanism which, when used properly, would eliminate the bending motion until such time as I was cleared to resume that activity. My kids thought that was pretty humorous as they knew I was probably not going to use the crazy thing. In fact, the little rascals set me up for a test as soon as I maneuvered into the house. They had sprinkled a few bits of paper just inside the garage door and it was only the screeching of their mother's voice which prevented me from tidying up the floor. She would hold me to the "rules" for sure and that was a good thing.

Luckily, my surgery had been completed before the Christmas Holidays started. Not so luckily, I obviously could not travel to my hometown for family festivities. We were very disappointed but not for long. In cahoots with my sisters and their families, my folks orchestrated a car caravan to our home so we could all be together! For one week the thirteen of us celebrated our Savior's birth together. It was a wonderful time as the nieces and nephews all got on splendidly and really enjoyed each other's company. I held the chair of honor in my La-Z-Boy while everyone shopped, attended movies, played video games, and ate great food prepared by my sisters and Mum. We even got to eat out for Hibachi supper on Christmas Eve. With all the watchful eyes keeping tabs on me, I did not get away with anything on the main care list! It was a precious time together as we had much to celebrate.

Moving along, that New Year of 1991 found me in my usual impatient state of mind for more action than being housebound allowed. I felt as though I was idling too long, and it was time to shift my vehicle into a higher gear to move on down the road. It was time to dust off my desk, rearrange the files which had accumulated while I was absent, and proceed down the smoother road in front of me having kicked pain to the curb.

By now my surgeon understood my type A personality and had given his approval for full-time workload with the promise to know when to call it a day. Everyone breathed a sign of thanks to our Lord for sustaining us.

The Prophet Isaiah best expresses how I felt emerging from the dark tunnel of another rough stretch. Isaiah 40:27-31 (MSG),

> *"Why would you ever complain, O Jacob, or whine Israel, saying God has lost track of me. He doesn't care what happens to me?" Don't you know anything? Haven't you been listening? God doesn't come and go. God lasts. He's*

Creator of all you can see or imagine. He doesn't get tired out, doesn't pause to catch His breath. And He knows everything, inside and out. He energizes those who get tired, Gives fresh strength to dropouts. For even young people tire and drop out, Young folk in their prime stumble and fall. But those who wait upon God get fresh strength. They spread their wings and soar like eagles, They run and don't get tired, They walk and don't lag behind!"

What has always amazed me is that every word written in the Bible thousands of years before my birth is still current and powerful today. Verses I had heard as a child, then again as an adult, have come alive through each traumatic roadblock I have been forced to navigate through. If there is anything I have learned it is the truth that even though I drive, God is the wheelman who steers and directs. When I am willing to let Him set our course, I don't have to put a vice grip on the wheel of my life.

With a new hip, no pain, and a fancy wooden cane to replace the well-used crutches, I pushed ahead with my return to work. Just as before, the snarls of Detroit traffic were not nearly as irritating as I was beginning to have a new appreciation for the privilege of a more normal existence. It was like having a new set of tires, a full tank of gas, and freshly cleaned windshield through which to view the world.

Our family settled into a pattern we were familiar with as the kids progressed in their sporting endeavors both at school and in club team play. Jane was thoroughly enjoying her part-time children's librarian position while juggling carpooling, sports practices or games, singing in the choir at church, and maintaining the boat for our weekend getaways. I think she often looked forward to her role of boat deck hand and first mate as it satisfied her need to organize and clean. Well, at least that is how I saw it.

Seriously, I am most grateful that she did enjoy assisting me with the boat care as oftentimes I could not have physically kept up with the work required to keep the vessel in tiptop shape.

After a long day at work, it was nice to drive to the marina for a quick skimming across the waters of Michigan's southeastern shores at full speed. What did you expect with that childhood nickname of "Rev"? Had to live up to my name!

This would be a good time to interject a life lesson here. During my younger years living at home, my dad had worked to instill in me the importance of keeping my bicycles, hockey equipment, and cars in good working order. He had taught me that it was good stewardship to keep whatever I owned or used in the best condition possible. I probably grumbled at this, but as I began to pay for "things" over the years, I gained a greater appreciation for what he was attempting to instill in me. "An ounce of protection equals a pound of cure," so stated the American inventor, Ben Franklin. Glen Revell would have agreed!

Because of my dad's leading, I made every attempt to teach my own children simple lessons of valuing possessions without worshiping them. They soon learned that we operated as a team to maintain what we enjoyed—house, bikes, cars, swimming pools, and anything else our hard-earned monies had obtained.

Ours was a fun-filled summer and it seemed as if we could all finally breathe a little easier when monthly checkups with Dr. Karanes held no negative findings in the cancer area. Could we possibly finally be in the clear? We could only hope!

Endnote

1 Steve Saint, (2010), https://www.goodreads.com/quotes/499173-your-story-is-the-greatest-legacy-that-you-will-leave.

STEM CELL TRANSPLANT

Unfortunately, our hopes were soon dashed like a blown car engine, when in midsummer, the sign suddenly posted in front of us read, "Caution Fallen Rock."

My disease had once again become active, and I was faced with additional treatments which now presented the attending oncologists with some very serious decisions. Because my original diagnosis was so advanced, the Buffalo doctor's chemotherapy plan of action had been very aggressive and was followed by weeks of widespread radiation. At that time, there were not many options available. The regiment had been to hit it hard but there had been no guarantees of a cure.

Now there were additional questions to be answered.

How much more chemotherapy could I tolerate?

What new drugs were available?

What were my odds of survival?

It was a somber day when Jane and I met with Dr. Karanes to review her findings and determine what was our next move in combating this destructive enemy bent on my demise. She kindly but clearly laid out for us the different scenarios available at this time.

1. Wait and observe.

2. Treat with current dosages of drugs available.

3. Agree to undergo a new, experimental procedure called a Peripheral Stem Cell Transplant.

A what?

A new treatment regimen for combating stubborn lymphoma cancers which was being studied and tested with the hope of arresting the progression of the disease to the point of reaching a cure.

A cure!

In the six years since my original diagnosis, no one had ever mentioned that word nor even suggested that anything like that could be attained.

Could that even be possible?

At this point, the first two options seemed like the safest choices and were very tempting. However, to possibly be disease free was very appealing to me.

Using carefully worded details, our doctor continued to walk us through the entire process of finding a bone marrow match whereby someone would donate compatible stem cells which could then be introduced into me with the hope of growing healthy cells.

These new cells would help my body make enough red blood cells which carry oxygen and nutrients throughout the body, or platelets which are responsible for the formation of clots, or white blood cells which fight infections. In order for this to occur, I would need to have every last minuscule bone marrow cell destroyed before the new cells could find a safe place to work their magic and begin reproducing. This was accomplished through the use of extremely strong chemotherapy drugs infused over a six- or seven-day time frame. At that point, I would not have any immunities left for protection from even the slightest germ.

The new donated cells would be introduced through my heart catheter and sent on a mission to seek out the spongy, fatty tissue inside my bones. If they were not rejected as foreign substances, they would begin the rebirthing process to become new blood cells full of life sustaining components. It would be like flushing out a car's radiator to rid it of all accumulated impurities then introducing new antifreeze resulting in a smoother running motor. A major system flush out but not in the quick Jiffy Lube method.

I should apologize for all the continued references to cars, but that is my heritage. Blame it on my grandfather and his two sons for starting me on the Ford adventure years earlier.

The downside of all of this was the time between bone marrow destruction through more powerful drugs and the evidence of new growth within the blood. This was to be an experimental treatment for my type of cancer and there were very few success stories for best practices to follow. Having worked with the assignment of developing best practices in the car business, I understood all too well the ramifications of uncertainties and risks involved. I would be literally submitting myself (and my family) to a complex regiment with many unknown twists and turns. My life car would once again be accelerating into the darkness of a long tunnel carved through a very large, looming mountain. Once I was on that road, there would be no turning back until I either emerged triumphantly on the other side clutching the checkered flag or be zooming along the streets of Heaven enjoying its smooth surfaces in some kind of custom designed Ford. Well, my Father God is building my mansion so there must be something special waiting for me in the big attached garage!

The decision was up to us, and we left the office ladened with information for our personal review. There was much to discuss with the kids, but the decision had to be made soon so the donor search could begin. Without the transplant, there was a slim chance I might have five more years of living even if the disease could be controlled somehow through conventional methods. Now I was being offer a forty five percent chance for extra years and maybe even a cure!

If I was honest, I had been fighting this dreaded malignant invader for nearly seven years and I was growing weary of all the mental as well as physical scrimmages. Maybe it was time to wage all-out war with every possible weapon available. Time to once again claim the promises in that Bible verse our family had been resting on, 2 Timothy 1:7 (KJV),

> "For God hath not given us a spirit of fear, but of power and
> of love and of a sound mind."

For many years, we had lived with our fears like driving on icy roads, slipping, and sliding while barely creeping along. Suddenly we were dead stopped at a major crossroads where a decision was required. Left or right? Forward or reverse? Such a choice required lots of prayer, so we rallied our family prayer warriors as well as the dear friends in our church and Home Team.

It was time to drop off that nagging passenger named "Fear" and follow Holy Spirit's map as instructed by Psalm 46:10-11 (MSG):

"Step out of the traffic! Take a long, loving look at me, your High God, above politics, above everything. Jacob-wrestling God fights for us, God-of-Angel-Armies protects us."

The warm days of our summer that year moved slowly but surely into the crispness of the Michigan fall with its amazingly vibrant colors and cooler temperatures. Even in the city, we were surrounded by such unbelievable beauty as each tree quietly pulled from its stored-up energy enough strength to fill our skies with flowing banners of leaves resplendent in every heavenly color imaginable. Bright scarlets, shimmering golds, soft oranges, bold bronzes, and every color in-between mixed with the rich hews of various evergreens. It was a reminder that God's creation was still operating in unison and according to His purposes. Man was simply a spectator to the phenomenon of this change in nature which had been occurring since the very first moments of Creation.

Even though there was great uncertainty for my immediate future, I could still witness the steadiness of God within the changing of the seasons in nature. Everything He created worked together for His purposes.

That became my prayer for what we had decided as a family. I would agree to the transplant procedure regardless of the uncharted roads we would be required to travel. It was a very serious, life determining decision which was not taken lightly, but I will add a little of that Revell humor here by suggesting that maybe this is how a crash test dummy feels every time he is placed within the confines of a test vehicle. No guarantee of the outcome! No assurance of emerging on the other end of the test whole and functioning with all parts attached!

Trust me when I state that it was by far the most important decision of my life outside of my choice to accept Christ's blood sacrifice on the cross to pay the sin price required to cover my future. Through that teenage acceptance, I had been promised an eternity in Heaven joyously worshipping Jesus right alongside billions of other believers. A signed and sealed assurance to be rewarded when I died.

But even with that promise written in the owner's manual in my soul's handbook, I was aware that this newest earthly medical option would be a pretty rigid struggle up some very treacherous paths containing lots of angled twists, blind turns, and bottomless crevices.

So, blessed with multitudes of prayer warriors all around us, pledges of support whenever we needed, and my employer's full cooperation in once more allowing me a Medical Leave of Absence, I informed Dr. Karanes and her outstanding team of professionals that it was a "go" for this experimental cancer regiment. We were ready to trust our Lord's leading to set our sights on procuring a cure!

WE WERE READY TO TRUST OUR LORD'S LEADING TO SET OUR SIGHTS ON PROCURING A CURE!

Almost immediately, the transplant group went into action. Jane and I had several preliminary meetings to cover the process in even greater depth. We needed to discuss the financial arrangements with my insurance company and my employers as this was to be a very expensive process. Far more than just routine cancer treatments, nuclear scans, hospital stays, and blood work.

Ford Motor Company had never had an employee faced with this major cost decision, so I needed to have every detail presented to them in a professional manner. Their decision to agree to cover the required expenses was a great relief to me. Without their approval, my family would have had to find hundreds of thousands of dollars or abandoned the whole hope of a cure.

Another tribute to God's faithfulness in supplying everything in His timing and for His purposes.

The next step was to place my medical history and information into the National Bone Marrow Donor Registry with the hopes of finding a bone marrow match through "Be the Match" data bank. Such a procedure through an unrelated donor is called an Allogenic Transplant.

This registry was and still is the organization through which doctors match donors to patients based on their human leukocyte antigen (HLA) tissue type. HLA are proteins, or markers, located in most cells in the human body. The incredibleness of God's creative mind is boldly on display with the fact that the immune system uses these markers to recognize which cells belong in that body and which do not. The necessary match can only come when the cells match as close as possible to prevent rejection by the HLA. A perfect match is highly unlikely, and the search can be similar to finding a needle in a haystack.

Family members of the patient are tested first with siblings being the best possible match because they share the same blood pool so to speak. If that proves unsuccessful, then the search moves to the actual registry. A match found here is based on the reality that someone volunteered to be tested as a potential donor thus offering to possibly save a life.

Both my sisters, having forgiven me of the threatening knife incident in our Verona childhoods, readily agreed to be tested through blood samples taken. This method of testing has since been replaced by a less invasive technique of swabbing DNA sample inside a potential donor's mouth. Unfortunately for me, they did not match close enough as neither did my children nor my parents. True to her fighting spirit, Jane even was tested but to no avail.

With the unsuccessful donor matches giving them no other choice, the transplant team proposed the next best thing for me. I would become my own donor, referenced as an Autologous Transplant. This was a whole different approach and would require several more steps ahead of the actual infusion of my own cells. Harper Hospital had been performing bone marrow transplants, but it had never undertaken such a specialized cell harvesting and infusion.

Would I be willing to be used as a test case, a human guinea pig to put it in laymen's terms, a crash test dummy in a somewhat controlled setting?

It was time to submit myself to the mysteries of medical science and possibly open the door for other cancer victims to have second chances for disease free living or extended years.

Selfishly, I wanted many more years to enjoy my children and grow old with my wife. It was a renewal of that previous request I had made back in Buffalo when first diagnosed. Just a few more years, Lord!

However, this time the stakes were a bit higher and the road in front would be even narrower, hemmed in by sharp walls of uncertainty. But God was still working, still moving, still on call, still listening, still seeing me right up to this very moment when I was fearful and uncertain of the number of my days as He had ordained on February 11, 1950. His timing was perfect, absolutely perfect as I was now in the right state, the right city, the right hospital, with the right doctors for such a time as this. He was about to build another milestone from which our family would reference all future events.

So, with the decision in place for my chance at a cancer cure, everyone around me accelerated into action with preparations for my October hospitalization at Harper. Because I was submitting to a transplant using my own stem cells, these cells would need to be cancer free and in infant stages not yet designated as specific white, red, or platelet cells. My bone marrow was cleaned up as best as possible with more chemotherapy infused through a new Hickman direct heart line catheter. This required another surgery to insert the device into my chest and heart muscles.

Seemed like a simple procedure and it was. Well, almost simple!

Being a Christ follower, I don't consider myself unlucky as the world might define luck. However, it was becoming a habit for me to reject the "normal" and never do the "ordinary, standard" when it came to issues of my health. This was to be one of those times. Several days after the surgery, I became aware of an odd feeling in the left arm which, of course, I did not mention to the wife. When will I ever learn that my practice of keeping silent when it came to my health would never be a wise choice?

By that time, in the middle of the night, when I was making that weird pain noise, burning up with fever, and sporting a swollen left arm with sausage shaped fingers, my caregiver was on full alert to a dangerous situation. Very quickly we made the trip to Harper where it was determined I had developed a serious deep vein thrombosis (blood clot) in my arm and would require a regiment of blood thinners under watchful eyes of medical staff.

Trust me when I say I was not a happy camper to be spending July 4th weekend in a sterile hospital room when our plans had been to spend the time on the boat making family memories before the transplant.

Once I was out of surgery for the removal of the catheter, Jane hurried home to pack the kids up and zoomed across the Ambassador Bridge into

Canada with the quickly organized plan to have the kids stay in Verona with their cousins for however long this little crisis would require their parents to be lounging around in the hospital.

She made the six hours round trip from Detroit to Waterloo, Ontario to meet Dad and Uncle Chet for the kid hand off. In record time and with an eye on the rearview mirror for those ever-present Ontario Provincial Police vehicles, she wheeled her little red Focus into the now all too familiar parking lot. Imagine her surprise upon entering my room to find me laughing loudly over some verbal antic shared by our dear friend, Dick DeWitt, who had also made a mad dash from Buffalo, New York to be with me!

He had left his own family holiday plans to come. It was even more amazing when he announced that he would be driving back to Buffalo that very day. He just wanted to encourage me and my family. What a friend indeed!

Once the blood clot swerve in the road was resolved, I received another catheter and we all returned to the pre-transplant preparations which now would require me to inject myself every day for the month of August with a specialized drug known as Granulocyte colony-stimulating factor or just GCSF. It is a glycoprotein that stimulates the bone marrow to produce granulocytes and stem cells to be released into the blood stream. These would be cancer free and become the nucleus for my new lease on life. After my wife's first attempt to inject the drug into the skin on my stomach resulted in a huge bruise, I took over the jabbing of myself. The oranges she practiced on did not have the same feelings as me!

Once the cells were given time to grow, they were ready to be harvested. The actual collection process would be the very first time the cancer team at Harper had used an apheresis machine to isolate stem cells. It was a four day in hospital procedure intently monitored by my doctors as well as the manufacturing representatives.

Lucky me! I was the star of the show!

Much to everyone's surprise I am not a doctor, so I have tried to simplify the descriptive pictures covering the details of this bone marrow and stem cell harvesting process. Without insulting anyone's intelligence, my attempt has been here to just state the basic facts as I witnessed them. From the viewpoint of the patient trying to understand the stem cell extraction method, I found this to be very helpful as explained by the supervisory team. Imagine a tornado whirling around in the air full of objects of different density. As it spins, the lighter objects are spun off first followed by the denser ones. In comparison, the blood cells have been amazingly designed so that they separate when strong, circular force is applied. Now, there is probably a more medically detailed explanation, but this one satisfied my need to know. The Triune Three Creators thought of everything—even the density of the tiniest human cell!

Bonus fact here! During the extraction process, only the needed blood cell components are stored in sterile infusion bags to be used later while the unused components are returned to the donor. Or in my case, me!

Not only were all eyes at Harper watching, but even my hometown newspaper got wind of the story. The Kingston Whig Standard called us for an interview which resulted in an article in the regional section of their paper. The short but concise story entitled "Verona Man First for New Marrow Transplant" created a great deal of community interest which was an encouragement to my Verona family as many folks offered prayers of support for all of us.

Four days of blood processing resulted in a significant amount of healthy stem cells to be frozen until I was ready for them to be infused back into my circulatory system. One more medical procedure completed.

Now our family calendar only had one date circled in red, October 15, 1991. This marked the day I was scheduled to enter the hospital with absolutely no guarantees. It felt as though I was driving my car unto a high-speed proving track designed to test every part of my vehicle. Each component would be stretched, evaluated, measured, and tried with the intent of creating a high-powered machine equipped with new components running along smoothly.

Naturally, my mind was full of questions and doubts as I acknowledged the "Change Lanes to Exit" sign illuminated in front of me. No one could question my belief that a divine plan was in place for every cell of the body. There still existed anxiety for the unknown and the process of signing all the medical release forms only increased my concerns. It was a scary time, but my family clung even tighter to that special verse given to us way back in 1984.

2 Timothy 1:7 (KJV),

> *"For God hath not given us the spirit of fear; but of power, and of love, and of a sound mind."*

We would not deny our fears as coming from the evil one but would repeatedly remind ourselves that our Lord's care was the best power to draw from, the deepest love to claim, and the divinely held source of sound minds. He would not fail to work through every detail of the transplant regardless of the outcome so that it would bring glory to the Father. Even if...I did not survive, my soul was assured of its salvation, and I would complete my earthy journey still trusting.

Finally, all details were in order for me to kiss the kids goodbye and drive downtown Detroit once more to enter the hospital. True to their unconditional love for me, my folks had once again put their business in Glenda and Sandy's trustworthy hands and joined us for the long haul ahead. I knew the level of my own fears but can only imagine the unspoken intensity of their concern as we entered uncharted waters together.

I was soon settled in a tenth-floor private room which would be my residence for an unknown time. Seeing my name listed on the report board across from the bed made the reality of the situation sink in. This was really happening!

Now it has been previously established in the pages of my story that I am a man who likes order and structure. I am not a control freak yet do function best when things around me are in the scope of my control to the best I can possibly manage. My success at Ford is proof that things work better when someone is in charge.

So, it did not surprise my family and upper management when I requested a computer and keyboard to be setup in my room so that I could continue as long as possible in handling my responsibilities at the office across town in World Headquarters. The hospital directors approved, and we were able to soon have a small desk with chair ready for me to connect to the telephone system. Remember, Wi-Fi was not even an option yet! Hard to imagine but true.

Probably the medical team had a bit of a chuckle over this unusual way to conduct business while being hospitalized as they were privy to what physically lay ahead for me. They sensed my need to keep some semblance of control in my life for at least a few days. Remember, I was the first person to undergo this new procedure, so it was all new territory.

Once my body began to be attacked by the aggressive chemotherapy coursing through my veins, Jane stepped in to read my correspondences and type my return advice. However, that soon became impossible for me to handle which resulted in the computer being silenced and relegated to a far corner of the cavernous room I occupied. That part of my life was on hold along with everything else I had known or presently knew.

For the most part in the writing of this life journey, the details have been shared through wordy composition. Executive summaries have only been permitted in just two sections. The rest of the narrative would present the intricate details of what I had lived through so God's faithfulness can best be understood. Therefore, let it be noted that I am making an exception here in the transplant retelling as the many necessary medical procedures with their complex details would exhaust even the keenest reader. (Actually, my co-writer gave me permission!)

With that in mind, here is the chronological unfolding of the next thirty days. (My mini-Executive summary!)

- October 15—entered Harper Hospital, extensive blood draws and testing began, bladder balloon inserted to protect lining of bladder. Daily walking regiment established.

- October 16 to 20—Strong Chemotherapy infusions commenced under close supervision. Bone Marrow is being destroyed. Side effects mounting in severity.

- October 21, 22—Rest Days. No chemo. Only blood draws.

- October 23—Stem Cell Infusion Day under direction of Dr. Karanes and her team. White blood count was zero. No immunities to infections. Extra Air filter machine powered up in room. Masks required on everyone. No visitors outside of family.

- October 23 to November 2—the waiting game began. Daily blood draws. Would the cells decide to reproduce?

- November 3—First sign that white cells are increasing!

- November 10—Blood counts strong enough for discharge from hospital as the first person to be allowed to do so less than 30 days after transplant.

There it is! The most dangerous 26 days I had ever lived up to this point in my 41 years of existence.

End of my summary! But not end of the story, so we shall continue once again filling in the details of this most difficult journey.

Through it all, I had experienced many negative physical issues with total hair and rapid weight loss, painful swallowing, unimaginable weakness, loss of appetite, and an unexplainable cessation of my desire to even speak or express myself. The last unusual side effect continued for nine days but was explained as my psychological response to severe changes in my body. Depression was not something I had ever experienced until now.

It came upon me like a soundless wind which swept across my consciousness. I was not prepared for its force in my mind.

Lucky for me, the wife was a talker who carried on all necessary communications with staff, alerting them to my needs. At home, my folks were faithfully attending to the children's daily routines as well as visiting me every day.

As my energy level evaporated and I lost interest in anything happening around me, I tried to just withdraw somewhere within myself by refusing to shower or walk the hallways. That was not going to be acceptable to my wife, the Pit Bull, who became my personal drill sergeant. She and my folks tag teamed each other for morning and afternoon visits so that

I was never alone. This worked to my advantage for the morning visiting team would not put any pressure on me to do my "drills." But when their relief person showed up, it was a different story! Would she never give me a break?

There was no slacking off from personal hygiene or completing the daily hall walking. She informed me that we were not going to give up, not now, not ever! Visitors were limited to only immediate family and extra precautions were in place to protect me. These were hours of deep emotional struggles mixed with pain, tempered by blind faith, but supported by thousands of faithful prayers spoken from every corner of the globe.

Speaking of prayers, both Jane and I experienced a gradual change in our prayer patterns during this time. Over the years, our usual style of communicating with our Lord Jesus had been similar in format consisting of laying our requests before Him followed by a smattering of thanksgiving for His goodness.

Suddenly everything changed as our prayers seemed trite, so inadequate, so futile! Was He even hearing our feeble attempts to communicate our feelings and fears? Could He be aware of our physical and spiritual weariness?

OUR PRECIOUS SAVIOR UNDERSTOOD OUR FRAGILE STATE

Of course, He was, even when we could not see or feel it. Our precious Savior understood our fragile state. He could identify exactly our weariness as He too had walked dusty roads of loneliness, tiredness, great pain. What a comfort to know He was walking beside, behind, and before us covering each step with His unconditional love. Even when our prayers seemed to evaporate into thin air or could not be expressed, He was fighting our physical and spiritual battles.

God was working every second of every hour through every day we were struggling. He was sustaining us through the thousands of prayers He was hearing from the obedient voices of our families, friends, entire churches, and even strangers as they joined together in expressing our needs. Over and over, we were encouraged by the reassurance that when we could not pray, they were interceding and petitioning on our behalf. We were actually experiencing the Apostle Paul's teaching from Romans 8:26 (MSG),

> "Meanwhile, the moment we get tired in the waiting, God's Spirit is right alongside helping us along.
>
> If we don't know how or why to pray, it doesn't matter.
>
> He does our praying in and for us making prayer out of our wordless sighs, our aching groans."

We were so physically tired in our own ways. As I was fighting on one front, my wife was carrying the weight of caregiver, wife, mother, librarian, and daughter-in-law all wrapped up in one big demanding package. It was a daunting task even for one as strong as her. She was our family's brick, but gradually small cracks were beginning to develop which would need to be addressed. Right in the middle of all this stress, the clothes dryer decided to stop functioning and the refrigerator struggled to keep food cold! Could anything else go wrong?

That is just what my wife yelled at God from the depths of her closet as she sat in the dark letting Him know she was just about at the end of her rope! Her cry of helplessness was just what He was waiting for so she would begin to fully trust Him, not her own strength.

This all came to a milestone moment when my mum ended up in the Emergency Room at another hospital diagnosed with a case of severe vertigo after having been rushed there by an ambulance from our home. The attending physician told Jane and Dad that Mum needed full bed rest and close monitoring. My poor folks were so upset that this had happened at this time. Finally, Jane got them settled at home then rushed out to the garage to hurry down to my bedside as I had left messages wondering why my morning visitors were late.

Well, the day was just going to get even better as Jane discovered she now had a flat tire on her car!

True to His perfect timing, God had one of the neighbor ladies observe my sobbing wife sitting on the driveway behind her crippled car. The lady's husband changed the tire as his wife and another dear friend comforted my discouraged caregiver. For her this was a definite breakthrough, a cleansing away of pent-up frustration buried within the dangerous pattern of ignoring self needs when caregiving. Working through her closet frustration moment.

The tire was fixed. The dryer was replaced. The refrigerator's cooling system still had two weeks left on its five year warranty so the repair cost was covered. Thankfully, Mum made a swift recovery. I was still suffering in isolation with no assurance of the future, but God was using these small blessings to keep us focused on trusting His timing and purpose. We were learning to be thankful in the midst of trials or situations. To hold a pity party for ourselves was a big temptation as well as trusting only in our own strengths.

With that thought in mind, I would like to remind myself of one of the good things that happened during this stressful period. Before the transplant began, we had decided that we would use a picture journal to record for our children and future generations the events as they unfolded. Why would we do this if the end result was sad? Our reasoning was that even in death, my life was a victorious example of Jesus' never-ending peace as I trusted Him for the promise of an eternity with Him. My loved ones would know that Psalm 138:8a (NLT) was true!

> *"The Lord will work out His plans for my life—for your faithful love, Oh Lord, endures forever."*

To this day, that photo album is still a part of the family memory treasures reminding anyone who views it of just what I walked through. There are numerous pictures of my hospital room wall decorated with many posters sent to us from well-wishers as well as a cheery, stuffed green frog which hung on my IV infusion machine. Mountains of cards came to me and were placed on a shelf right next to a large container of Good 'N Plenty candy supplied by the Greer family, dear friends from church. I have mentioned that visitors were limited but it was great to have several pastors stop by to pray with me and my folks.

There were also photos which visually recorded just how quickly I had physically spiraled down until the actual day of transplant which was then proceeded by days of waiting. Because I was hospitalized through the month of October, there were even photos of young cancer patients dressed in their Halloween costumes complete with medical masks as they came to my room for trick or treating. Those were the days when all bone marrow recipients were housed in the same area regardless of their ages. It was a somewhat unsettling time as we were all aware of each others' struggles with this savage disease of cancer. I think my family was more aware of the successes and failures of treatments in the lives of my fellow patients, but they kept much of it away from me. Just as well. My world was pretty closed in for a reason.

Everyone was holding their breath as it would become evident quite quickly if the cells were fully engaged in rebuilding my basic survival structure. It was a fearful time for sure!

Waiting was never my strong point so one can only imagine how difficult it was for me to be held in the grip of suspended time!

The first days after transplant seemed to crawl along with no promising results or changes in my physical condition. Eating was a struggle, showering was exhausting, and there was little energy source to draw from. These were the precarious moments of truth for my body's decision to accept or reject the new cells.

Then remarkably, my blood counts started to display better results. From all the medical records we still have from those days, I can actually pinpoint October 26 as the day positive things began to happen.

Eureka! Praise the Lord!

I began to regain physical strength and an appetite. Each day the medical team observed through blood draws how the new stem cells were evolving to rebuild the vital framework of my existence as found in my immunities. Within my body there was evidence of a miracle forming. It was obvious that God was working His supernatural, creative wonders.

That frightening path upon which I had been creeping along was beginning to slowly emerge from out of the darkness into patches of sunlight and more solid footing. I was not out of the woods entirely by a very long shot, but at least my new cells were growing and reproducing. The infection caution signs were still posted, and we knew they would be in place for several months to come. But my physical vehicle was being restored.

At this point, my folks returned home to Verona for a well-earned rest from the stress of walking with me and my family through such dark days. Words are just so incapable of expressing my gratitude for their sacrificial love. Even as I look back over all the years of my life, I can see their unselfish dedication to protecting, teaching, nurturing, guiding, and supporting me through every turn or twist in front of me. Please, Lord, help my children and their children be able to say the same of me someday.

Finally, the day arrived on November 10 when Dr. Karanes was satisfied that all my blood counts were strong enough for me to leave the hospital for the journey home! Can you imagine the excitement running through us all to realize that what everyone had prayed about was coming to pass? I had survived driving to the end of life's narrow lane and could now make a sharp turn at the sign labeled, "Right Exit." For me, that directional word seems a positive affirmation that we had made the right decision about the transplant.

Our celebration of this ever-emerging miracle was of course joyful and well-earned, but tempered somewhat by the discharge papers which spelled out all the precautions we would need to take for the next several months. I hardly glanced at them! My caregiver had proven herself to be totally dedicated to religiously following all instructions for my home care. Her "pit-bullishness" had been honed over the years and she would protect me as best she could.

Soon my hospital room was packed up. For the first time in many weeks, I was dressed in street clothes! The kids and Jane were ready to usher me to the car, but there was one moment where the evil one, who had fought so hard to destroy me, threw a bit of fear into my mind and I hesitated to leave the confines of the four walls which had been my rest stop. What was out there in the real world which might be my demise? Would the refurbished vehicle I was now sitting in be able to protect me from the scratches and dents one always acquires when moving along through life?

Taking a deep breath and accompanied by all the well wishes from the attending medical staff who had expertly cared for me, I headed home! It was a milestone for them and for us!

What a joyous celebration awaited the four of us as our car pulled into the driveway! All our neighbors had gathered with welcome home signs! They had decorated the garage door with a happy face made out of paper plates! I was overcome with emotions as the reality swept over me that I was truly loved and that they had taken such great care of my family and home in my absence. Several of the ladies had even deep cleaned our entire house as instructed by my doctors.

With an exhausted but thankful sigh, I sank into the comfort of that much appreciated La-Z-Boy recliner and realized this part of the journey would be accelerating slowly into the next phase of healing. Now the chair gets no credit but remember this was the place where I rested and began to be revived, regenerated, and restored in the past. It just represented a physical place I could be reminded that my Lord Jesus had and was still watching out for my physical and emotional needs.

THE PRAISES OF HUNDREDS OF PRAYER WARRIORS RESOUNDED IN HEAVEN AS WORD OF MY HOSPITAL RELEASE BECAME KNOWN

The praises of hundreds of prayer warriors resounded in Heaven I am sure as word of my hospital release became known. The phone was ever ringing with the congratulation calls from around the world it seemed. Well-wishers sent more cards and wonderful meals continued to be dropped off. It was a bit of a nuisance that in spite of being at home, I still needed to wear a protective mask when people stopped by. But that little glitch was a small price to pay for being home.

Our family routine soon settled back into school and sports for kids, limited part-time library duties for Jane, and the close monitoring of my daily health conditions. Due to my early hospital release, the doctors had cautioned us to be very vigilant in recording and reporting to them ANY changes in my daily health. Even a hang nail or small cut could invite infection. My bone marrow was still gaining strength. Believe me when I say my home-care nurse was observant and attentive to everything. Nothing escaped her notice or detailed recording to be reported to the powers that be! For this I will always be thankful even if it did drive me nuts sometimes. I was tired of all the hovering being done but had learned that this was for my own good.

I would like to say that all went well over the next four months, and I was able to just motor on a straight road with the top-down enjoying sunshine and cool breezes, but there were still struggles to be overcome. I was not a little bummed when it was announced to me on my first follow-up visit two weeks after my release that the final step in the transplant process was seven spinal injections of chemotherapy to destroy any cancer cells hiding in the spinal fluid or brain. Well, wasn't that just dandy! Seems I had missed that part of the pre-BMT discussion!

It was explained to me that the wonder of creation had designed my spinal cord to be a sealed membrane so that the original chemo drugs could not have penetrated it. Therefore, within it could be minutely, destructive cells just waiting to migrate. Not only were these injections necessary, but they then required another bone marrow biopsy as a reevaluation of all my cells contained within. Hopefully this would be the final maintenance check scheduled for a long time!

Even though I did not relish those further tests and procedures, I submitted to it all by trusting the decision making of my specialty team of brilliant medical doctors who had literally held my life in their hands many times previously. They did not want all their hard work centering on the potential for a cure, not just for me, but for thousands of other cancer sufferers, to be done in vain. If I survived with no relapse, it would be a victory for all of us! Now was not the time for me to pull over to the side of the road and shut off the engine.

Over the next four months and to the delight of everyone, my body began to make progress in strength, endurance, appetite, and mental sharpness. We have all seen pictures of vehicles driven crazily to the very edge of high cliffs then teetering precariously with front wheels touching nothing but air. Well, that is an apt description of exactly how I felt many times before, during, and after the transplant.

Now, I began to feel my loving God build a strong bridge under me by which my life car tires could slowly creep forward. Each suspension support came in the form of every healthy twenty-four-hour distance forward from November 10 as constructed by the invisible workings of my new stem cells. When it seemed my recovery was not moving fast enough to satisfy my childhood "Rev" nickname, I reminded myself to be patient. Of course, there were also three other people living at the house who kept my impatience in check whenever it was observed that I was not following careful precautions.

How do I remember that protection detail from so many years ago? A clear picture pops up of a large, water swollen, very much dead opossum floating in the winter cover of the backyard swimming pool around which my wife and kids were standing. Said creature had taken an early spring dive and held his breath too long thus creating the unpleasant job for someone to retrieve his soddy carcass from the brackish water. I immediately went for the pool skimmer pole with the intent of solving the smelly problem.

I am sure the entire neighborhood heard the shrill screeching command of my wife, "Put that down! Are you kidding me? You are not to touch that creature nor the water!"

Guilty as charged!

The problem was solved by someone else, and I beat a hasty retreat back to my chair, nursing my wounded pride but fully reminded of the infection dangers still lurking around me.

Good intentions all around on my part and the household guard!

No one wanted a relapse or medical hiccup at this crucial time in my healing.

There would be several such reminder moments over the next four months as I was pretty much housebound and masked up. As you can imagine this got old very quickly, but there were times of welcomed reprieve one of which stands out clearly. Because I could not be exposed to others for a few months, I could not attend my church. This grieved me greatly as I deeply valued my church family as represented by worship, preaching, Sunday School classes, and care group. It was a sad time for me when the family left for Sunday church. I dreaded being alone.

Well, God once again had His plan in place for supplying what I desperately needed. Into my life came a fellow believer who offered to come to my home on Sundays to share in personal worship and Bible Study. It was amazing as this man was an active member of the Detroit Tigers and was offering to give up family time right before he was scheduled to leave to spend months in Florida at Spring Training Camp. Out of his love for Christ and me, he would do this. Wow! What amazing timing and what amazing times followed as we opened the Word and prayed, seeking the Lord's perfect peace.

Not only did he share of himself, but his wife and four daughters opened their home to the four Revells for Christmas Eve dinner complete with prime rib and a visit from Santa Claus. It was a wonderful time of laughter, some tears, and being embraced by love. Christmas in Verona would have to wait until the next year, but we were able to enjoy the Holiday festivities while staying close to home.

The New Year of 1992 was ushered in at our house with great anticipation on our minds that this was a year of new beginnings, new adventures, and new life! Every successful clean blood draw and physical exam was one giant step toward my goal of returning to work at Ford. It was my deepest heart's desire to once again dress in my business casual clothes, back the car out of the drive, and head down the busy roads to Dearborn and the office which had been reserved for me by my employers.

I craved the action and motivation my job offered with its demands which had always challenged me to be a better employee, a more creative manager, a committed-to-excellence team member, and a mind set on the goal of future career development.

This stem cell transplant side trip had forced me to relinquish my dreams and aspirations for my future at Ford until such time, if ever, I could once again join the ranks of the corporate world. Believe me there were many dark moments when I was fearful that my job would be removed from me thus ending my career.

But in words far too inadequate, I express to you that never once did my employers even hint during my physical healing time that my job was being phased out and I would be required to resign. From the very Senior Managers down, these people had stood by me at every turn and twist throughout my entire ordeal. Medical procedures I had endured were so new that they could have very easily refused to cover the tremendous costs which would have forced my family to abandon the whole idea or find private funding. In the best estimate we can muster from actual billing forms we still possess, the rough base price of my transplant was at over $300,000.00, an astronomical cost at that time. This is a true tribute to their loyalty to me as a valued employee. Now I was more than eager to repay their generosity by resuming my responsibilities as soon as possible.

That opportunity finally came in March when my medical team, under the superior leadership of Dr. Karanes, determined that I was now fit to return to full-time work. Those much-despised masks could be burned, the nuisance of a heart catheter could be removed, the weekly appointments could be replaced by monthly checkups, and the bike I had been riding as physical therapy could once again be parked in the corner of the garage.

As the new bone marrow and stem cells were functioning with renewed vigor, I could trade in my old worn-out jalopy of a body for a sleek, high-powered sports car completely powered by high octane fuel and running on Pirelli performance racing tires. The green flag had been waved in front of me, so I wasted little time accelerating into the lane marked "Express"!

I was overjoyed to once again pass-through security at the Ford Credit doors and, with the sincere greetings of "Welcome Back" expressed from every person I passed, entered the office with my name on the door just like I had done twice before after health issues.

But this time, things were different. I was different!

One can't experience what I had experienced having to face the actuality of potential physical death and not be changed. The temptation was to only look ahead and never look back at what had transpired in the last year. It would have been true to my organizational mind to have immediately placed that entire medical experience in a file labeled

"Closed" and inserted it at the back of my brain's filing system. No one would have faulted me if I never spoke of all the suffering and uncertainty which I had endured. But I was learning that every day of my life, all 14,965 days of them counted up since my birth to October 23, 1991, was a testimony of God's fathomless love for me. That day was a huge personal milestone marker which I would refer to for the rest of my life.

Many times my words fail to express what I want to share with others so this is a good time to set down this reminder as found in Psalm 23 (TPT),

> "Yahweh is my best friend and my shepherd. I will always have more than enough. He offers a resting place for me in His luxurious love. His tracks take me to an oasis of peace near the quiet brook of bliss. That's where He restores and revives my life. He opens before me the right path and leads me along in His footsteps of righteousness so that I can bring honor to His name. Even when your path takes me through the valley of deepest darkness, fear will never conquer me, for You already have! Your authority is my strength and my peace. The comfort of your love takes away my fear. I'll never be lonely, for You are near. You become my delicious feast even when my enemies dare to fight. You anoint me with the fragrance of Your Holy Spirit; You give me all I can drink until my cup overflows. So, why would I fear the future? Only goodness and tender love pursue me all the days of my life. Then afterward, when my life is through, I'll return to Your glorious presence to be forever with You."

Wow! There it is in black and white.

This ancient declaration of praise to God stills rings true. Verses I had heard over and over for my entire life would powerfully express just how I felt.

To some it may seem trite to talk of God's love, but I knew without a shadow of doubt that only because He walked with me, carried me, upheld me, comforted me, wept with me, and covered me with His mercy, had I survived.

Assuredly, family had always been precious to me but now it was even more so. Why was I being given a second chance to make a difference in the lives of my wife, children, and extended family members? Who was watching my daily walk with my Savior to see if I truly trusted Him to supply whatever I spiritually needed? My perspective had definitely been altered through what I had endured.

Work also took on a whole different nature as I looked at business with a new set of criteria. What really was important? What really was worth stressing over? Where can I make a difference in the lives of others? Why have I been given new hope? Renewed vigor? That other second chance to make a difference in the lives of others? There were no concrete answers, but I figured my journey so far had a purpose beyond what I could imagine right then. So with renewed enthusiasm for accomplishing good things at work while spending every moment out of the office with my family, I anticipated healthier days ahead into the summer and fall months.

For the first time in over a year, I felt like my "car" was finally operating on all cylinders while running down a pretty straight highway at a steady speed. Every new medical checkup was approached with an extreme anxiousness that would only be alleviated by those wonderful words, "All Clear" as spoken by Dr. Karanes. Her smiles were almost as big as mine whenever the testing reports were reviewed with no cancer present. My entire physical system had been miraculously healed.

Once again, my amazing Creator had touched the minutest biological cells in my body to rebuild, repair, and revitalize. He, who knew me from even before my actual conception, had channeled His healing energy through remarkable medical minds, caring hands of health care workers, and the relentless prayers of many. You might say that He had quietly performed a frame-off restoration.

I probably need to explain what actually is a frame-off. With the plan of increasing the functionality, appearance, or value of a vehicle, the restorer will disassemble an entire unit right down to the frame. He (or she) will then rebuild the body using all new components with the sole purpose of creating a vehicle which resembles the original design in its pristine condition.

It was not an instantaneous healing but rather a gradual process unfolding every day I could take a breath on a new cancer free morning. I mean no insult here to anyone who believes in instantaneous healing moments following intense prayer. It is not my intent to belittle such miracles as they do happen over and over many times. They are truly miraculous and blessed. However, I am also confident that it is God's choice to heal in His time and for His purposes. It is not the believer's role to order Him to perform in a certain manner. His plan for me has always been to keep trusting throughout each health crisis I have faced. He is far more interested how I trust, not how I feel.

Where I see hopelessness, He sees fulfillment.

Where I feel pain, He knows the benefits.

Where I express helplessness, He shows strength.

Where I vent frustration, He gives encouragement.

Where I crumble under fear, He upholds with unseen wings.

I think Oswald Chambers best described this new form of faith building I experienced (and continue to experience) when he wrote,

> "Faith is deliberate confidence in the character of God whose ways you may not understand at the time."[1]

So, filled with a gradual strengthening of my physical body as well as the maturing of my personal faith, I set about taking each day as an added blessing. It was rewarding to once more join the ranks of the corporate world at Ford Credit. Business meetings did not seem quite as laborious nor work related travel out of the office nearly as stressful. I had only to be reminded of where I had been just a few months previous. These were bonus days for sure.

Even the beauty of the Michigan fall that year was not lost on me nor was the joy I felt whenever my family was together, whether at Cindy or Matt's sports events, their various school programs, a late evening boat ride on Lake St. Clair, or just enjoying a lazy Saturday around the house together.

An added bonus for being back at Ford was the new responsibility my team and I had been given to handle all the customer correspondence and complaints for Edsel Ford II, the great grandson of Henry Ford who founded the company in 1903. This required regular meetings with him and his staff to review customer issues.

Being a hands-on manager, he was always interested in my ties to the Canadian based Revell Ford Lincoln Mercury dealership as established by my grandfather, my dad, and his brother. This was evident when one day my Uncle Harry was attending some type of dealer meeting in Dearborn and just happened to share an elevator ride with Edsel who, upon formal introduction, warmly remarked, "... so you are Uncle Harry. Dale has mentioned you numerous times." Edsel was a fine man to work under and I count it a privilege to have known him.

This now brings me to the next leg of this incredible legacy journey I am sharing with you. I could just wrap it all up with a few phenomenally powerful wise statements and put an end to this story. But there is so much more Holy Spirit wants me to lay in front of others as a tribute to the mighty workings of God and the compassion of Jesus, my Savior.

My story is set down specifically for my descendants to know who I am, where I've been, what I have faced, and who walked with me every step of the way. I want my legacy to not be simply that I reached a certain level of success as the world measures it, but that the struggles and victories have all been working for my good and God's glory. It will be an added bonus to have extended family, friends, and other acquaintances view my personal struggles through altered eyes while understanding the importance of a personal relationship with Jesus Christ. He alone promises eternal life in Heaven as well as rest for the burdens we carry while winding our ways through the present dangers of the here and now.

His very words from Matthew 11:28-29 (TPT) pledge this:

> *"Are you weary, carrying a heavy burden? Come to Me. I will refresh your life, for I am your oasis. Simply join your life with Mine.*
>
> *Learn my ways and you'll discover that I am gentle, humble, easy to please. You will find refreshment and rest in Me."*

With that said, I will move along in my life "adventure" to a very significant day in the spring of 1993 when arriving at what I assumed would be an ordinary Friday at the office, I was surprised by my upper management director's summons to his office. Must be some urgent company business which required my personal involvement. Imagine my surprise when it was presented to me that I was being offered a lateral move which would require a relocate out of Michigan. It would change my title, change my responsibilities, and change my family's address to Omaha, Nebraska! A place smack dab in the middle of the county surrounded by corn fields! In fact, their favorite collegiate team was the Nebraska Corn Huskers for Pete's sake!!

After recovering my breath and agreeing to consult my wife, I drove home in a state of turmoil. What I had dreaded throughout my last health crisis had happened or so I reasoned. Upper Management had reached a collective decision to offer me a position designed to place my career on a "forever" siding, way off to the side of the main traffic pattern of Ford business thus removing me as a liability in case my health fell into crisis again.

I remember walking into the house to break the news to Jane and did so with tears in my eyes. It was the personal derailment of my career. Bless her heart! She never missed a beat in reassuring me that God had never failed to bless us wherever our family landed, and He was not going to start now! Her mind was already packing the house. Her curiosity was already in high gear as she jumped wholeheartedly into discovering all the details of life in Omaha!

Just imagine all the new adventures our family would be given. If she had any second thoughts, I never knew because it was always her pattern to make the next place a special place without having any regrets upon leaving the old place.

Endnote

1. Oswald Chambers, "Devotional Reader: 52 Weekly Themes" www.azquotes.com

2003 HARLEY DAVIDSON SOFTAIL
100TH ANNIVERSARY EDITION

OMAHA, NEBRASKA

With such positive support from my spouse, I agreed to the position and set about working through the details. If this was the sidelining of my career, then I was determined to make the best of the situation for the sake of my family. The bigger challenge was to trust God's timing on this one. Because I had not personally instigated the relocation, there must be something Holy Spirit was not making clear to me. Slowly I was learning that it was not important to have the inside track on what lay ahead for my family because by now we had many memories of blessings and miracles erected as milestones special to every place we had called home.

My new title would be Customer Service Center Manager which carried with it the extensive duty of overseeing a call center responsible for all retail customer interactions as related to vehicle loans and leases. My staff handled customer service complaints to executive level management and written or telephone contacts with customers. Our call volume exceeded millions of inbound and outbound calls each year. I was to fill the role of Crew Chief, to use a car racing term, while orchestrating the design as well as construction of an expanded office space to accommodate the doubling of staff personnel from 300 to 600. Having successfully completed a similar project for the Buffalo office, I was excited to tackle this venture.

In addition to this, I reviewed all aspects of operations and implemented "best in class" strategies to move Ford Credit to world class customer satisfaction by benchmarking other world class companies. To do this, I was able to recruit and hire many very talented managers and team leaders who shared my passion of striving for excellence.

Space does not allow me to mention everyone who contributed to the success of the Omaha operation; however, I would like to highlight the accomplishments of one individual who remains to this day as a valued family friend as well as an accomplished businessperson. I was privileged to have Donna Marasco join my management team in the vital role of "Chief of Staff." She ably assisted me in executing our vision of operational excellence. Her keen organizational mind combined with that desire for excellence was supported by a solid base of personal integrity. Ford Credit was a stronger service system under her dedicated leadership and her support of me as her manager never wavered.

On a lighter side, I remember one specific business trip we all enjoyed when I took my senior leadership team to Walt Disney University to study their customer strategies and training methods. A great learning experience with some fun thrown in! Creative leadership has to make room for rewards and fun sometimes or the troops get discouraged under the workloads.

It may seem like I accomplished all this in the three months before the family joined me so I will clarify that my co-writer does jump ahead to fill in details I may have left out. Remember, I am the executive summary guy. She is the detail scribe! Takes a team to tell a story!

What was my family doing while I was tackling all these early tasks in Omaha? Well, true to her form, Jane was knee deep in the relocation details of setting up the packers and movers, filing numerous request forms for medical history from all our doctors and dentists, resigning from her librarian position, collecting school records, and once again, preparing our household possessions for transport as soon as school was released for the summer.

Thankfully, the past moves have taught her to be diligent in acquiring all medical records, X-ray films, doctor's reviews, and hospital reports. She is almost obsessive about this, but it has proven to be invaluable over the years. One such incident reinforces this. At one point during the next seven years after my transplant, the medical team working with my rechecks needed to determine if I should have another bone marrow biopsy. I have previously explained how horrendously painful this test is and I was fearful that it would need to be repeated. To my rescue came my Pit Bull who asked how this could be avoided. Our fine team of cancer doctors at University of Nebraska Medical Center wanted to view the original slides from my previous biopsies as a study of my lymphoma history.

Did we have said slides in our possession? No, but we did have files full of paperwork which supplied us with the actual dates of all my biopsies, so armed with this, Jane called the Detroit hospital and was able to locate a lady in medical records who discovered that the requested slides and reports were scheduled to be destroyed two weeks from that very day.

Information was expedited and met the satisfaction of my present doctors, so I was given a reprieve from the one test which frightened me every time. God had once again intervened on my behalf through a little detail He had been teaching us. Trust the one who watches out for even a sparrow's life!

As I have shared several times already, relocation moves are each unique with their own persona. Some flow smoothly while others are a jumble of miscues or blunders. If we are counting, this would be our seventh company sponsored relocation (that means Ford paid!). All things were progressing nicely with kids at school and Jane subtly supervising the packing team as they moved throughout the house expertly consigning its contents to sturdy cardboard boxes thus assuring their easy transport by the huge moving truck parked in the driveway. All was going well until the kids arrived home from school to observe the entire contents of their bedrooms packaged in several large boxes sitting in bare walled rooms. Cindy took one look at this and promptly burst into tears realizing this was actually happening. Everything she cherished was about to change. Everything she prized was confined in these four or five boxes.

Her brother I think was just as sad but quietly resigned to the inevitable. He held in his emotions like his father while his sister expressed hers with pretty obvious feelings like her mother. As my Aunt Bonnie Ball would have said, "She did not lick that up off the ground!" A wise saying we have used many times over the years!

The situation was quickly resolved through a phone call between Detroit and Omaha as the children's Mum informed their father that the Embassy Suites just down the road would be their address until the moving van departed three days later. It was too much to ask our teenagers to witness their home being displaced as well as dealing with all the goodbyes. Detroit had been such a mixed bag of emotions for us all, and yet it would always supply us with great memories of God's faithfulness through all the good or not so good times.

Thus, it was that one day in early June, I rejoined the family to bid goodbye to the moving van with its heavy load of all our worldly treasures and begin the drive out of Michigan toward the Midwest. Seems like most of my journeys so far had been heading East or West!

The journey was progressing nicely with the kids dozing in the usual teenage years travel-induced coma as their parents conversed quietly. Chicago rolled past the windows, and we were soon entering the vast fields of Iowa with its endless rows of corn stretching sometimes as far as the eye could see. Occasionally, a farm would appear alongside the highway to remind us there were folks living amongst all this corn.

About then the 16- and 14-year-olds awakened from their naps to realize the landscape had changed significantly from the city streets we had left to rural scapes! Between the two of them they renamed the area, "Hicksville!" and proceeded to declare at every new farm or field that expression. Unfortunately, we also saw and smelled some immense pig farms fully baking in the hot summer sun. Finally, their mum strongly suggested that they refrain from the word usage whereupon they restructured their comment to declare, "Humville!"

Give them credit for showing respect for authority but still lodging their opinion. This was not a good start for the Midwest relocation!

Of course, it did not help the situation when, upon driving into Des Moines, Iowa to locate a hotel for the overnight stay, we passed the very large and bustling Convention Center whose immense front billboard announced the convergence of the World Pork Exhibition! This was not missed by our observing protesters! It was somewhat amusing to hear their comments regarding this new world view! They had only experienced corn as on the cob or pigs in the shape of bacon!

Fortunately, things did improve somewhat for the female member of this grumbling duo as she and her mum sat in the hotel parking lot waiting for Matt and I to reserve a room. As she was slumped in her backseat corner throwing a small pity party for herself, there suddenly appeared next to our vehicle the looming presence of an extremely magnificent fire engine red Ford F350 truck with shining chrome detailing. It rolled on huge dually tires and sported a custom designed door signage which advertised its owner's profession—Hog Farmers! Out of the vehicle stepped two young men resplendent in full cowboy attire complete with finely crafted boots, expensive formfitting jeans encircled with leather belts secured by silver belt buckles, crisply pressed white dress shirts, and wide brimmed Western hats! Our daughter sat up and took in every detail of their persona as they ambled across the parking lot into the hotel lobby. She then stated, "Well, maybe this isn't going to be so bad after all!"

We have laughed over this incident many times and did get Cindy's permission to include it.

The rest of our trip into Omaha was uneventful and actually unfolded nicely when we introduced the kids to their new home complete with spacious bedrooms and a bathroom for each of them. This house was a new construction, so we had been able to pick some of the finishing features. It was to be the home where Cindy said was the most enjoyable because it was not filled with cancer fears, medical emergencies, and constant doctor appointments. It was a great place to just relax and enjoy pain-free moments. A chance to focus on life in the normal lane for a change!

Much to their surprise, Omaha was a beautiful city with many interesting and positive aspects which included a low crime rate as well as more conservative political viewpoints in governmental as well as educational policy making. The seemingly endless corn fields had given way to reveal a city bustling with new businesses, many team sports programs, a revitalized downtown complex with even a French cafe, the sprawling campus of ConAgra's food brokering conglomerate, Mutual of Omaha Insurance's stately buildings, Union Pacific Railroad world headquarters, Father Flanigan's Boys Town main campus, and the world class Henry Doorly Zoo, to name just a few more visible signs of a growing economy which welcomed new ideas as well as fostering history. It was the home of the NCAA Division 1 college baseball World Series and each year successfully hosted thousands of avid fans. There were plenty of things for teens and adults to enjoy.

As was our family's routine when relocating, we sought out a church which would become our community of believers. Westside Church, a Southern Baptist governed facility, got the nod from our teens. They were very encouraged to meet other teens from their high school and immediately became involved in youth activities. This would become our worship spot where we would find dear friends, prayer warriors, opportunities to serve others, outreach events similar to the Buffalo church, and more importantly, fellow believers who loved Christ. It was by no means a perfect church. That does not exist anywhere! But its mission statement was sound, and its people did not lack enthusiasm for sharing the love of God with others.

Speaking of the kid's high school brings up an interesting story. When we first arrived from Detroit, we had driven the kids by this very large facility just down the street from our new house. One of them commented,

"Why would someone build a factory in the middle of a housing area?" Imagine their shock when we told them it was not a factory but their new school!!! This school had over 2,000 students in four grades and was bigger than my hometown and Dale's added together when we were their age. This was definitely going to be a new experience!

Not only were they going to be attending this very large school, but it was also a public facility. As their last two schools had been private, we had looked into sending them to a Christian school. But on further review of available programs in the area, we determined that their best opportunities for a balanced academic preparation would be better met at the public level. It was not an easy decision but one which suited our family at the time. Matt helped cement our choice when he commented, "Guess it is time to trust your Christian instructions as parents." Wise words from a ninth grader!

After a week in a hotel, we were soon reunited with our household goods and settled into the new place. Cindy was a newly licensed driver and very happy to take over the wheel of her father's new car which had somehow been promised as an enticement to accept the Midwest move. It was a white Mustang GT convertible with red interior bedecked in the latest options! WHAT was I thinking???

It certainly garnered her some attention at Millard North High School when she arrived for the July volleyball camp run by the Varsity coach. As luck would have it, the football players were also having camp at the same facility at the exact same time so... she was not without the admiration of the entire team!

What WAS I thinking?

Both kids were quickly accepted into their chosen sports club teams and that certainly helped to smooth over the sadness of leaving Detroit. Over the years of our relocations, they have had to adjust to new team members, coaching styles, playing schedules, academic requirements, and fitness routines. They were like sponges soaking up the intensity of their volleyball and soccer commitments on club and travel teams. Within the first couple of weeks in Omaha, Cindy was attending a volleyball camp at University of Nebraska's Lincoln campus as a member of Rivercity Volleyball Club and during which we had our first serious experience with an active tornado!! She spent several hours hunkered down in a stairwell with the other gals while we watched the wind hurling around patio furniture and anything else not tied down!

Welcome to the Midwest!

Shortly after, Matt joined a select soccer team and we headed off to St. Paul, Minnesota for a weeklong Olympic style World soccer tournament where he played against teams from Mexico, Germany, and many other countries. It would be the start of four years of great soccer for Matt during which he excelled as a defense player at Millard West High where he transferred in his junior year. He became a leader both on and off the field and never failed to give his very best at practice, competitive events, and academically. It was such a joy to watch him mature from that little blonde-headed five-year-old kicking a soccer ball around with his first team in Buffalo into a six-foot, two-inch young lad quietly leading others.

Cindy successfully joined the Varsity Volleyball at North High team after excelling at grueling tryouts. Under the direction of her intense but wise coach, she stepped up to the challenge of elevating her skills to meet the rigid requirements expected at this level of competition. Her dedicated love for the sport worked in unison with her amazing commitment to others. She, too, brought such joy to me when I reminded myself these were the extra years, I had asked God to give me way back in Buffalo.

As an extra bonus, God tossed in another blessing when it became apparent that "Hicksville" had become "Home" for our two teens as they settled into their new life amongst the corn!

It was soon obvious that these were going to be extremely busy years for us both at home and at Ford Credit Omaha. The call center's new expansion was completed, and my staff celebrated the official move in with a grand celebration. We were even honored to welcome Edsel Ford and other senior management from Corporate as special guests. It was an exciting time for sure.

Hopefully without seeming to be a boaster, I will add that I was very proud of what had been accomplished in such a short time in this hidden jewel of a Midwest city. Our gleaming facility, with its cutting-edge technology surrounded by modern office equipment, went a long way in replacing the old view that Omaha was just a large cow town surrounded by those famous cornfields.

With the new space now available to accommodate more employees and the call center business expanding across the United States, our office was soon hiring people to handle all the accelerated call volumes. This was not missed by the Nebraska state Governor's office which then followed that Jane and I were invited to a reception hosted by the governor for companies expanding into the State. After the beautiful lunch served on the mansion's extensive gardens, we enjoyed our first University of Nebraska Corn Husker football game! Wow! What an experience as thousands upon thousands of enthusiastic fans filled the beautiful stadium. Everyone was attired in red! It was a sea of red!

Let me state here that I grew up watching the intensity of Toronto Maple Leaf hockey fans, but their love of a sport paled in comparison to the fervor of these football fans! Even their shoes, purses, and jewelry boasted the Husker red! It was an unbelievable sight when upon the home team scoring its first touchdown, hundreds of red balloons were released into the air and the screams of rejoicing were deafening. In fact, the whole state's football loyalty seemed to consolidate on Husker game days into one massive display of emotion. Win or lose, they stood behind their gridiron warriors.

When I look back on all that unfolded in the Omaha move both in my family's life and the company business, it quickly became clear that what I thought was a career offramp was in reality, a divinely orchestrated personal road map upon which had been detailed exactly what was planned for me. Just as I led management staff meetings by drawing their attention to preplanned agendas, all powerful God was drawing my attention to the intricate working of His purposes in my life. That little skinny kid from Verona certainly had come a very long way from fishing poles, hockey sticks, paper routes, and pumping gas.

Whatever I am sharing is not to blow my own horn in an attempt to elevate myself above any other man. All the credit for any positives in my life must be awarded to the handiwork of the power greater than me. I have an unimaginable legacy to pass on to my descendants, but none of it can I claim as having come from my own efforts.

Here is what is true!

Psalms 118:14-17 (NLT),

> *"The Lord is my strength and my song; He has given me victory. Songs of joy and victory are sung in the camp of the godly. The strong right arm of the Lord has done glorious things! The strong right arm of the Lord is raised in triumph. The strong right arm of the Lord has done great things! I will not die; instead, I will live to tell what the Lord has done."*

It is truly amazing to rewind the life journey I have been allowed to live and see the miraculousness of God removing those "Dead End" street signs that had been posted by the evil one always bent on stopping my witness.

If I had a vault full of money or a vast Texas-sized estate supported by a huge investment account to leave to my heirs, it could never take the place of a legacy of personal integrity and a continued dependency on God's grace during difficult struggles. When the "world" measures a man's worth, it counts only what is owned or earned. If I have learned anything over the span of my years, it is that my value as a person must be weighed on the scale of how I faced crippling health issues, how I handled difficult people, how I managed what I was entrusted to me by friends or family, and how I practiced daily dependence on my Lord.

Just as the value of a road vehicle is measured by the aid of a special book called the Kelley Blue Book which rates material worth based on vehicle reviews and ratings, my life, too, is measured by a priceless book entitled *The Bible*. It has been my comfort and guide while trusting its words even when I don't understand. When I feel as if I can never measure up to God's standards, my Lord Jesus gently reminds me of who I am in Him. He acknowledges my earthly success in passing but is far more focused on how much I love Him and trust Him. Even if.......is really the bottom line.

Now, after this brief off-roading in my thoughts, I will keep the story line rolling along. Having struggled through so many difficult moments in the past twenty-one years since my original cancer diagnosis, my time in Omaha was probably the first chance I had allowed myself to take a deep breath and begin to actually "live"—to make plans, to set longer life goals, and to believe that maybe this silent, but stealthy enemy could be left in the rearview mirror.

My new medical team consisted of the world renowned and highly respected lymphoma specialist, Dr. James Armitage. He and his team at the University of Nebraska Medical Center in Omaha would now be in possession of the volumes of medical records and pounds of X-rays Jane had brought from Detroit. Their expertise in monitoring my follow up cancer care had been highly recommended by Dr. Karanes and we were blessed to have access to them. It was a smooth transition as I was cancer free during our entire time under their watchful eyes.

I have already mentioned the blessing of the bone marrow tissue scans being rescued two weeks before they were scheduled to be destroyed. Seems like a small thing to note but only by someone who has never had a bone marrow biopsy. Each medical victory of clear blood and CT scan test results was a blessing I could record in my legacy travel log!

As a result of the absence of any personal medical complications for me since 1991, our family was able to create more valuable memories which were not overshadowed by dread or uneasiness. We could begin to figuratively relax somewhat from waiting for a "mechanical malfunction," a "tire puncture," or a "blown engine" on the family vehicle! The dispirited memories of painful times would never completely disappear, but their powerful grip on our emotions would be loosened by Jesus' never-ending grace.

Some of Cindy and Matt's earliest memories would have been of their dad always being in some dejected state of physical adversity and their mum unselfishly engaged in his care. Now we could relax somewhat in our Midwest surroundings and enjoy some good times together. Through careful management of our finances after having concentrated my mental energies elsewhere for many years, I was able to invest our moneys more wisely which allowed for some benefits.

We were able to join a newly established country club where I could refresh my golfing skills. Where once my hands had tightly held a wooden hockey stick with its curved surface designed to send a small, round, black puck on a straight path into a netted goal, they now gripped a skinny metal shaft attached to a weirdly shaped head also designed to deliver physical force onto the surface of a round white object to send it straight into another goal—a small hole cut into a grassy spot. Please take note of the word "straight" here as it is key to understanding the challenge of this new sport.

The old activity on ice had its unique requirements of balance, power, strength, accuracy, and endurance. All these I had been able to perfect through the years while moving on thin blades attached to leather boots. It should then follow that this new sport of walking in leather shoes on solid ground with no physical opponents accosting my person to impede forward progress while in pursuit of knocking that tiny ball straight into the designated hole should have been nearly a hole in one every time.

Truth be told, my golfing skills would never match those of Arnold Palmer, but the sport captured my attention and challenged me each time I stepped onto the course. It also opened the door for me to spend quality time with seven fellow golfers who quickly became some of my dearest friends.

Together with them, we fondly named our band of brothers, The Golfing for God Guys. Our individual skills ranged from well-developed to not so well-developed, but the camaraderie of our faith superseded the differences in our abilities. Bible studies together always were a major part of our golfing trip agendas wherever our travels took us.

We enjoyed such spots as Banff in Canada, Mazatlán in Mexico, and numerous courses in America as well as several challenging ones in Scotland and England.

This last trip was an amazing two-week extravagance which included our wives! They were more than happy to have us golfing in Europe as long as they too were part of the group. Of course, none of them golfed, but they certainly did enjoy the sights and sounds of all the fascinating places we stayed. I think they were delighted to "play" the high tea and tourist courses while we slugged it out amongst the heather of Scotland and the formality of English golf courses. On one of the latter events, we men were required to change from our golfing gear into our suit jackets, dress shirts, and neckties to eat lunch before resuming the next nine holes in regular golf wear! A very unique British experience.

I have conveniently forgotten the scores we earned during our golfing trips, but I will never forget the bond I felt with these men who were not perfect but were genuine and caring. We shared our sorrows as well as thousands of laughs while never taking the differences in our golfing skills too seriously.

My wife will readily admit that she never really grasped the quirky mechanics of golf even after lessons from a professional. (She may have been the first person who ever was asked to drop out of golfing lessons!)

She did make an observation once which was on point regarding the entire quest of golfing prowess. After one depressing day on the course where my scores discouragingly ballooned causing me to complain, she asked, "And you wonder why I have no desire to take up a sport where frustration is my companion? Was the day not bathed in sunshine and the birds singing as you strolled along the beautifully maintained course with its lush foliage and fauna highlighting meandering brooks of sparkling water? Did you not delight as well in the opportunity to dine on the hearty lunch expertly prepared in the stately club house?"

Well, she did have a point.

Seems my frustration over less than stellar golfing scores had created within me a negative attitude which I expressed on a regular basis. From that moment on after each golfing outing, I regaled her with the splendor of the natural elements surrounding the chaps and I as we calmly meandered through the strategically placed tee boxes, lush fairways, expertly manicured greens, unlimited sand traps, and dreaded roughs chasing that dimpled white ball with little regard for our final scores. Well, that might be stretching the truth a little! Actually, that is stretching the truth a whole lot!

The one sport my family did continue to enjoy together was boating as we were able to include the transport of our boat from Michigan to Nebraska. Our Omaha real estate agents had assured us that there were bodies of water which could accommodate our vessel. Well, that claim was not totally true. We discovered that the only suitable marina near us for the thirty-foot Sea Ray was located on the muddy, polluted Missouri River. It shared the space with sports fields and a very crowded public park. With no other suitable option, we rented a slip and attempted to enjoy the river. It was such a letdown after the majestic water expanses of the Great Lakes we had so enjoyed.

Little did we realize that our boating days in the Midwest would prove to be very short as not long after securing our boat slip, the river flooded causing that very dock section to drift away from its moorings. Three weeks passed before we were allowed to even see our boat let alone assess any potential damages.

Because of the increased pollution in the water from the flooding, we made the decision that our boating days were over. It was not a healthy place for me to be exposed to whatever was floating in the nasty water, so we sold the boat. Well, I will clarify here that I did agree to sell said boat for x amount of dollars and left the negotiating process to my fellow crew mate while I was out of town on business. She did successfully sell the beautiful craft but at a $6,000 reduction in our agreed upon price. Her logic rested on saving the monthly sale's lot fee and winter storage!

It was a sticky moment of miscommunication!

Oh well! Life has its moments of adjustments. Sadly, it was time to close that chapter of adventures on the water.

If you are tempted to feel sympathy for me as I added the no longer useful marine life jackets to the same dark box in the attic which contained my old hockey gear, please don't. For you see, I was soon captivated by a new sport which definitely fulfilled my need of speed. "Rev" Revell was still my unofficial nickname!

But before I regale you with the new adventure, I should mention that I was diligently still working for Ford Credit and not just out of the office on personal pleasure exploits. (The Revell household expenses still needed to be covered!)

The Call Center had now been firmly established in its new larger space and was successfully functioning with the continued addition of well qualified staff. It was my personal goal to develop many "best in class" customer service policies, and this was accomplished through the dedication of each manager, team leader, and individual service representatives. I was the front man, but they were the behind-the-scenes crew who earned us several business awards through dedication and hard work.

That hard work did not go unnoticed as my management team, and I set into motion many incentives for reaching performance goals. Of course, it was only natural that we tapped into a perfect automobile themed scenario by treating our winners and their spouses where applicable to all expense paid weekends track side at many NASCAR Motor Racing events! These were very popular prizes as well as our Perfect Attendance weekend jaunts to Kansas City, Kansas for overnights at the Ritz Carlton Hotel.

Over the years in management, I had learned that people work better when they feel that there are rewards for competence and loyalty. Our center was not just a workplace. It was a unique community of hard-working individuals who deserved fun activities, picnics, contests, and the one visit from the Easter Bunny dressed in full furry costume commissioned to distribute Cadbury eggs to every employee at their desks! Imagine everyone's surprise when the identity of costumed figure was revealed as being none other than Mrs. Dale Revell. One never knew where she would show up or what she would volunteer to do for a good cause. It was great fun for sure, but only done once!

Veering onto a side road here, I should mentioned that I had learned over the years that one has to be flexible and accept some moments of humorous introspection, or as my Mum would have said, "Don't be afraid to laugh at yourself!" This rang true for me twice when I remember coming home from the office one night to grumble a little to my wife that it had been proposed to me that we should have a lactating room made available at the Center. I chuckle to think what my facial expression revealed at that moment! I affirmed the proposal would be considered and then wondered what in the world that was—lactating. That word was not familiar to me.

That evening, Jane explained it was the official word for breast feeding. Well, how was that supposed to work in the office setting? More details followed with the process being explained to me. Several days later, I admitted that the whole idea was new to me, but we were able to set up such a room complete with comfy chairs and refrigerator. My resume now had a new bullet point—Lactating Room Manager!

You can imagine my reaction, when just a few days after the special room was operational, it was further proposed to me that we offer an onsite daycare for parents of young children and babies! Well, that idea was also discussed at home, and I firmly said, "There is no way we can have wailing toddlers running up the hallways ladened with sodden diapers or dragging favorite blankets while frantically searching for their parents."

Well, it was explained to me that was the wrong picture to paint as businesses were offering daycare at their facilities and rather successfully. We had another good chuckle over my imagined scenario, but thankfully our new building had no extra space for babies on site. Well, at least I was thankful.

Decision avoided!

Seriously, as I have previously mentioned, our center was awarded many well-deserved honors during those successful years of operation. One such prestigious award was the J.D. Power Customer Contact Award in 2001 and again in 2002. Our inbound call volume exceeded one million calls per month at that time. That is a great many "Hello, thank you for calling Ford Credit Company" for sure! It was also our privilege to host many outside groups who, in learning of our success in call centers best practices, traveled to Omaha to study our methods firsthand.

Subsequently, I was promoted to Director, North American Customer Services Operations. This new position included additional responsibilities of Primus Financial Services Customer Support and establishing an offshore vendor, Florida based Sykes Enterprises, to assist Ford Credit in better serving our clients through a Costa Rica call center. It was a whole new experience for me as I traveled many times to Central America region visiting with the large, relatively young, but highly educated staff.

My roots were in the cold winters of Canada with their brief summer spurts of warmth, so this new tropical climate exposure was fascinating. I was able to witness a very different culture of lush green landscapes, coffee plantations nestled amongst city buildings or perched on mountain sides, and palatial estate homes or humble dwellings sharing neighborhoods albeit each encircled with some form of privacy fencing. The hustle and bustle of San Jose was similar to any other big city I had visited, but unique in its Hispanic flare, while the countryside was enveloped in dense forests, small villages, mountainous terrain, as well as seaside communities with surfers and tourists in abundance. Over the course of the remainder of my business career, I was privileged to make thirty-three trips to this divergent country.

My travels did not end there. Along with keeping my eye on the bigger picture of directing and leading the North and Central America sides of the business, I was privileged to be selected to serve on an advisory board with other Ford Credit senior executives during a four-month period of time. Our mission was to formulate plans for an improvement in Ford of France's sales volumes. Our headquarters of operations for the assignment was in Paris, so I travelled there two weeks in each of the four months. It was fascinating and challenging work.

My fellow teammates were from Germany, South America, England, and France so there were many opportunities to study their types of business practices as well as exchanging new ideas. It was a very great honor to have been selected for this and once again I was reminded just how God had blessed me from those early crazy years of collecting accounts in Toronto to being part of a global focus group. At the conclusion of this assignment, we presented our recommendations to the CEO of Ford Motor Company Worldwide. This was just incredible when I once again remember thinking Omaha was a dead-end street for my career development.

God sure does have a sense of humor and I can just imagine the chuckles exchanged between Him, His Son, and Holy Spirit as they watched their plans unfold in my life. Their view was so much broader than mine would ever be! Seldom did a day go by as I worked behind my desk, sat in boarding lounges at airports waiting to fly across miles of sky, rode in taxis through big cities, or just sat quietly at home, that I was not aware of just how merciful God had been to bring me through many difficult years.

I WAS NOT AWARE OF JUST HOW MERCIFUL GOD HAD BEEN TO BRING ME THROUGH MANY DIFFICULT YEARS

Sometimes during those quiet moments of personal reflection, I wondered why I was given so many new chances at living. Why was I allowed to enjoy so many more career advances, family centered celebrations, exceptionally interesting places to explore, and cancer free months? Why were the days of my life extended? Why was I to live when others, family, or friends, did not? One thing I did determine is that I could never know the mind of my Creator.

My wise Mum remarked to me one time that she felt one of the reasons I was allowed to endure such difficult times with my health was because it was God's way of keeping me from developing pride in my accomplishments at work or personal life. She may have been right to some extent. God did not orchestrate my cancer diagnosis, but He did use it as a platform to demonstrate the importance of a personal reliance on Him.

Whatever I have accomplished in my lifetime has been through some degree of effort on my part, but more importantly, a reliance on Jesus' daily leading in my thoughts, pleasures, and goals. He has opened the door for me to be His witness to family, friends, and acquaintances who will, without a doubt, someday find themselves traveling on some troublesome route with all the proper directional signs ripped off their posts and lying face down in the ditch.

Without the struggles of my disease, I would have never known true dependency on Him for strength in the midst of chaos. Even when all was going well as it did for many years, I still needed to give Jesus control and honor in every decision I made.

One of those decisions I made at this time was to find ways in which to encourage others. This chance had afforded me when I was asked to serve on the official board at The Open Door Mission in Omaha. Here was an opportunity to make a difference in the lives of others struggling in everyday living. It was my pleasure to serve in this capacity for almost ten years. Even though I had never personally experienced lack of a job or limited financial security, I did know firsthand how crippling fear can grip the human heart. What a blessing to see lives changed through this amazing ministry.

Another interesting opportunity to serve others was offered to me when, out of the blue, I received a call from none other than Dr. Karanes, the physician responsible for my second chance at living. She was now Assistant to the Director of the National Marrow Donor Program based in St. Paul, Minnesota. There was an opening on their finance board, and she was offering me the position as a volunteer member. Without any hesitation, I accepted the offer. The uniqueness of this assignment was not lost on me as I realized that my Ford Finance background allowed me to offer a business expertise paired with the deeply personal experience of being an actual stem cell recipient. It was my honor to contribute to this organization for next the ten years.

Looking back on these volunteer settings helped me realize that there was a purpose for the continuation of my life which only God knew. Even if He never chose to share it with me in some blazing vision or dream, I could still be humbled in the realization that I did have the privilege of using what I had been allowed to battle through to encourage others. So much had been given to me during my struggles that it was time for me to give back. Because I had been cared for, it was time for me to care for others in any way I could. That may just have been another answer to the "Why me, Lord?" I have asked over the years.

Time marches on and so must I or this legacy journey will be a never-ending epistle.

While I stayed very busy at work, my family, too, was on the fast track. Matt and Cindy were focused on school and sports responsibilities as well as activities surrounding youth programs at our church. A short-term mission trip unfolded for Matt as he became part of a youth group serving in Nicaragua during school break. It was very rewarding time for him to experience what his folks had experienced in their early years of marriage through two work trips to Haiti.

In fact, I still have sitting on my home office shelf a reminder of his trip in the form of a small decorative clay pot he brought back to me. This particular, native crafted pot caused some excitement at the airport when, upon his arrival back into the States and while being questioned by Customs as to what he was bringing into the country, he said, "Oh, just a little pot." Well, it was an honest answer but caused a few raised eyebrows!

What seemed to come in just the blink of an eye, Cindy graduated from high school, and we geared ourselves up for the dreaded day when we would need to drop her off at college. She had accepted a scholarship to play volleyball at a northern Iowa school. When the day arrived, I cautioned her mum to not make the parting a difficult one by some loud emotional goodbye. Just give a hug, a pat on the back, and release her with well wishes

Seems I should have listened to my own advice for when the actual moment came to head back to Omaha, I was the one boohooing! Jane reminds me that I also said, "If she had asked me for money, I would have given her my whole wallet!" Guess I wasn't as prepared as I thought! It is always an unsettling moment when one's children begin to cut the ties to home and their childhood.

The next year unfolded with lots of fun times for us as we enjoyed traveling to college venues for Cindy's exciting and challenging volleyball games as well as cheering on the sidelines for Matt's impressive play as a member of his high school soccer team. He had made the decision to transfer to a brand-new facility and it proved to be a good experience.

Throughout our young adult children's lives, I have been blessed to observe their dedication to excellence in both individual commitment to skill development and team effort. They never wavered in their support of team members or a coach's instructions whether winning or losing. These were legacy moments which reminded me of my father's teaching to never give up and never alter personal integrity to match the moment. I watched with parental pride as my children walked out their faith in Christ and continue to do so as spouses and parents. They were (and still are) my prayer warriors, depression battlers, and discouragement slayers!

By spring of 1997, Matt was ready to graduate from high school and make the big leap to the college of his choice, Baylor University in Waco, Texas. His sister was making her own leap as she was getting married! Seems her heart had been captured by a young Omaha fellow, Christopher Washburn, who had caught her eye one night at Westside Church. Their mutual interests were friends, playing volleyball, and attending church so their days and evenings were filled with many activities which cemented their relationship. I should add that Chris was NOT a Midwest pig farmer, and he actually became one of our Ford Credit team members shortly after they met. By all counts, they were very young for marriage, but then what could Jane and I say as we too had been their ages when we said our wedding vows. Of course, we always added that we were very mature for twenty and twenty-one! Some may have disagreed with this bold statement.

For sure, it was a very busy time for our household as graduation ceremony came in May and the wedding followed in July. Each celebration needed planning and I was instructed to hand over my credit card with the biggest spending balance available and then just show up at each event. In other words, keep quiet, strap myself into the passenger seat, nod to the driver, and smile! I joke here, but seriously, these two events were such a gift from God as so many years ago I had asked Him to allow me to live long enough to see my children graduate from high school.

He certainly did allow me those extra years and then added additional blessings beyond my wildest dreams. I think the directional words of Psalm 37:3-5 (TPT) best describes here what I was learning during this time along my legacy journey.

> *"Keep trusting in the Lord and do what is right in His eyes. Fix your heart on the promises of God, and you will dwell in the land, feasting on His faithfulness. Find your delight and true pleasure in Yahweh, and He will give you what you desire the most. Give God the right to direct your life, and as you trust Him along the way, you'll find He pulled it off perfectly."*

I hesitated to quote these verses as someone may raise a question about getting what WE desire as promised. As an explanation, I will mention that way back in our Buffalo and Christian Central Academy days, Jane's beloved principal and dear friend Ruth Adams, explained this verse very clearly at the staff morning devotion when she announced that the Revells were moving to Detroit. It was a moment of selfish sadness for everyone, but she reminded all that God will give His followers WHAT to desire—more of Him and less of self. That is not to say He doesn't bless materialistically, but He is steady in His desire for us to be in agreement for His will not our own. A new car, a bigger house, a better job, or a healthier body is not what He deems as important when eternity with Him is His desire for us.

GOD GIVES HIS FOLLOWERS THE DESIRE FOR MORE OF HIM AND LESS OF SELF

So with a whirlwind of activity swirling through our house for graduation and wedding celebrations, we made mega long to-do lists, delegated errands, stockpiled mounds of food, and rolled out the welcome mat for family and friends. It was three months of joyful celebrations, albeit with mega organizational stress for the mother of the graduate who was of course the mother of the bride as well, for the bride herself, and for my credit card! However, I did not mind as these were such special occasions I had often feared I would miss out on by not being present.

Actually, the groom and I breezed through all the festive preparations pretty successfully! Seems the only tense moment for the bride and her mother was over the price of some glitzy pair of earrings at Von Maur. Problem was resolved when a cheaper replacement pair was found amongst the costume jewelry collection in the bride's jewelry stash from Junior High years. My bank account was saved at least for that moment.

True to their dedication to making family memories, my folks flew in to celebrate Matt's graduation which was a very proud moment for all of us. What a fine young man he had become!

Mum and Dad always enjoyed these good times as we had all experienced so many difficult times together in the years past.

Just two months later, we rolled out the welcome mat for treasured family and friends for Chris and Cindy's wedding. For this special occasion, many invited guests traveled from Ontario, Texas, Michigan, North Carolina, Washington and New York anticipating a weekend of festivities. The wedding came off without a hitch and more great memories were made. Once again, I was just overwhelmed by the goodness of God to allow me to enjoy every moment of these two special events on our family's life journey. It may seem as if I repeatedly mention the extra years, but they were (and are) such unfathomable gifts to me

In the years which followed from 1997 to 2001, I continued to successfully keep the wheels of progress rolling at the call center with ever increasing call volumes and new innovations for processing customer connections. It was extremely challenging work, but very rewarding as I was privileged to see the mechanics of this well-oiled "machine" functioning in a relatively smooth gear. Like any business, we had our downshifting moments with personnel issues and malfunctioning equipment, but the management team actively worked together to problem solve each situation. Were there conflict moments? Of course, but nothing which logic and common sense could not resolve.

And if we needed more concrete clarification, we had manuals full of Ford Credit operational guidelines to follow while balancing the unique dynamics of the Center's customer service teams. Frequently, it required a more personal touch, so every day I asked God for wisdom in addressing the challenges of directing what had been entrusted to my care.

Many times, I felt like I needed the wisdom of Solomon in negotiating situations! It was always given to me through the unseen workings of the Holy Spirit, gifted to me by my Savior, Jesus Christ. If I doubted that godly guidance could be present in even the smallest details of my life, I only needed to look in the rearview mirror of my life journey car to be reminded of the expanse of the faithfulness of my Creator. Through every turn and twist of my almost unbelievable journey, God was teaching me daily perseverance (endurance), deeper levels of positive character growth, and a steady-going hope.

Romans 5:3-5 (MSG),

> *"There's more to come: We continue to shout our praises even when we're hemmed in with troubles, because we know how troubles can develop passionate patience in us, and how that patience in turn forges the tempered steel of virtue, keeping us alert to whatever God will do next."*

With this confidence that God was always working something in my life, I greeted the 2001 New Year with a commitment to keep my eyes focused on His leading. With Matt at college and Cindy married, our household was now officially an empty nest setting for the wife and me. Ford business trips were still on my calendar, so Jane decided to try her hand at working full-time. She had been successfully substitute teaching occasionally over the past several years, but now plunged into a position at Matt's high school as the Attendance Secretary! She would be totally responsible for keeping meticulous records of the whereabouts during school hours of every student in the student body of over 1,600! It was a daunting and demanding task which required detailed computer inputting every day!

It was baptism by fire for my sweet wife who was, by her own account, hopelessly ignorant of computers. Her answer for any problem which presented itself was to hit the exit button and turn the whole machine off, just short of pulling the electrical plug out of the wall. What saved her many days was the excellent support she received from sympathetic staff who appreciated her efforts to complete her assigned tasks as well as bond with the students.

In the spring of that same year, we proudly celebrated Matt's graduation from Baylor University and looked forward to the arrival of our first grandchild in December. Cindy and Chris had purchased their first home in anticipation of the blessed event, and I needed to figure out what I was to be called by this wee child. Dale was probably NOT acceptable! Grandpa? Papa? Gramps? After some debate with everyone involved, I settled on the title, Poppy. This went well with Jane's choice of Nanny.

It was a joy to watch Matt successfully adapting to the world of Informational Technology in his full-time job in the Dallas area with his first grownup apartment. Soon he was zooming around town in his car, a new zippy 2001 Ford Focus, which represented the first purchase he made on his own. Remember, we had not had a purchased car of our own since he was 6 months old! It was a bit of a sticker shock for him to now have to make car and insurance payments. Adult responsibilities come on us all quickly!

Then, along with the entire world, we experienced in one way or another, the tragedy of the 9/11 events in New York City! It was one of those milestone moments which would forever mark us all. Everyone can remember where they were when the very first planes hit the twin towers. I was in my office at the center when Jane called me with a warning to quickly turn the televisions on as something tragic was erupting. What unfolded over that day could never be erased in anyone's mind. The stories are never- ending, because we were in Omaha where Offutt Airforce Base Command Center was located where President Bush would eventually end up being quickly relocated from Florida, I made the executive decision to close the call center so that my people could go home. It was a very tense time.

In spite of some criticism from my superiors in Dearborn over the closing, I made my decision based on the emotional condition of the entire staff who needed to be at home with their families or friends. Sometimes decisions require more than what the Procedural Manuals dictate as acceptable. None of us had ever been faced with the magnitude of such an event in our business and well as personal lives. I never personally questioned that closure decision. It was the right one.

Within a week, we were all back at work, but still reeling from what we had observed through news media and stories of   human loss as well as human triumphs of endurance and service to others. These acts of terrorism affected us all even if we were thousands of miles away from the actual attack sites.

We all struggled in some way to understand what had happened, put it into perspective, and move on in our daily lives toward some degree of normalcy. What helped our family do so was the anticipation of a baby's arrival which would bring us the reminder that God was still in control of lives, still working for our good, still tuned into our deepest thoughts, and still faithfully showing us all His care through Jesus' unending love!

December 7th finally arrived, and the Washburn couple became a family of three with the arrival of Lauren Elizabeth! There was added celebration as her birth came on the same birthday as her Mum and her

Mum's Mum! What an amazing occurrence that these three gals shared the same birthday, albeit a few years apart.

I was immediately swept up into the experience of grand parenting! When our children are born, we love them unconditionally, but there is always the underlying sense of the intense responsibility of preparing them for their role as well- rounded adults, able to function away from home setting. Sort of like the "pushing them out of the nest" practice. It is the role of parents to equip their children with good life skills.

However, I was soon to learn that when grandchildren are placed into one's arms, they completely steal your heart, and you never want them to grow up. You forever want their faces to light up when they see you! They accept your phases of growing older as wrinkles and creaky joints replace youth. They listen to your life stories and never say, "You told us that already!" Of course, they love to hear stories about their parent's youthful antics. They even laugh at your jokes!

At our house, they are free to eat whatever is in the cupboards or refrigerator at whatever time of day or night they choose. They can even have snacks at bedtime and coffee at midnight. All that is required of them is that they keep their attention off their cell phones and don't make jokes about the All-Bran box in the cupboard! It is such a phenomenon— grandparenting! Maybe because one can spoil them completely and then send them home.

Seriously, there is one area of parenting which definitely spills over into grandparenting and grows in importance with each passing year. I always prayed for my children as they were growing up but will admit sometimes the responsibilities of work and family activities limited my prayer time. This new role of being a grandparent coupled with the maturity of middle age and a sense of a morally changing world revealed that I needed to really concentrate on praying down wisdom for my children, their spouses, and our grands. I doubled down on my petitions to God for His overseeing protection of Lauren and any others to be added to my family.

Did you notice my use of a plural word here—"others"?

Well, not long after we celebrated Lauren's first birthday in December of 2002, we cradled her brother, Luke Andrew, in our arms. He arrived in March of 2003 and soon the Washburn home bustled with activity as Chris and Cindy were both working full time, singing in the church choir, playing some volleyball, and keeping a household running. As Jane had been helping out with the babysitting since Lauren was six weeks old, it was a natural progression that she continued to do with our second grand. I never heard her complain once about the early morning hours or late nights often required of her in being the nanny as I was traveling so much with business. What a privilege to be caring for these precious little people.

It wasn't all work and no play for me that year as I became very aware that this specific year had some rather interesting celebrations in which I could be involved. It just so happened that Ford Motor Company was celebrating its 100th anniversary of the automobile which carries its name. There was a grand celebration weekend event in Dearborn, Michigan so Jane and I made plans to attend. The whole event was just superbly organized, and we had a wonderful time.

There were original cars on display from every year Ford had been manufacturing vehicles—100 of some of the most amazing cars ever produced. The festivities were held on the lawns in and around the Glass House complex. Henry Ford would have been amazed at the growth of his original plan to offer mankind a better way to work and travel. I was very proud to be part of such a remarkable company which had been connected to my family for two previous generations.

There was also a second anniversary celebration that year which I became involved in with great excitement. Once again, it just so happened that Harley Davidson Motorcycle Company was celebrating their 100th anniversary of the birth of their product. What a better way to combine the two anniversary events than through renewing my love of speed and the memories of my college days zooming around on two wheels than by purchasing a new motorcycle? Not just any model but the Anniversary edition special Softail silver and black bike with leather saddle bags and unending chrome? This was my plan to honor both my company and my hobby!

It did not take much convincing that this was a fine plan, but just what would the wife have to say about this large expenditure and hair-on-fire adventure? I had always required my children to present a modified business plan for the rhyme or reason of some expensive shoes or clothing they wanted so it would be hypocritical of me to not do the same. While I still figuring just how to approach the bike idea, I took Jane to a local Harley dealership for a "look and see" just to get her reaction. Well, I guess I failed to warn the salesman that this was a sensitive moment because upon greeting us he announced, "Hey, Dale, great timing as I just got that one in you are looking at!"

Another one of those awkward moments!

Thankfully, Jane also loves adventure so after a mock tongue lashing, she joined the excitement of the moment. How very blessed I have been over the years that she welcomed my hobbies and embraced the adventures. Of course, she did have her requirements that we both be attired with the necessary safety equipment which included sturdy leather boots, proper helmets with built in speakers, leather gloves, leather pants, leather jackets, and sunglasses. I spoke not a negative word as it was an extravagant sport, but one

THIS TIME I HAD A LITTLE MORE MONEY TO UTILIZE—CALL IT A DELAYED MIDLIFE CRISIS!

which I was excited to engage in again. This time I had a little more money to utilize—call it a delayed midlife crisis!

Attired in our new wardrobes and astride the glistening Harley, we were soon gliding around the roads of Nebraska thoroughly enjoying the wind in our faces and the open road ahead. Well, I was enjoying this rediscovered sport while Jane was quickly learning the requirements of riding behind the driver on a motorcycle. Her weight, though not much, added to the skill required for me to steer the vehicle and even the slightest leaning opposite of my body angle would cause the bike to negatively respond. In other words, she was required to hug me close and "feel" the ride. This bike had a very narrow seat with limited passenger room, so I had a back rest added for her relief.

When the Midwest weather permitted, we zoomed all over some very interesting highways and stopped at new places to embrace the flora and fauna of the state. There were many miles of corn- fields but just as many small towns with their uniqueness to explore. Our kids just smiled and shook their heads at our attempt to recapture some of our early marriage memories.

It seemed that every week or so we visited the local Harley dealer to just check out the newest bikes and attire available. On one such visit, a craggy old, road weathered biker guy asked Jane if she had any ink. Innocently, she pulled a pen from her purse where upon he bellowed, "Oh ..., you are just one of them RUB bikers!" Someone close by educated her on the term as meaning a Rich Urban Biker. Actually, he was inquiring if she had a tattoo!

It was embarrassing for her but pretty funny to everyone else.

All humor aside, we did enjoy our new means of recreation in spite of numerous frowns from our friends who I think were secretly jealous of our newfound freedom. Sure, it was dangerous, but then one could always die from being hit by a golf ball or crossing the street. Well, that is how I reasoned it anyway!

Our little grandkids really enjoyed the sounds of Poppy and Nanny roaring up into their driveway on a sunny Sunday afternoon. My folks were not so enthusiastic, but it just gave them more chances to sharpen up their prayer arrows to shoot Heavenward!

Motorcycling, working, grandkids, golf, and church filled my days now as milestone moments kept occurring to remind me that each breath, I took was an added bonus from the Father. In November of 2004, Jane and I rejoiced when Matt announced he had found the one Texas gal he was going to love for the rest of his life! Wendy Jo Wilbur had swept his heart up in her arms! We were (and still are) totally thrilled when we met her over lunch at Bahama Breeze where she ordered dessert first! Yes! She was a keeper!

Once again, many Revell family members traveled to Dallas for another grand celebration to be held at the lovely Paradise Cove wedding venue right on Lake Grapevine. Great day was had by all! As an added bonus, our grandchildren count was increased by the addition of Wendy's two precious children, Sierra and Sebastian! They embraced us as grandparents, and we were more than thrilled to encircle them with lots of love and laughter.

Like Cindy's, Matt's home was full of activity and good times whenever we visited! Under their parents strongly united leadership, the children attended Gateway Church and a Christian Academy where the basics of Christian living were reinforced. Their new home was always a place of Biblical teaching, group meetings, family meals, and a night's lodging for weary souls or those who might just need a handful of comfort. It was such an added bonus for us to see their generous hearts and true commitment to the needs of others. That continues to this very day.

Back at the home front in that Fall of 2004, our Omaha bunch was just settling into a familiar routine of management work for me, grandbaby sitting for Nanny, Pottery Barn work for Cindy, and call center employment for Chris when a change occurred which would affect us all. After much prayer and private discussions, Cindy and Chris had realized that Ford was not the place he wanted to spend the remainder of his career. It was steady work, but there had to be something more challenging for him to focus on for personal development. We understood and agreed to pray for God's leading. There were many different options for such a bright young man.

When recalling this time in our family's life, I am once again reminded of our move from Buffalo to Detroit and Principal Ruth Adam's reference to God giving us what to desire in our hearts. He promises to satisfy those desires when we are focused on what He wants, not just what we think we want. Chris desired God's very best for his little family and was willing to walk the path chosen for them.

None of us could have ever imagined the adventures awaiting them as they decided that Chris would, at age 28, enlist in the United States Army as a combat engineer. Their travel road of choice was going to be filled with relocations and deployments as well as all that military life required. They would be strapped into a fast-accelerating vehicle navigating through every possible road condition imaginable!

Ahead for them would be the adjustment from civilian to military life with its celebration moments and separation times of deployment. It was an active time for soldiers as the USA was at war in Iraq. But how God led them to become the strong warriors in His spiritual army is their amazing story to tell. I am resisting the temptation to share just a fraction of what occurred for them as it is their story, not mine, which someday they will put on paper, I am sure. It is remarkable testament of God's faithfulness. From Strykers to the Pulpit is all I am saying!

By now, Jane and I had moved to a brand-new house on west side of Omaha after having sold our Franklin Street house before the "For Sale" sign was planted in the front lawn or the video officially listed on the sale's agent web site! How did this happen so quickly?

Well, one Sunday afternoon we had toured a model home out of curiosity. During our visit, the saleslady mentioned it was being put on the market the next day to clear its builder's inventory. Without a moment's hesitation, we agreed to buy said house and would seal the deal the next day. First thing Monday morning, we contacted an agent to come list our present house and she quickly did so. Upon the return to her office to complete the paperwork, she met a walk-in client who was desperate for a home. After viewing our unabridged video and seeing the details, the lady bought the house without delay. She never even walked through the house until after she had placed the offer. We quickly finalized our new house purchase and then ran around the neighborhood, explaining to our dear neighbors why there was now a "Sold" sign on the lawn.

Just what God was up to this time as He directed us to steer down this newly paved stretch of road became pretty clear when in October of the next year, Chris headed off to his Army basic training after they had sold their home. Cindy and the children moved in with us until he would be posted to their first base posting. The new house was perfectly designed for two nearly retired grandparents, one retail working Mum, and her two little people. Oh, yes, must not forget Alpine, their Mainecoon cat with his wealth of long hair and Golden Retriever personality. God knew we would need a big space to contain extra furniture, piles of children's toys, and a cat's litter box! He, who owns the cattle on a thousand hills, had supplied us with 4,000 square feet of four large bedrooms, mega closets, full basement, three car garage, and a huge backyard. It was all new so there were no things to change except our address, once again!

Those were fun-filled months of craziness surrounding two cute, active grands along with their rambunctious cat who took over the entire house with their laughter and never-ending motion.

Once the Washburns were reunited with Chris and relocated to Fort Lewis Army Base in Tacoma, Washington, I found myself sitting at my desk at the center pondering something new—Retirement! By now I had been a loyal Ford Credit employee for nearly 33 years with so many unbelievable experiences. So much had occurred within those years! It was almost mind boggling to think of where I had started with Ford— in Verona as the child of a car dealer—to where I was sitting now— the director of many people while managing huge budgets alongside developing new business in many countries.

How had all this come about?

I could never question the power of God's plan for my life. I was just one believer amongst billions living and millions already passed on to Heaven. Just a young lad from a small Canadian town skipping rocks across Rock Lake while never giving a thought as to where my life roads would take me. I wondered if that is how David from the Old Testament felt at my age as he recalled his own humble beginnings as a shepherd boy practicing his slingshot skills while tending his father's flocks.

I know there is little comparison between us as he became the King of Israel and some called me the "Prince of Verona." But still, we did both rise from simple beginnings destined for what God was designing us to become for the glory of His name.

We just needed to trust Him with each step we took, even if circumstances unfolded in unusual ways, mysterious ways, or even unbelievable ways.

Proverbs 3:5-6 (MSG) best expresses this truth,

> *"Trust God from the bottom of your heart; Don't try to figure out everything on your own. Listen for God's voice in everything you do, everywhere you go; He's the one who will keep you on track."*

With this reminder of just who was holding the road map of my life in His very strong and capable hands, I began the process of preparing for the trip down the street marked, "Retirement." Of course, there was an official termination of employment manual to be followed which made the whole process a smoothly orchestrated procedure. Official paperwork was soon winging its way to Ford Corporate with the chosen date of November 2005 as my final month at the Center. I had formulated an exit plan which would best serve the timing required for my replacement to be named and a smooth leadership transition to occur.

Everything was rolling along as planned until one small glitch arose in the scheme from an unrelated source. Remember that infected hip replacement from my Detroit years? Well, it seems that after fifteen years of non-stop functioning as my bionic partner, it too decided to retire! It would need a "retread grip" which would require a full replacement. Traveling back to Detroit for the excellent services of my original hip surgeon was not practical so I was referred to Doctor K.G. at the University Medical Center, the same facility where I was currently receiving my annual cancer checkups.

Does the Lord God care about every minuscule detail of our lives?? Does He orchestrate all good things?

Let me tell you that He surely does for this specific hip surgeon was closely associated with my original doctor and possessed the exact expertise required to replace the weakened hip with its complicated history of infection damage. It should be noted that this would be the only medical issue for me that my family would have to maneuver through in all our years in Omaha.

The timing of this second long operation came at just the right moment in my retirement schedule. Post-surgery recovery would bring me right up to November and then I could officially bid my career with Ford a fond farewell. Ahead would be a new avenue to travel with a refurbished tire on the aging car I figuratively found myself encased. Maybe I should use the term "maturing" vehicle as I anticipated many years of good living with all body parts mechanically functioning well at this stage of my life.

As the official days approached for both the surgery and my job leave-taking, it all seemed a bit unreal. Going again under the physical knife of an orthopedic doctor and his surgery team was not my idea of an enjoyable side trip, but the prospect of being free from leadership responsibilities with its quirky turns and twists, did cause me to secretly smile! I was ready to move into the next stretch of roads and propel myself into a world I had only been able to observe from afar.

Before I could actually invade my wife's kitchen and assist in process improving her daily life or activities (humorous assumption on my part), I was the guest of honor at a retirement dinner attended by many upper management people whom I had worked under and with over the years. It was a great celebration and made even more memorable when a certain fellow, whom I have previously mentioned, stood to publicly apologize to me for his comments regarding my choice to abstain from alcohol consumption all those years ago in Barrie, Ontario. He further commented that he admired my depth of character and high standards of integrity. He appreciated that I had not buckled under pressure to alter my personal beliefs in order to fit into the culture surrounding me.

This leaves me with the commitment to encourage those in my family who will undoubtedly be faced with the "to drink or not to drink" alcoholic beverage question to stand firm in what you know is right and what will reflect a life under the influence of only one thing—the steady intoxication of Christ's presence and Holy Spirit's guidance. I have often expressed my belief that all problems related to alcohol consumption start with the first drink!! Just as nothing good happens after midnight, neither does anything good come from drinking alcohol.

Now if I wanted to appear really spiritual here, I would quote Psalm 32:8 (MSG) which reads,

> "Let me give you some good advice; I'm looking you in the
> eye and giving it to you straight."

There! That is my honest opinion, and I am sticking with it. An opinion formed from observing many of the negative effects drinking has caused in the lives of family, friends, and acquaintances.

With the retirement party behind me as well as the six weeks of homebound rehab drawing to a close, I supervised my wife's efforts to once again sort a household, pack and label a garage full of boxes, arrange for a moving company, and say goodbye to our Midwest life. Hoping for a quick sale, we wasted no time in placing the house on the real estate market. Winter was upon us so that meant winterizing the entire household water system to prevent frozen pipes. It had been a wonderful home and God had richly blessed us with amazing friends and neighbors whose friendships we would carry with us forever.

The new home being constructed in Florida was on schedule for completion in December, so my ever-loyal folks had invited us to stay with them in their Clearwater Snowbird home. We were very blessed with their willingness to share their special place with us, albeit for a short time. They included us in their activities of regular dinner parties, drop-in visits from neighbors, senior events at their church, and evening card games with whomever was available.

I should clear up any confusion here regarding who exactly played cards as it is well-known in my family that I am a card-carrying member of the "I don't play cards" club. Only upon the soulful pleading from a grandchild do I break rank and participate. All that game playing I leave to the enthusiasm of my dear wife!

All in all, it was great time to once again listen to my parents reminiscing through stories of days gone by. Often times the younger generations make fun of older folks recalling their life experiences and yet, there is much to be learned in remembering the past. After my beloved Dad and Mum left us to enter into their Heavenly home, I fully realized how important their life stories were in reminding me of how God leads, directs, challenges, disciplines, rewards, and basically all-around loves each of His children. Poor is the generation who makes light of the details of the past, even if they are told and retold!

At this point, the actual physical move was unfolding as planned and even had an extra surprise thrown in. Upon hearing of my departure from Ford Credit, one of our largest off shore vendors, Sykes Enterprises, approached me with the prospect of my working for them! Would I be interested in assuming the role of Director of Client Services for their

North American Client Account Operations through its Central America call centers?

A very interesting offer!

I should clarify here that these were the very same call centers which had serviced my Ford Credit business several years before! If I agreed, Ford Credit would now be one of my client responsibilities as I would be their connection to call center operations in Costa Rica and El Salvador. It would be like working for a different race car owner.

After discussions with Jane, I agreed to begin working for them the first week of December 2005. Seems my retirement had lasted less than two weeks! Once again, I shake my head in wonderment at the mysterious ways God works. We can never outguess what He has planned for us.

After getting an all clear from my hip surgeon at the six-week checkup, we accelerated our out-of-state move into high gear. Once again, our household belongings found their way across state lines via a large moving van which also contained a specially constructed wooden box designed to securely transport my 2003 Anniversary Edition Harley on its longest journey yet. It was important that it arrive unscathed. I did have my priority in the right order even though the wife might have disagreed. I jest here!

"GOD WILL NOT LOOK YOU
OVER FOR MEDALS, DEGREES OR
DIPLOMAS BUT FOR SCARS."

—ALBERT HUBBARD

2012 HARLEY DAVIDSON ULTRA SCREAMIN' EAGLE 110

SUN CITY CENTER, FLORIDA

Florida was a welcomed destination as winter weather quickly swept across the vastness of Nebraska. Unfortunately, Jane had to spend her birthday that year supervising our big move as the wind chills hit the teens and snow swirled around. It was my misfortune to be on my first Sykes employee official visit to the Central America call center amid the heat of the tropics. Well, maybe it wasn't such a misfortune after all. I did reward her for such a personal sacrifice by taking her with me on several future business trips back to San Jose, Costa Rica.

Sykes Enterprises in Tampa, Florida became my new work site when I needed to connect with the physical office staff, but it was a pleasure to now be part of that new business concept of working from home. Of course, I was required to travel to visit our centers which accounted for the thirty-three trips to Costa Rica I made over the next three years. Just as we had in ever previous corporate job setting, we enjoyed the adventures of working in different geographical locations surrounded by interesting people and distinctively different cultures.

An interesting part of my many travels in Costa Rica was the occasion of participating in a team building activity with some staff personal at the center. It was to be a full day of fun events centered on a relatively new business practice of interacting outside of the office setting with the purpose of strengthening relationships around the team concept. Our day started with a bus ride into the lush, tropical mountains for a zip lining adventure through massive trees! Scenery was beautiful and the excited screams of the participants as they zipped from high point to high point repeatedly filled the rainforest jungle. Great fun!

After lunch, we were driven to a local river site where our teams donned helmets, zipped up life jackets, and received instructions for the next event—White Water Rafting. Seemed like a relatively safe process to climb into a large raft accompanied by a skilled oarsman and journey down the river before us. Well, said river only appeared to be lazily moving in front of us until we hit the first rapids.

Then it became very clear to all that THIS could well be our last days on earth! This was NOT a calm river lazily traveling to the ocean. This was a full-blown white-water rapids nightmare of a high ranking in the degree of rapids! We were swept into raging currents and frothing water over and over. At one point, one our team was violently swept overboard and completely disappeared from our sight. Only now did we understand those somewhat vague cautions at the beginning of our trip. Hang on, stay in the boat, and IF you are ejected out, just relax, and let the current carry you to shore or calmer waters. Sure! Sounds like a plan!

Team building happened very quickly as we all breathed a collective sigh of relief when our team member finally appeared ahead of us, bedraggled and exhausted but safe. What an experience for sure. Maybe we should have planned on a round of Putt-Putt golf or ping pong match!

On a side note here, this trip would carry with it one additional memory for me, not just because of the near drowning part, but due to the five days I spent in hospital after returning home. Seems I had potentially been bitten by a malaria infested mosquito while cavorting around the jungle trees and rivers on team building! It was never fully diagnosed but did cause some worries for my wife who learned just what I had been involved with on this last business trip. Gee, I think I just forgot to tell her what was planned!

Stupid me, why did I never learn to stop keeping things from her? She was extremely upset with me, and I guess I could not blame her. Caregivers never give up their sense of responsibility for the well-being of their loved ones, I guess. Even in foreign countries!

But true to her love of traveling and not wanting to miss out on a new adventure, Jane later accompanied me on several Costa Rica trips (Or maybe because she wanted to keep an eye on me). She, too, was impressed with the people, their desire to preserve the natural settings around them, and especially their famous coffees.

I worked and she played! Seemed like a perfect arrangement in her eyes. We were even able to entice some of our Omaha friends to join us at a Pacific coast resort for a week of vacationing fun. I will save the details of that trip for book two!

When I was not traveling with business, I could be found puttering around my garage making sure not one thing in my Man Cave was out of place or dusty. In a stroke of genius, I had installed a pretty cool overhead rollup screen door so that the irritating mosquitos and the nasty love bugs did not impede my industrious commitment to polishing my bike or car.

It did take some adjustments to the Florida humidity and heat, but a large garage fan assisted in the process. I had music for my listening pleasure, a small refrigerator filled with sports drinks, lots of yellow cleaning towels, a steady Amazon delivery of detailing materials, and walls lined with posters of favorite bikes, signs, and cars.

THE ELEVENTH COMMANDMENT "THOU SHALT NOT DRIVE A DIRTY VEHICLE"

Some may have thought that my blood ran motor oil thick, but I think it was just in my DNA to love order, clean cars, and motion. I always believed that the Eleventh Commandment—"Thou shalt not drive a dirty vehicle"—had been deliberately deleted from the original tablets by Moses who did not operate even a chariot!

When I was not tinkering around in my immaculate garage, I was joining my wife as we became members of the Faith Rider Motorcycle Ministry at Bell Shoals Baptist Church in Brandon, Florida. This was a large Southern Baptist Church with a long history of Christian presence in our area. We were thrilled to join this merry band of bikers who had been formed with the dual purpose of fellowship and outreach to anyone associated with the popular motorcycle lifestyle with its often "colorful" participating membership.

As the old biker fellow in Omaha had correctly labeled us as Rich Urban Bikers or RUBs, we certainly had some very vivid misconceptions of motorcyclists in general which were quickly corrected when we began to worship and serve with these seriously dedicated believers with their varied hair styles, degrees of beards, unusual church attire, and trend setting tattoos. We had our own meeting room and designated parking spots so that all the bikes were parked together whenever we gathered to worship.

It was quite an adjustment for us as our church attire soon consisted of blue or black jeans, leather vests with our ministry logo boldly displayed, leather boots, and biker helmets. Gone were the usual Sunday best suits, fancy dresses or pants, street shoes, and Easter bonnets! We adapted well to this new Sunday-go-to-meeting garb, but my parents had a bit of a difficult time accepting that this was proper church clothing!

Once they realized the serious commitment and genuine faith of our group, they positively adjusted their concerns for our spiritual health. We were not cult members! Just loud and excited about bringing the love of Jesus to people drawn to the noise and power of motorcycles. Many of these bikers needed to see Christians in a new and positive light after experiencing some type of negativity from judgmental religious people.

Our involvement in Faith Riders was very rewarding as we assisted with planning and serving at monthly bike night events, various motor cycle rallies, church functions, and even funerals. Our membership was rich with hearts willing to support whatever and wherever we could to further the joy of the Gospel. We engaged the public at many exciting events such as Dayton Bike Week, local Harley Davidson dealership bike nights, our sponsoring church events like Trunk or Treat, Juvenile Diabetes fund raisers, and our annual mini rally event at the James Haley VA Hospital in Tampa, Florida.

This last-mentioned service opportunity was our very own premier event which was birthed in Jane and I after an exposure to the traumas caused by battle injuries to military service members. As only He can do, God miraculously brought a family we loved through a very difficult time when their soldier was injured in Iraq and the wife was able to stay at the Fischer House in Germany as she assisted in her husband's care until he could come home. This "house" is a free facility which offers comfort and residence to caregivers assisting their injured soldier at military hospitals around the world.

In coordination with the leadership at the hospital and the House staff, we determined that this could be a great opportunity for Faith Riders to use the draw of motorcycles by hosting a parking lot event at the James Haley Hospital to support, through good free food and fellowship as well as donated gifts, these wounded soldiers and their families. It opened the door for us to connect with those receiving treatments as well as their dedicated doctors and nurses. We were even allowed to carry meals into the hospital and deliver them to non-ambulatory soldiers who could not leave their rooms. Many lives were touched, and hearts encouraged by our volunteers.

In blessing these wounded warriors and their caregivers, everyone in our ministry had a deeper appreciation for what their service to our country had cost them. The whole day was christened, "Thank A Hero," and certainly lived up to its title.

It is also worth mentioning that the generosity of our members did not stop with this event as many of our group joined thousands of other bikers in Washington D.C. at a massive Memorial Day weekend motorcycle rally called "Rolling Thunder" which was organized in 1988 to support servicemen who were left behind as prisoners of war in Vietnam. At that time, 2,000 riders from all over the world formed up in the Pentagon parking lot to circle the National Mall in a respectful tribute to the 58,318 names of the brave soldiers listed on the Vietnam Wall. Since then, it has become one of the largest displays of American patriotism where, in 2018, nearly 500,000 riders joined forces to honor all American military members who had lost their lives defending our freedoms.

For us, it was a once in a lifetime privilege to ride from Florida to D.C. with more than 200 other East Coast bikers. In several large cities, our long caravan of rumbling, fast moving bikes was escorted by local and state police to allow the entire group to remain together through heavy traffic. It was a thrill to hear the sounds of vehicle horns blasting and see folks waving as we zoomed through on our north bound mission.

As an added bonus at the end of the whole event, Jane and I transported our bike and ourselves back to Florida on the Auto train out of Virginia to Orlando. That was a pretty cool trip in itself as we had a tiny but adequate private roomette boasting dimensions of about four feet by seven feet! Tight fit but functional. Restroom and showers were shared down the hall which brought back camp and college memories, but the wonderful dinner served on china and linen in the dining car made up for that. The process of loading vehicles and motorcycles into their respective train cars was fascinating as the crew was well aware of the value of each vehicle to its owner and had a very well-organized process. For sure, we have great memories of the entire weekend.

I just can't leave this trip without recalling a humorous happening on our first night in D.C. A small group of us did an impromptu walk-about downtown near the massive white government buildings. Upon reaching the steps of the Supreme Court, three people from our group challenged each other to a foot race up the steep steps leading to the massively impressive front doors! Well, about the time they reach the top, a security guard informed the rest of us that he could shoot the three as they had now committed a federal offense! Obviously, he did not as our three impulsive climbers quickly returned to join us. Oh, I should mention that one of the three was my wife! That should not surprise anyone who remembers the Easter bunny story from Omaha.

Undoubtedly through the Faith Rider Ministry during the years Jane and I lived in the Sunshine State, we were repeatedly blessed by the generosity and servanthood of our fellow bikers.

Deep and lasting friendships were packed into our "memory" trunks to be recalled later when our personal journey roads led us in different directions.

As in all stages of life, our life clocks just kept ticking away, so before I had time to even pause, the year 2008 was on my desk calendar. My business responsibilities soon required me to expand my travels to Manilla in the Philippines nearly 9,115 miles as the crow flies from Tampa. That must have been one tired crow as I sure knew how tired I was at the end of my first 19-hour flight there.

It was a memorable flight not just for the time in the air but also because a very elderly person actually died before our plane landed. Strange occurrence for sure!

I was happy to disembark but already dreaded the long trip back home. In spite of this, Manilla did prove to be very interesting. After my one-week exposure to life on this side of the world, I gained a greater appreciation for my home base.

As I had prayed for, the return flight was uneventful but no shorter unfortunately. Strange how that works!

When I had recovered somewhat from the jet lag caused by so many times changes, I seriously questioned the reality of having to make those trips every month as this was the new directive from my employer. A decision needed to be made, so one morning I caught my wife on her way out the door for her haircut and color appointment and we briefly discussed the situation. Now, one should understand that one does not stand between my wife and her hair appointments unless it is a medical emergency or national crisis! She politely heard my thoughts then quickly prayed for God's wisdom before rushing out the door leaving me to ponder the whole second retirement decision.

How surprised she was to receive my phone call twenty minutes later informing her that I had officially resigned and would once again be back in her kitchen fully ready to help her organize her life. Her response was epic, "Oh my stars! God answered our prayers that fast?"

He surely had and I was officially allowed to exit the corporate expressway I had traveled on for thirty-six years! It was a great feeling!

From this moment on, I was free to unload from the trunk of my life vehicle all the suitcases which contained business suits, pressed dress shirts, fancy ties and shoes. My leather brief case was tucked away in the office having been emptied of all papers or files connected to work accounts. My office was reorganized to now showcase family pictures and memorabilia from years of service to the two amazing companies for which I had been privileged to work. The various wall art within view of my desk was like a big shadow box telling a wordless story of where I had been and what I had been allowed by my Lord to experience over the years He had granted me to live. They were all reminders of His faithfulness in directing me along every path I was destined to travel.

Now new paths were ahead of me, new milestones to mark along the as yet uncharted road. What was I to do with all the empty time slots on my personal calendar? While I was as excited to be officially retired, I wondered just what I was going to do each day after my regular morning coffee and bowl of oatmeal faithfully prepared by my wife. Just what did a retired executive do to fill the hours of the day? How many times can one sweep the garage, clean the cars, vacuum the house, run the dust cloth over the furniture, check the stock market, and take the wife to the grocery store? My honey-do lists were swiftly completed with precision accuracy by my standards. Now what?

Well, I did not to have to wait long for an answer to my question as God had orchestrated my retirement to come at just the right moment for Him to use me in a very special way. His timing is always perfect, and it was soon evident that He had been planning for me to be jobless (in a good way) with loads of free time on my hands.

Once again, I was reminded that He does work in mysterious ways and uses willing hearts to fulfill His commitment to display His love for people.

Proverbs 20:24 (TPT) best explains this truth.

> *"It is the Lord who directs your life, for each step you take is ordained by God to bring your closer to your destiny. So much of your life, then, remains a mystery!"*

He was about to send me and my wife on some pretty incredibly challenging adventures which would have us trusting Him over and over as we accelerated around some crazy curves, zoomed up steep mountainsides, or crept along narrow lanes. I speak figuratively here, but what was ahead for us over the next three years did require some degrees of physical maneuvering as well as drawing from past personal experiences to accomplish God ordained missions.

Before one thinks we went undercover as spies, let me reassure you our tasks were all on the up and up, even if they were a little clandestine in nature.

What had been presented to us through a phone call from our beloved Dr. Karanes was the opportunity to become volunteer couriers for the National Marrow Donor Program operating all over the world offering hope for other human beings in need of bone marrow or stem cells to save their lives from the ravages of cancer. If we were willing to be trained and use our personal time to transport the necessary blood products from donor sites to transplant locations where patients were desperately waiting for a second chance to defeat this horrid disease, the NMDP staff was ready to accept us as vital members of their team. My ten-year tenure as a volunteer member of their finance board had officially ended so they knew we were now available.

We were stunned at this offer with its perfect timing!

How could we refuse such as tremendous opportunity to be entrusted to successfully carry precious, life-giving cells to suffering people who were undoubtedly praying for a second chance at life? Our family had stumbled along this same horrendously dark stretch of road of uncertainty way back in Detroit and could readily grasp the desperation for anything to give us hope of a longer life for the person we loved. It would be one of the greatest privileges offered to us and we did not for a moment hesitate in saying yes.

What followed was making formal applications, being vetted for any negative behavior in our past, signing the agreement papers, and then being trained at an all-day in-service on the detailed mechanics of volunteer transporting of human blood products, bone marrow and stem cells, to wherever the donor and recipient matches occurred. The actual carrying process was controlled by concise paperwork with many layers of details which needed to be closely adhered to at each step of our transport.

When a match was identified from the volunteer donor list managed at NMDP headquarters in Minnesota, couriers were contacted and could select which "trip" best suited their availability. Once the details of calendar time at donor site for pick-up and delivery location had been determined, the real leg work kicked into full gear.

We would be required to pack extremely light for our quick trips with the precious, time-sensitive cargo packed in a chilled cooler but safely stored in its original collection infusion bags. There were concise steps to be followed for security reasons so the cooler itself was carried in a larger canvas bag labelled very carefully for identification at airports or hospitals. We were required to check and double check all medical documents which accompanied the products to guarantee all data was correctly tagged for processing at the transfusion site which was a hospital or medical center in the city of final delivery.

The blue bag was never to leave our sight. It was never to be left unattended. Its contents were never to be revealed except to American TSA officials at local airports and foreign Customs officials for overseas deliveries. We never knew the donor or recipient. Each trip had a time cap of two to three days depending on location of donor pick up and final destination drop off.

The organizational responsibilities for each delivery trip were demanding with the reliance on potentially unreliable air travel, missed train connections, and delayed security checks as well as taxi availability in bustling cities. It was fast paced from beginning to end and required the volunteer to be calm, organized, and able to handle local as well as foreign travel situations. The whole process was not for the faint of heart or anyone not able to make quick adjustments in personal comfort or changing circumstances.

The priceless cargo each volunteer courier carried represented possibly the final chance for the recipient to spend additional years with family and friends. Just as I had been gifted additional days through the wonders of stem cell transplantation, these cancer fighters too deserved to have this fresh hope available to them.

With this all explained, I can proudly share that over the next three years between the two of us, Jane and I made forty-three volunteer courier trips in the USA and Europe. We did not travel together. We did not miss one plane connection. We did not have any mishaps. We did not miss any appointments or deadlines. We did not experience any physical hinderances.

Our Heavenly Father's hand was all over these successful missions.

Our journeys took us on multiple careening city taxis, long airplane rides, fast moving trains, and miles of leg work. The entire process could be compared to entering the "Express Lane" on a busy freeway at an accelerated speed for a short period of time.

Fortunately, on several occasions when we had parallel trips to Europe, we were able to meet up post-delivery in London to spend some time together exploring that fascinating city. I should clarify that the only cost to us as volunteer couriers for the trips was our time and any personal purchases we might make or additional hotel costs when we stayed over our two-day recovery limit.

It is very easy to firmly state that this once-in-a-life time chance to serve complete strangers was gifted to us by our all-knowing God Himself and we were thrilled to be part of a greater picture of hope.

At the end of each successful delivery, we breathed a prayer for God's mercy to rest on the struggling recipient, his or her attentive family, and the dedicated medical teams. Even though we would never personally know the outcomes of all our deliveries, we did rest assured that there were (and are) cancer survivors out in the greater world enjoying extended years with their loved ones because of our willingness to step outside our comfort zones.

As I recalled these unique opportunities for using my extra gifted years in some greater way, I had to consider that one question which rolled over and over in my mind. Just why was my life spared so many times on this odyssey I had been on since February 11, 1950? It was a great mystery, but I just kept trucking along with the assurance He was using for His purposes wherever I was along whatever path He allowed me to walk. He was (and still is working) His good, acceptable, and perfect will.

Proverbs 19:21 (TPT) reminds me of this:

"A person may have many ideas concerning God's plan for his life, but only the designs of God's purpose will succeed in the end."

Now, when I was not jetting around on courier trips or planning the details of our next cruise on the high seas (we had embraced big ship cruising as a new leisure sport), my spare time was spent acquiring the latest version of Harley Davidson's customized vehicle in my garage. At one point, there were actually two bikes side by side occupying their special spots. The wife frowned at such extravagance, but quickly withdrew any objection when she remembered the cost of her monthly haircut and color. Out of self-preservation, I would never have mentioned that!

Changing gears here, I should mention that my health remained under the scrutiny of oncologists at Moffitt Cancer Center in Tampa where I received in-depth yearly checkups. Each visit with its testing and lab results was a nervous time for me as it is for every cancer survivor regardless of how many years since remission. Some people use the term "cancer free" when describing their condition, but it has never been my practice to use such a bold term. This is not to be interpreted that I don't believe my Creator can give me a cancer free body because I know He can.

For me personally with my past history of reoccurrences of active cancer cells, I prefer to identify myself as having NED—no evidence of disease. So it was that for the duration of our time living in Florida, I could celebrate that I was NED. In combination with my NED years in

Nebraska, I had now reached a milestone of nearly 25 years since my stem cell transplant.

Each of those cancer free Octobers has been a time of celebration and reflection on God's great faithfulness to me and my entire family.

I also was blessed to have the expertise of a well-respected orthopedic surgeon in Florida who would monitor the health of my newly replaced hip. It should have come as no surprise to us when our first visit to Doctor H. confirmed that once again God had led us to just the right physician for my care as said fellow had trained under my original hip surgeon in Detroit and alongside the Omaha doctor. It was a small group of experts, and I was privileged to be their patient! Can you see the thread of divine planning throughout my entire life? I sure can and rejoice in it over and over!

Actually, my only health issues of some concern came in the form of a diagnosis of CAD, coronary artery disease, which required a heart vein stent and adjustment to my medications as well as my diet. My cardiologist told me to eat grass, his term for a better diet of less fats and more greens. I gave said diet a try but determined there was more to life than salt free or fat free eating. Moderation was the key, and an occasional Canadian butter tart was surely a mental health booster no one would deny me.

Speaking of mental health booster, I will say the best two helps I received during this time were the arrivals of our two youngest grandchildren. In 2006, we welcomed our own Texas rose, Skylar Jade Revell, into the family circle at Matt and Wendy's house and then celebrated the arrival of 2009 Florida born, William John Washburn, as the third addition to Cindy and Chris's clan. We were (and are) so blessed by these two grand kids. They have brought us such joy and love.

Our grandchild count was at six over a wide stretch of ages, so we anticipated enjoying all the varied experiences and emotions of children from infant to teens. It was exciting times for us and challenging times for their parents. As I have previously mentioned, there was a freedom to alter those parenting practices which governed raising one's own children. Suddenly there were no bedtime schedules, no rules for eating all one's food on one's plate, no shoes off at the front door, no assigned household jobs, and no denied reasonable requests. Even the infamous wooden spoon collected dust sitting in a closet. Matt and Cindy would have a comment about this, I am sure!

As well as enjoying my grandkids and the new road speeding away from corporate work settings, I concentrated on expanding and refining my mini fleet of personally owned vehicles. To save wordiness here, I will just give a brief bullet point summary of just what came and went from my garage over the course of several years. Each one was a treat to own and operate. To the shock of friends and family, I even broke away from the Ford line of cars to experience the competition's products.

- New Harley Davidson Customized Touring Motorcycles in 2006, 2007, 2010

- 50th Anniversary Edition Used 2003 Burgundy Corvette Convertible in 2009

- 2007 Used Army Green Jeep in 2010

- New Black Two-Door Willeys Jeep in 2011

- New 2012 Black Grand Sport Corvette in 2012

To some people reading this list, these may seem to represent a lavish lifestyle, but I had been careful with our investments and thus was able to budget our expenses to accommodate the "extras" we enjoyed.

Stewardship of what God had blessed us with was of greatest importance and we never "robbed from Peter to pay Paul."

Our bottom-line loyalty always was toward the Ford line of automobiles, so with my retirement benefits, we could order two new cars each year. A comfort one for the wife and a sporty model for me which resulted in many high-powered Mustangs edging out the Jeeps in the garage. Those ponies left the others in a massive dust cloud!

When looking back at the milestone memories in our years of living in Florida, I will always remember with great fondness a most wonderful motorcycle trip I was privileged to participate in. One of our best friends, Gary Langley from Nova Scotia, Canada asked me to join him and six other others in a two-week trip. We would be biking from Salt Lake to Yellowstone National Park then on to Sturgis, South Dakota for Bike Week followed by rides through Colorado's Rocky Mountain National Park before returning to Utah. I was thrilled at the offer and made plans to professionally ship my 2010 Screaming Eagle bike out to Salt Lake City where I would meet up with the others.

What an adventure this proved to be! Hundreds of road miles embraced by thousands of magnificent views of unimaginably beautiful mountains, lakes, and small towns unfolded in front of us as we accumulated over 2,800 traveling miles on our tripmeters.

Each day afforded us lots of excitement and challenges as we maneuvered through every type of road condition, mountain height, valley depth, and weather situation imaginable to a traveler. By God's grace, we had no mishaps or close calls while riding on these high powered, two wheeled cycles. At one point, we had close encounters with buffalo who wandered near to us as we parked along the roads of Yellowstone.

There is even a shocking, out of character photo taken on a rugged South Dakota terrain of us middle-aged guys posing with our shirts off trying to be tough looking biker lads roaming around the Badlands. Not a pretty sight but too funny!

Upon my return home from this trip of a lifetime, I discovered that my wife had been a busy gal in my absence. She had been approached by a local real estate lady looking for new listings in our community of only senior citizens. Would we ever consider selling our present home? Jane explained this was not on our agenda at the time but thanked her for stopping by. Minutes later the same lady returned to leave her business card just in case. Well, now the wheels of my wife's mind started turning. Maybe we were ready to sell and this was just the nudge we needed to think seriously about moving closer to our church and back into a community of mixed age family type housing.

Much discussion followed over the next few weeks as we needed to make a decision.

At about the same time, we were contacted by a local newspaper editor who was interested in the details of our NMDP courier volunteering experiences and wanted to write a human-interest story. What resulted was a very nicely written article titled, "A Survivor Pays It Forward, One Flight At A Time," in the December, 2011 issue of the Sun City Center Observer. It was a great opportunity for us to draw attention to the importance of being a bone marrow or stem cell donor as well as highlighting the importance of serving others.

It wasn't long before we sold that home and moved to our second Florida residence—another new place built for us by a Texas based builder. We thought of it as our "forever" home as it was tucked away in the city of Brandon, just east of Tampa and was a great base for church activities, our courier trips, and any other adventures we might plan.

An added bonus was the relocation of Cindy's family to our sunny climate for Chris to complete his bachelor's degree, Masters of Divinity, and two year Pastoral service requirement in anticipation of a call back into the Army as a chaplain. He also served as a Reserve Chaplain for a local Army Medical unit.

Well, just as He has proven over the years, God was still orchestrating so many details in my family's life which would be pretty amazing. Our new location placed us next door to a retired Army colonel who had served on the front lines in the Vietnam War, so his stories were remarkable and fascinating. He had memories of somewhat bad experiences with various military chaplains during his service years, so when we introduced him to our son-in-law who was now serving as one of the pastors at our church, he was somewhat skeptical.

However, God used Chris's humble and steady walk with Christ to display a genuine and unselfish testimony of a spirit-filled life to this watchful man. The Colonel mentioned many times how impressed he was as he observed our family interact with each other as well as this young chaplain's walk with his Savior. This whole relationship would never have been possible if we had not moved from our comfort place to our new home. Another example of an encounter designed by God to further His love.

Not only were we seeing God's hand in the connections we made in our new neighborhood, but we were able to continue our NMDP courier trips as well as visiting family in Michigan and Canada.

Life was smoothly rolling along a pretty straight stretch of highway with few curves or directional changes. We enthusiastically enjoyed many overnight visitors as well as drop-ins from grandkids, friends, and those Canadian Snowbirds eager to escape the cold, raw winter days.

It was with not a small degree of sadness that my beloved parents were not able to enjoy our newest home setting as their failing health did not permit them to travel very far from Verona. They were so disappointed when their Florida home, full of wonderful memories, had to be sold thus ending a part of their lives which had given them much pleasure over many years.

We were even privileged to have yet another newspaper, The Kingston Whig Standard in Kingston, Ontario, Canada, contact us for a possible story of our NMDP courier trips and my cancer survival. As it was, we were in Verona visiting family, so the interview was handled in person at the newspaper office. We thought probably it would be a short section tied back to that first small article they had printed way back in 1991. Imagine our surprise, when upon opening the newspaper a few days later, February 16, 2012, we discovered that the headline story on the front page was a long article entitled, "Sold on Stem Cells," below a color photo of Jane and me! My parents were overjoyed and so proud! All their earnest prayers and support of me had come full circle! They fielded many calls from well-wishers as it seemed all of Verona enjoyed reading a true miracle story about one their own young lads.

Unfortunately, but as time does to each of us, their health slowly deteriorated to the point that Dad entered a palliative care facility where, remarkably, he stayed for nearly fifty days under the gentle care of medical staff and family. Jane and I were able to spend every morning with him after we had made the daily Tim Horton coffee stop for his favorite donut and double cream coffee. Through God's grace in keeping him alert and verbal, he became a real testimony of a spirit-filled Christ follower who prayed out loud for his children and grandchildren by name every night. He even asked the nursing staff if he could pray for their personal needs.

What is even more remarkable is that he had always suffered with deeply felt fears all his life until he was reassured by Holy Spirit that God would always love him unconditionally. This blessed gift of freedom came when he was 90 years old and had been reading the Bible every day to Mum whose eyesight was poor. He requested to be baptized and it was a glorious occasion when this occurred.

Throughout my life, my dad had always been quietly reserved and burdened under a dread that he was not good enough for entrance into Heaven, even though he was a strong believer. What a joy it was now to share his last days with us knowing that he was at peace within his soul. God had blessed him with salvation reassurance so when he left us on August 1st, 2014, in his 94th year, we mourned for our loss, but rejoiced that he was with his Lord.

His spiritual legacy to me is his unwavering trust in God's faithfulness right up to the moment he drew his last breath. The treasury of my faith is overflowing with the riches of having had a father who disciplined me, cared for me, laughed with me, taught me, and prayed for me.

I have been richly blessed by an earthly father who never wavered in his support of me. That is what I pray my descendants will be able to say of me. He prayed for us and walked in faith, even if life handed him some difficult roads to travel upon.

Even though the folks could never return to visit us in Florida, we did not lack in company. We enjoyed each guest who entered through our front door. However, there was one group of visitors we did NOT enjoy nor welcome to our property. Florida is well known to be the residence of choice for some very rude and destructive creatures who discovered that our new lush back- yard was an ideal place to forage for a delicious meal of grubs and worms. At their leisure over the course of an evening, these "guests" could destroy an entire yard in their quest to find food! I speak here of the famous hard-shelled Armadillo, a creature who is ugly and a carrier of leprosy virus to unsuspecting persons.

In a gallant effort to preserve our lawn and flower roots, we waged an all-out offensive against these destructive critters. Short of using a shot gun to completely obliviate them (and get ourselves arrested!), we used every imaginable trick known to man. Nothing worked including commercially purchased fox urine or heaps of hot chili powder spread around the yard. In desperation, we had an expensive wrought iron fence installed as well as bright motion detecting flood lights, but even these did not deter the enemy from rooting around inside the fence! What was the solution?

Well, one night when we were awakened by a rather large critter dining on the delicacies of grubs even as the bright light illuminated his banquet table, I arose from my bed, and armed with a baseball bat, crept out of the house to challenge said beast in one final battle. It was him or me! One can just imagine the scene as I stealthily advanced across the yard while attired only in my boxer shorts. With one loud cry and a powerful swing of the bat, I descended upon the mulching destroyer.

Through bulging eyes, he took one look at me and proceeded to swiftly squeeze his big armor-plated body through the narrow fence rails and clatter away into the wooded field. I triumphantly returned to the house to be greeted by my wife who was in a hysterical laughing fit over the picture of my valiant effort and battle attire. We had a good chuckle over this, but the very next day decided to install a chicken wire fence outside the lower edge of the iron barricade to further stop another invasion of unwanted pests. It finally worked, but had cost me a new fence, new lawn, and some embarrassment! Well worth the effort!

With this mini crisis behind us, we settled in to appreciate life as I was in good health, fully retired, happy to be serving wherever God sent me, and enjoying our offspring and their children. We anticipated many, many years of sun-filled Florida living.

This was all about to change and in quite an extraordinary way we could never have imagined. Leave it to Father God to have even more unusual turns and twists planned for my life journey! Who could have predicted the next two years happenings?

In July 2015, just as I was settling comfortably into the driver seat of my "life" car cruising along at a relaxed speed, it started to gradually accelerate and for good reasons which unfolded pretty quickly.

Our entire family rejoiced when Chris received the official call from the Army to return to active duty in the position he had been working toward, Army Chaplain. Their new duty station would be, of all places, Fort Lewis in Washington State which was the exact post they had moved from 6 years before! What an affirmation of His perfect plans for each of His loved ones?

With this news, the organizational gears of everyone involved shifted into high gear as there was much to be accomplished. After the movers departed from the Washburn Florida house to carry a van full of their household treasures to their new home, we caravanned with Cindy and the children on our way to a new adventure for them.

Of course, a stop off in Texas to spend a couple of nights with Matt and Wendy's family, was scheduled into the travel plans. This brief journey stopover would prove to be part of an even bigger divine plan when, on our first evening together, Matt mentioned to me that we should move to Texas. At about the same time, his mother-in-law said the same thing to Jane as they relaxed on the patio.

What followed was probably one the most amazing unfolding of a "God" plan in our lives. The very next day, as if led by some unseen force, my wife and I located a new community being developed nine miles from Matt and Wendy's home. One of the builders was the same company who had just built our second home in Florida. By the end of that day, we had chosen a house plan, picked the lot, paid the deposit, and signed all the official papers. With the stroke of a pen, we were committed to moving to Texas! It was all done without a moment's hesitation and that evening, we announced it to all the family gathered who were dumbfounded and yet ecstatic!

Our heads were spinning with the relocation details, but we continued our trip out to Joint Base Lewis McChord to help Washburns get settled and covered all the return miles back to Texas with Jane's pen filling notebook pages with moving details for what needed to be accomplished soon.

Once we had stopped off again at Matt and Wendy's to finalize the new house details, we scurried home to Florida with the need to list and sell that home. It was vital that our real estate person get us a good price with a quick sale as we did not want to be moving during the winter months looming ahead.

Well, it is astonishing how that part of the plan unfolded!

The agent we choose was a lady who lived in our neighborhood whom we had never met before her first meeting at the house to do the walk through and set up the listing contract. As we had learned through our married life to be the best practice, we had prayed that God would lead us to the one agent He had ordained to be the best for us. Well, let me tell you that He did answer our prayer in an unbelievable way!

After walking through the house, this lady said, "I am not going to list your house because I am going to buy your house. This is exactly what my husband and I have been looking for!"

Astonishingly, in less than three hours, we had unofficially listed the house then officially sold it! Even more of a blessing, her company waved the usual high real estate fees. When her husband came just a few hours later to give his approval, he wanted to buy almost half our furniture.

Believe me when I say that whatever plans man thinks he can put on paper for the future don't have a chance of surviving when God the Father puts His divine purposes into action. We tore up all our previously written plans and just stood in awe of how our lives were rolling along as we sat in the passenger seats with Him driving straight and fast!

It was fun and exciting to see Him at work!

"YOUR GREATEST MESSAGE WILL BE SPOKEN BY YOUR LIFE NOT YOUR LIPS."

—STEVEN FURICK

ARGYLE, TEXAS

Once again six weeks later, I was headed down the roads marked "West" toward a whole new adventure in the Lone Star State of Texas with my sidekick settled into the passenger seat and my latest black Jeep securely strapped onto a flatbed trailer behind the Explorer. Could this be a taste of what the adventurous pioneers must have felt when they hitched their wagons to horses in anticipation of life in a new place? Thanks to man's ingenuity, my horsepower was a little stronger than theirs and the miles ahead not as treacherous, but our excitement equaled theirs, I am sure.

While I have compared our trip west to those old road weary travelers, there is one area in which there is no comparison. Their relocations took months, even years to accomplish whereas ours took us just under seventeen hours. My goal was to reach Matt's home as quickly as possible with only the necessary gas, food, and restroom breaks scheduled into the timetable. Having traveled with me over hundreds of thousands of miles in the 45 years of our marriage, my understanding wife knew this was the usual plan as it did fit my young lad nickname of "Rev" from Verona days.

What a shout of celebration filled the car, when the big "Welcome to Texas" sign appeared ahead of us! This second largest state in the Union was the land of long horned steers, world's best BBQ, spicy Tex-Mex cuisine, a month-long state fair, rodeos, oil fields, blue bonnet flowers, cowboy boots, ten-gallon hats, guns, country music, hot summer winds, scorching heat, big expanses of modern cities, unique small towns, huge cattle ranches, the Alamo, and the Dallas Cowboys!

Of course, least one think I have placed my favorite football team above my family, I will add that this expansive land was also the home of our amazing son, his precious wife Wendy, and three of our six energetic grandkids who welcomed us with warm hugs while still in awe of how God had led us in the past four months. Also rolling out the welcome mat were Wendy's parents, Bill and Sandy Wilbur and our dear friends from Buffalo, Dick and Marvel DeWitt, who also had found Texas living to be irresistible. In His attention to every detail of our lives, God had once again blessed us through friends and family so that our new state of residence felt like home from day one.

Four months later, our home construction was completed and we were able to moved from the rental apartment into what would now count as our 18th address change since 1970!

As my wife would exclaim, "Oh my stars!"

Who could have ever imagined so many relocations, but each one had its own particular reality for me and my family. Each one had resulted in experiences and memories we could never have envisioned nor ever forget.

Just like every other move we had made; it was not long before we had established our connections with a new church community in which to worship as well as those vitally important medical people to care for our health needs. Upon the recommendation of Dr. Karanes, we engaged the services of an oncologist at Baylor Cancer Center in Dallas for my yearly follow-up rechecks. By now, I had become somewhat of a rare case as I presented to the medical team the uniqueness of being a 31-year lymphoma survivor as well as an experimental peripheral stem cell transplant survivor 24 years ago. They had not seen many people with my survival history. It was a celebrity status I could have done without, but it was a living example of the power of prayer and the mystery of God's plans unfolding in my life. Each testing result of NED, no evidence of disease, was a blessing which I carried with me for the next 365 days.

So it was, with very thankful hearts for good health, we set about to continue our adventures in traveling, cruising the high seas, establishing new friendships, serving at our church, and exploring the grand state around us. By now, I experienced another small bout of vehicle "foot fever," a dormant ailment from my boat ownership days in Buffalo, which could only be cured by replacing the two door Jeep in my garage with a shiny, larger, new four door model. More room for passengers I explained to the wife. She just shook her head and climbed aboard to enjoy the rides which only occurred on clear, rain free days and never through off-road mudding jaunts. Too much mess to clean up later! It was strictly a mall crawler!

Of course, our greatest joy of Texas living was the freedom we had to spend quality as well as quantity time with Matt and Wendy's family who lived a scant nine miles from us. How thrilling it was to not just be occasional attenders at football, volleyball, softball, basketball, track, and field day events of the Texas grands, Sebastian, and Skylar. We were regulars who added our loud voices of encouragement to those of the home team crowds. We even had the pleasure of spending the day as gallery spectators for Sebastian's state golf competition. Added to this was the unique opportunity for both of us to coach Skylar's sixth grade volleyball team! It was fun, challenging, and very rewarding. This ran parallel to the multiply trips we flew across those invisible paths in the skies to the Pacific Northwest to create more memories with Cindy and her family through Luke's football, Lauren's volleyball, and young Will's soccer or just family hiking trips in the majestic mountains of Washington State.

Our new Texas residence also gave us the pleasure of attending the beautiful destination wedding in Galveston, Texas of another granddaughter, Sierra Hays, to Alex James. With their marriage we welcomed three precious great grandchildren—Lexi, Sage, and Cadence. We have been so very blessed with our family members whom we pray for everyday in the tradition of my parents and Jane's parents. It is the greatest privilege as well as responsibility to cover them all with prayers for God's protection and their individual life choices as they travel along their own life journey.

Overall, my life during the next three years was pretty calm and satisfying as Jane and I motored along each road of choice following the big sign posted up ahead marked "Through Traffic."

No big bumps or potholes or traffic jams or detours altered the course of our motion.

Our saddest time came on June 8th, 2016, when we had to say goodbye to my precious Mum as she greeted her Savior face to face in her ninetieth year of earthly life. She was my lifelong prayer warrior, wise mentor, daily encourager, strict but necessary disciplinarian, and my loudest cheerleader. Every birthday card I ever received from her (and Dad) always included the phrase, "We are so very proud of you." And they meant it!

She was not perfect, but her life exemplified a deep-seated trust in her God. Some of the legacy I have to pass on to my descendants can be credited to that unwavering commitment.

About this time, we even began to write an autobiography based on my past cancer experiences and filled with tons of descriptive details painting a picture my miraculous story. It was to serve as the fulfillment of the Legacy Man prophetic word given to me at my Quest experience.

An additional prompting to start this memory process came to both Jane and I through the prophetic words of our pastor, Robert Morris, who reminded us that we each have a story to tell of God's faithfulness through good and not so good times. He strongly suggested that each Christian's story is a living testimony and should be told. Undoubtedly, it would be a labor of love filled with moments of exuberant rejoicing as well as times of painful recollections through many mental, physical, and emotional trials.

For sure, we will never forget one painful and frightening accident which unfolded on a sunny morning in June of 2019 as Jane and I were enjoying a leisurely jaunt on Rock Lake—that very same lake of my childhood adventures. This was our usual summer retreat from the intense Texas heat and it was a pleasure to spend the time with my Canadian family. Unfortunately, our summer fun and fishing pleasure was short lived!

As I was attempting to pull-start the boat motor, something unexpected happened and I was abruptly thrown backward into the water! The acceleration of the engine into high gear pushed the boat into tight circles around my struggling body which was not encased in a life jacket. Big mistake on my part! Simultaneously, Jane was hurled into the back of our small boat where she scrambled to keep the vessel from running over me. Adding to the intensity of the moment was her realization that there was blood gushing from a nearly severed little finger on her left hand!

What had happened?

Furiously treading water, I yelled quick instructions on how to slow the motor and steer the boat over to where I grabbed unto its slippery side. It was then that we both realized there was no way she could haul me back inside. We were both in a state of extreme panic!

Realizing the desperate situation we were in, Jane strongly expressed a verbal plea to the Lord that He had better do something quickly as there were no other boaters near us nor anyone on the shores who could render aide. Almost immediately, Jane's eyes located an old wooden dock with a white swim ladder attached some 200 yards from us. Well, it must have been quite a sight to see us zig-zagging through the murky waters with me dangling from the side of the boat and Jane, with her injured hand wrapped in a dirty yellow towel, attempting to maneuver us to the shore. To this very day we do not ever remember seeing that old dock before that moment and my wife is convinced it was placed there for just a time as this by the all powerful hand of God. I am not arguing!

Once back on board, I was able to resume control of the blood-spattered boat, survey my dear First Mate's hand, and then quickly head back to the house. That twenty-five mile trip to the closest hospital was one of the fastest trips we have ever travelled into Kingston. The degree of Jane's injuries was soon realized—a badly cut finger with crushed bones, a fractured forearm, and torn hip muscles. It was determined that surgery was necessary to save the finger, so our summer holiday abruptly ended and we returned to Texas two days later.

The Lord went ahead of us to prepared an amazing hand surgeon who successfully perform not just one but two reconstruction surgeries complete with a microscopic sized steel plate with four tiny screws. Six months of intense physical therapy followed, but given what could have happened, we were both thankful. It was not lost on everyone that the entire accident could have had a more serious ending. I had never planned on Rock Lake being my final resting place!

True to the Revell humor in crisis situations, I should add that my sudden man-overboard move had resulted in the loss of my favorite ball cap, my new eye glasses, and my brand new fishing rod! But all was not lost as my expensive Apple phone and Apple watch survived the extending dunking!

In His amazing grace and with His deep love for us, God had once again rescued us, guided us, and provided for us in a moment of fear, stress, and uncertainty.

THE TRIUMPHS OF SUCCESSES AND THE AGONY OF STRUGGLES HAS NOT BEEN LOST TO ME ...

For this last reason, I have not shied away from sharing the victories as well as the battles. The triumphs of successes and the agony of struggles has not been lost to me even if I did not understand the reason why each occurred. Recently, I found my notes from my spiritual 2015 Quest experience and this sentence jumped out at me. I had written,

"The one theme that really impressed me was the father's responsibility in blessing his children and grandchildren. The legacy we leave them is critical to their understanding of our Heavenly Father."

That is my reason for sharing my life journey! That He would be glorified!

Psalm 107:43b (NLT),

"They will see in our history the faithful love of the Lord."

Not only has He been faithful to me, but there is someone else who has also been by my side for nearly my entire life. On August 22nd, 2020, Jane and I celebrated fifty years of marriage! An incredible milestone which marked our devotion to each other through every moment of our time allotted to us by God. We have stood beside each other through so many wonderful (and not so wonderful) experiences. I like to think of her as my own classic car—an investment, cherished, well preserved, valued above all others, and a one-of-a-kind model. She has become my nurse, my caregiver, my pit-bullish advocate, my mischievous adventure seeker, my confidant, my tear wiper, my prayer warrior, the mother of my children, and my very best friend. How richly I am blessed to have her beside me.

It seemed only natural for us to celebrate this anniversary as we had never considered divorce as an option through any difficulties we might have experienced. Strange as it seems, 50 years together is a pretty amazing record. To our surprise, we were once again interviewed for a news article for a local magazine centered on our town in Texas. A reporter, from the Argyle Living Magazine, came to the house and spoke with us about being married so long. She was amazed at the details of our life journey and in October of 2020, there appeared a full page retelling entitled, "The Secret of 50 Years of Marriage." Once again I will state that every Christ follower has a story which can reflect the glory of God and the love of Christ through its telling.

Now, usually at this point in a story, there is some type of conclusion or summary followed by the words, "The End." The action ceases. The hero successfully destroys the enemy and navigates his car toward the beautiful sunset filling the sky as the hidden orchestra plays some majestic music.

All is well!

Having been totally honest throughout this autobiography, I will now state that I am living proof that this is not always the case. I have been writing in past tense form as we have figuratively traveled together down some pretty smooth and scenic roads with the occasional necessity of maneuvering around potholes or bumpy ruts. I have endeavored to keep the focus upon my God's faithfulness to me, even if ...

Well, I must now share that I am once again presently in one of those uncomfortable and highly stressful stretches having been suddenly forced to veer off that "Through Traffic" lane onto a narrow road marked by two disturbing signs labeled, "Detour Ahead" and "Construction Zone."

This personal narrative must now be written in a present tense form of wording as I suddenly find myself and my family in yet another health battle. Sadly, this one is just as intense and disturbing as my very first cancer diagnosis way back in Buffalo in 1984.

Without me being conscious of it and hidden deep within my body, a menacing disease had become lodged in the kidney draining tube designed to remove waste products after the filtering process had done its valuable work. It was only through the quick action of our family doctor, who had observed a dangerous elevation of creatinine in my blood during a routine study, that we found ourselves under the care of a urologist and surgeon. What transpired then was a mad rush to correct the drainage issue. It was a shock to everyone when it was discovered that the mass causing the blockage had destroyed the kidney itself to the point it was not even functioning.

As a side note, let this be a warning to anyone who makes the foolish decision to avoid regular physical checkups and blood test regiments. They do take time and possibly extra expense but can be a life saver. I am living proof that ignorance is not the best medicine. Without Dr. B's close observance and sounding of alarm through my regularly scheduled six-month physicals, this book you are reading would have become a biography instead of an autobiography!

What proceeded to unfold was the removal of the destroyed kidney and blocked ureter tube as well as biopsies which confirmed the diagnosis of a very rare form of aggressive ureter cancer which would need to be just as aggressively treated with chemotherapy. Sadly, my years of NED, no evidence of disease, were over.

In all honesty, I will unashamedly acknowledge that we were in a complete state of shock at this reoccurrence of more cancer with its advanced stage. The nature of its origin is unknown, but the effect of its potential destructiveness was very evident to myself, my wife, my children, and the extended family or friends who had walked with us through previous years of cancer battling.

Nearly 30 years had passed since I had been a cancer patient, but the memories of those experiences seemed to just rise up in front of me like a very bad chain reaction accident in the middle of a busy expressway. Once again, my shocked wife had to break the news to me as I recovered in post-surgery and we wept together for such devastating news which would send us down a familiarly depressing path we had hoped our feet would never travel again.

I use the word "depressing" here because, if I am to continue to be completely honest in my legacy journey, it follows that I must share that depression has become an unwelcome yet present travel companion. Has my faith faltered? Have I wrestled controlled of my emotions from the hands of my Savior? Have I sinned in allowing depression to ride in the back seat of my "life" car? Have I faltered somewhere in my living that has resulted in this trial?

The answer to such questions is simple for me.

Even though the way is dark ahead of me, I belong to my Heavenly Father, my Savior His Son, and His Holy Spirit who all love me unconditionally and see every detail of where my mind is now, the condition of my physical body, and how my soul is struggling. They will not abandon me, forsake me, nor judge me! They will help me walk through this rut of depression thrust on me by the evil one.

I can make no claims of superhuman strength or mind-over- matter thinking as every day has become a struggle both physically and mentally. But I can claim the strength I have found through the multitude of family and friends who are daily praying for me as well as the reassurance I find in the words of Scripture. Words which I have heard and read for my entire life, but now take on even greater importance. Words woven into songs which remind me of God's presence and Jesus' comfort to my weary soul. I have found my worship and prayer life closely tied to Contemporary Christian music which I play constantly in our home and in the car. I am amazed how God has blessed me through songwriters sensitive to His leading in their creativity of lyrics and melodies.

With that said, I must push on to eventually put semi closure on the present journey I am on.

So in 2020, right in the middle of the Covid virus crisis which started in 2019, I found myself sitting in an examination room at Baylor Charles A. Sammons Cancer Center in downtown Dallas, Texas. Beside me sat my faithful wife with her ever present notebook open to a page full of questions to be asked of Dr. Thomas E. Hutson, director of the Urologic Oncology Program, Co-Chair of the Urologic Cancer Research and Treatment Center at Baylor Scott & White Health and a Professor of Medicine at Texas A&M College of Medicine.

Once again, God had quietly intervened in my new, unforeseen life crisis as He had led us to contact my lymphoma doctor at Baylor for his recommendation of an oncologist who could best address my situation. He immediately directed us to Dr. Hutson right at that cancer center where all my medical history was already on file. Some would say how lucky I am in this, but I testify that this small milestone marks another moment when God supplied exactly what I needed. It is not luck as the world would view it. It is the love of a Father for His son.

I am actually living out the words recorded in Psalm 37:23-24 (NLT),

> *"The Lord directs the steps of the godly. He delights in every*
> *detail of their lives. Though they stumble, they will never*
> *fall, for the Lord holds them by the hand."*

This fine doctor's credentials are beyond impressive, and I am privileged to be his patient. He is internationally recognized as a brilliant physician and cancer research doctor, but the best bonus of his presence in my life is that he is a vocal believer in Jesus Christ. We share the same faith, and it is a strong assurance to me that he has God's ear in what treatments would be best for me. I am richly blessed to be under this watchful care. My God is so good!

Dr. Hutson quickly assessed my complicated medical history with its new twist, and he determined that a chemotherapy regiment of Gemcitabine and Carboplatin was the best course of attack. By this time from March to November of 2020, I had undergone five major surgery procedures, many dreaded blood draws, several ultrasounds, and vitally important CT scans.

For the staff at Baylor, I have been labelled their Unicorn, a one-of-a-kind individual with many complex problems which all have to be considered at each step of my care. Through no fault of my own, I have become like an Audi A8, one of the most difficult luxury cars to maintain and repair. Only certain specialty mechanics can service such a vehicle and return it to road worthy status. How blessed I was (and am) to have an amazingly brilliant medical "repair" crew handling the details.

What was before me was an attack plan for monthly infusions of very powerful drugs specifically designed to seek and destroy those tiny but deadly cancer cells secretly roaming around inside of me. I am reminded of a game my Verona childhood buddies and I would play called Hide and Seek. The call-to-action cry was, "Ready or not, here I come!" How appropriate for this new stretch of highway I was forced to travel. Physically, it was necessary. Personally, I was not ready for more of what now became fresh in my mind as the devil reminded me of all the suffering and pain from my past cancer histories.

How was it possible we had this cloud covered mountain in front of us again?

Adding to the fact that I never seem to do the "usual" in my health situation, at February's checkup in 2021, my doctor determined that we would need to stop the infusions in order to protect the one remaining kidney struggling to do its job. Miraculously, March's CT scan showed NED, no evidence of disease, and my kidney functions were stable. Praise the Lord for some good news!

With this excellent report causing great rejoicing, we traveled to Washington State to celebrate Luke's high school graduation as well as Aaron and Lauren's beautiful wedding.

It was as though God wanted to send us a special blessing on the day of the wedding at the Army base in usually rainy Tacoma when majestic Mount Rainer broke through her usual cloudy cover to present us with a glorious backdrop for wedding pictures. She rises above every other natural element at the height of over 14,000 feet, has her own weather system at the top, and is very stingy with clear views for those in her shadow. But on that June day, her Creator swept aside her clouds to make our gathering a very special time. The wedding pictures set against this beautiful natural backdrop are stunning! It was a wonderful occasion for celebration. Another graduation and a wedding milestone gifted to me by my God as part of those bonus years I had asked Him for way back in 1984.

Back home in Texas, the intensity of the summer heat descended upon us and also the scheduling of my annual colonoscopy which had been derailed for a year or so. Now let me just say that I know of no one who looks forward to this awkward but important procedure. I am no exception as the preparation process is unpleasant and the whole thing somewhat embarrassing. It would have been very easy to postpone the whole thing with an excuse of taking a break from medical tests.

However, once again, I am very thankful that God's timing is not my timing, as through the preparation for the test, I experienced blood in my urine which required the attention of my urologist who grasped the seriousness of the situation, preformed yet another unpleasant bladder cystoscopy test in the office where he discovered a newly formed tumor was present. Less than 24 hours later, I was in surgery again to remove a bladder cancer tumor which had somehow survived the last rigorous chemotherapy.

Everyone was seriously disappointed with this continued disease progression. My family and I felt like we had boarded a roller coaster for some endless ride of emotional ups and downs.

What in the world was happening as obviously the usual drug therapy had not done its job? This sad situation erased the NED status I had briefly celebrated as this new situation plunged me into a whole new field of concern. Back to Baylor we went to now hand my medical team another problem to address.

Dr. Hutson quickly laid before us the options of stopping additional treatments for now or agreeing to continue fighting with the use of an immunotherapy drug called Keytruda, a medicine that works with my own immune system to attack and destroy advanced cancer cells. There could be serious side effects that we were made aware of, but the hope was it would work its magic to stop tumor growth.

Because it would be like a raging battle within me, my sighs of weariness became louder and more frequent as I contemplated the future. I was beginning to understand how even the great King David of ancient Israel, who had commanded armies and ruled millions of people, could still pen these words so close to how I feel so many times lately.

Psalm 38:7b-9 (NLT),

> *"And my health is broken. I am exhausted and completely crushed. My groans come from an anguished heart. You know what I long for, Lord; You hear my every sigh."*

But thankfully, with great patience and love, God reminds me of the verse He had shown us way back in 1984 when we found ourselves passengers aboard a swiftly moving vehicle with broken headlights careening down a steep embankment into the dark.

2 Timothy 1:7 (KJV),

> *"For God hath not given us a spirit of fear, but of power, and of love, and of a sound mind."*

It is time once again to trust God's faithfulness to never leave us powerless as we daily leave that evil deceiver bent on my destruction standing on the side of the road as, under Jesus' power, we speed away. It is not to suggest that doubts and anxious moments are not creeping into my thoughts. I do not want anyone to think I am super spiritual because every day I beg God to give me new strength to just get through that day. The intensity of my weakness both physically and emotionally often frightens me.

So it was with hope for remission, I started on a Keytruda regimen requiring a once per month infusion for four months. Blood tests gave readings in all hematology areas so that each infusion could occur on schedule. The daily side effects I had to endure were extreme cold, excessive fatigue, and loss of appetite as well as depression. It was a struggle most days, but I kept walking around my neighborhood and staying hydrated to combat negative effects.

We even gave in to a "senior" moment and ordered an electric blanket for our bed to combat my chilled physical body. Jokingly, my dear wife exclaimed, "Oh my stars! We have become our parents!" A much-needed humorous comment to break the seriousness of my struggle.

Our laughter was short lived as right before the fifth Keytruda infusion, I had a CT scan to get a clearer picture of the tumor sizes under this attack by the immunotherapy drug. To put it bluntly, the news was not good as two tumors had grown and had now encased the one remaining ureter to the point that the attached kidney could become as useless as the one removed last fall. So once again, we enlisted the surgery expertise of my urologist to insert a tiny, snake like stent into the kidney to help drain itself into the bladder and hopefully, prevent any more blockages. Also, I had to gear myself up again for a new heart port to be installed before yet another surgery. It seems as though every time I drive forward a mile, I am thrown into reverse by some uncontrollable force.

Let the records show that this latest surgical procedure is number nine for me since March of 2020. Mine is a very familiar face at Flower Mound Presbyterian Hospital, Texas Interventional Radiology, and Baylor Cancer Center. Someone even humorously suggested that I should have a frequent user card at these places with benefits.

Sick joke, but very true!

This new engine failure on my life journey vehicle meant that the much hoped for disease destroying Keytruda had to be stopped and I was offered another newly FDA approved drug, PADCEV (enfortumab vebotin-ejfv) which recently showing good results in stopping the progression of advanced bladder or ureter cancers. It is not like chemotherapy but rather a prescription medicine used to attack cancers which have spread or are inoperable after previous standard treatments have failed. Disturbingly, I now fall into that group of people.

At this point in my legacy journey, I feel I should explain that it is not my desire to spin a tale of pain and suffering, however it is my desire to keep focusing on those milestones of my Lord Jesus' faithfulness in providing me with new medical advancements developed by the brilliant minds of research and medical professionals. This newly designed drug actually attaches itself to a cancer cell, burrows inside, and then releases destructive chemotherapy into the very heart of these active cells to cause their demise. It is worth a try, and we seem to be reaching the end of the list of things to "try."

Along with its powerful medicinal strength, this new drug also carries with it a different set of side effects which can be debilitating. These must be closely monitored so it is a good thing I have a super attentive support system in place at home. No detail of my physical state goes unnoticed. I am blessed to have a caregiving spouse who records details important to my care. Hers is not an easy task but one done out of deep love for me for which I am exceedingly grateful. I am also blessed to have the powerful prayers of my children and their children, as well as countless other family members and friends.

So, and this is a big so, I presently find myself and my beloved family once again tightening the seat belts in this battered up transportation SUV in which we find ourselves traveling. The view out of our front windshield captures a disturbing prospect of another large, sinister looking mountain we must climb to reach a summit of good health and continued memory making years. As much as we fight it, weariness and its backpack filled with dread does try to hitchhike a ride with us. We are creeping along following a newly posted road sign labelled, "Proceed With Caution," unsure of the number of the days God has ordained for me to live on this side of Eternity.

Thousands of words ago, I started on a journey to share my life legacy with whoever picked up this book. It has been a labor of mixed emotions and humility as I have purposed in my heart to be honest and genuine in relating the deeply personal recollections of a carefree young lad from Canada who would never have believed what lay ahead for him! What adventures, joys, sorrows, fears, failures, dreams, nightmares, triumphs, defeats, challenges, and victories would be mine to experience under the watchful eye of my loving God.

Now it is time to put closure on this written adventure.

Realistically, I could find some famous quotes, declare some profound insights, or create some inspiring words which would mark me as having attained some degree of lofty emotional heights through life experiences. But once again, God has quietly brought my focus back to His faithful presence as my Creator. He sent His son, Jesus, to be my Emmanuel (God with us), my Counsellor, my Healer, my Protector, my Friend, my Shield, and most importantly, my Savior with His sacrifice of Himself thousands of years ago.

GOD HAS QUIETLY BROUGHT MY FOCUS BACK TO HIS FAITHFUL PRESENCE AS MY CREATOR

No other conclusion could put the final touches on this legacy journey of mine like these words found in two ancient but alive verses from the Old Testament in the Bible. Some unknown choir director wrote in Psalm 42:5-6 (NLT),

> *"Why am I discouraged? Why is my heart so sad? I will put my hope in God! I will praise Him again—My Savior and my God!"*

Each day of my present struggles, I can relate to those emotions as well as those expressed by Job, who also experienced remarkable successes as well as unbelievable trials, and still was able to declare,

Job 23:10-12, 14 (NLT),

> *"But He knows where I am going, and when He tests me, I will come out as pure as gold. For I have stayed on God's paths; I have followed His ways and not turned aside. I have not departed from His commands but have treasured His Words more than daily food. So He will do to me whatever He has planned. He controls my destiny."*

I will stop the retelling of my legacy journey with this—

I am a child of the Living God.

I will place my life in His ever-faithful hands.

I will trust Him who loves me unconditionally
and will never leave me.

Even if ...

Made in the USA
Monee, IL
10 June 2023

35475712R00187